FINANCING PUBLIC UNIVERSITIES

HIGHER EDUCATION DYNAMICS

VOLUME 18

SCOPE OF THE SERIES

Higher Education Dynamics is a bookseries intending to study adaptation processes and their outcomes in higher education at all relevant levels. In addition it wants to examine the way interactions between these levels affect adaptation processes. It aims at applying general social science concepts and theories as well as testing theories in the field of higher education research. It wants to do so in a manner that is of relevance to all those professionally involved in higher education, be it as ministers, policy-makers, politicians, institutional leaders or administrators, higher education researchers, members of the academic staff of universities and colleges, or students. It will include both mature and developing systems of higher education, covering public as well as private institutions.

For other titles published in this series, go to
http://www.springer.com/series/6037

FINANCING PUBLIC UNIVERSITIES
The Case of Performance Funding

by

MARCEL HERBST

Zurich, Switzerland

 Springer

Library of Congress Control Number: 2008939500

ISBN 978-1-4020-9502-3 (PB)
ISBN 978-1-4020-5559-1 (HB)
ISBN 978-1-4020-5560-7 (e-book)

Published by Springer,
P.O. Box 17, 3300 AA Dordrecht, The Netherlands.

www.springer.com

Printed on acid-free paper

Contents

Executive Summary

The reform movement has spread like wildfire, often without careful analysis of the results [it has] produced or the preconditions for success.

Donald F. Kettl (Kettl, 2000)

Mass Higher Education and Universal Access Tertiary education is a success by most standards. In Western nations, student numbers have greatly expanded during the past half century: while roughly 5-6% of the relevant age groups were enrolled in higher education institutions in the years following World War II, current participation rates vary between 25% and 60%, or even more. Higher education institutions were instrumental in the pursuance of a social agenda which is central to modern democracies: they attended to equity concerns and have opened their doors to previously under-represented groups of their respective societies, such as economically disadvantaged children, women, minorities, older students; they assumed an equalizing and citizen building role; and they paved the roads to prosperity — both for the graduates themselves as well as for the societies at large.

Fiscal and Funding Crises Expanding tertiary education systems require resources. Unlike many other industries, higher education is labor intensive and, hence, even unit costs are rising; the search for capital intensive operations or options is in its infancy; and possibilities to move institutions to locations where labor is cheaper defeat the very mission of higher education. While higher education creates wealth — and implicitly tax income —, and while higher education is commonly viewed as a motor of economic development, returns on investment in the higher education sector are characterized by time-lags of decades, and governments are under great strain to fund higher education at levels deemed necessary or accustomed: too pressing are the demands of competing state obligations and too seductive the political agendas which call for tax reductions. The very success of higher education has brought the various systems to a brink where retrenchment is a common course of action, frequently accompanied by slips in the quality of education and research. Although all Western systems are touched by these trends, European higher education systems, because of their governance and management structures, appear to be affected more significantly.

New Social Contracts Higher education systems were bound to their respective societies by social contracts which assured, in general, adequate resource bases for the institutions in exchange for educational and research-based services. Research universities operated on the premise of various rights bestowed on them: the freedom to teach, to learn, and to research — subsumed in Humboldtian higher education systems under the terms of *Lehr- und Forschungsfreiheit*. In the US system, universities also have the right to choose who to admit to studies of higher education. Although no institution was completely autonomous, governments — during periods of democratic rule one should add — respected this social contract which was based on trust: trust regarding the adherence to institutional roles and missions, and trust regarding non-interference into the internal affairs of the university. The fiscal and funding crises of recent years has now prompted a reevaluation of the original social contracts, and new contractual arrangements are being drafted and tested. This has led to contrasting developments. In Europe and in countries shaped by European traditions, block grants are being used to extend the financial autonomies of institutions. These grants not only demand greater accountability on the part of institutions; they also frequently imply performance funding measures. Conversely, in the US the customarily looser strings which tie state and public institutions together are being tightened.

Symptoms of Strain Apart from the apparent difficulties in funding higher education at levels deemed appropriate, a range of strain symptoms within European higher education systems are coming to the fore. These strain symptoms are directly related to funding issues but implicitly also to governance and management issues: mass higher education has not only opened the doors of universities to a broader and more diverse spectrum of people, it has also impersonalized education and widened the social distance between faculty and students; outmoded pedagogic approaches are used, perhaps out of necessity, and program options which cater to the diverse student population are limited; mass higher education has become associated with wasteful drop-out rates, longer study periods, and late graduation times; career prospects for younger scholars and for women have been curtailed. While these symptoms of strain are widespread, affecting institutions around the globe, European institutions appear to be affected most strongly: European institutions as a whole have not been able to regain the international status that they enjoyed before World War II, and their attraction for foreign students — from overseas as well as from within Europe — is limited; the relative quality of European research appears competitive only in a narrow spectrum of disciplines, and the regional economic impact of European research universities lags behind those of the US.

Problem Diagnoses There is no shortage of diagnostic attempts to analyze the situation, but there are clearly diverging views on how to see the problem situation in a systemic way. Current reform measures are mainly based on the treatment of two classes of ailments diagnosed: the first class of courses of actions address a lack of standardization in course and study formats as well as an insufficient coordination between differing higher education systems by what is known as the Bologna Process; and the second class of courses of actions try to rectify an insufficient market orientation as well as flawed governance and management practices of institutions or higher education systems by novel modes of management and, in particular, by performance-based budgeting or funding measures. Both treatments appear to oversell current reform efforts: the first because its range is limited; and the second because other, tested, measures are available which appear more effective in bringing about desired ends and are not associated with potentially harmful effects.

Public Management Reform Debate Reforms and reform measures within higher education have to be seen against the backdrop of a general reform debate, which has affected Western nations for the past two or three decades. Higher education forms one of the many problem areas which call for solutions in our modern, complex societies, and comprehensive — and in a sense ideologized — solution approaches

become visible to address these problem areas. Higher education reform proposals are frequently steered by an overbearing notion of
how to reform public management in general and higher education
systems in particular. Public management reforms follow a definite
trend, and possibly even a fad, whose origin lies outside academia.
They touch a broad spectrum of disciplines, from policy sciences to
economics and law, but their integrative, encompassing view finds
no correspondence in the more fragmented academic world, and the
reforms themselves have failed to attract major academic support.

New Funding Modes Funding or budgeting modes form a central package of measures related to public management reforms, particularly
in the field of higher education. Funding or budgeting modes not
only serve to allocate resources for given ends; they are also increasingly being used as governance or management tools in situations
where institutions operate at the fringes, or outside of markets. In
such cases, where an absence of competitive elements is being decried, performance-based funding or budgeting modes are advanced
to create an environment of quasi-markets. Universities, and in particular public institutions of higher education, often appear to be in-
sufficiently competitive, thus supposedly in need of such measures.
This has made them targets for a paradigm shift that replaces direct
governance and management by indirect, formula-driven directives
tied to input, output, or performance indicators. In the present context, performance-based budgeting or funding modes are based on
contractual arrangements between public authorities and higher education institutions or systems — performance contracts, *Zielverein-
barungen* or *Leistungsaufträge*, et cetera — and may serve as an exten-
sion, or an add-on, of Management by Objectives (MBO). The new
funding or budgeting modes appear to be politically driven and have
a far greater resonance in nations characterized by a traditionally
strong governmental role in the steering of higher education, a corresponding culture of weak institutional leadership, and by an oli-
garchic faculty.

Implications and Side Effects Performance-based budgeting or funding
use performance indicators to allocate funds. Performance indicators, by themselves, cannot provide a proper rationale for resource
allocation: additional information is necessary for sound decisions.
Resource allocation which is functionally tied to performance indica-

tors foregoes the information as to why performance is as assessed or measured. Furthermore, linking performance measurement or performance assessment to resource allocation may affect the quality — and reliability — of performance assessments. Performance-based budgeting and funding modes are implemented with a range of aims: they are used as agents of change in an environment perceived to resist change, as a means to raise efficiencies of operations and to reduce public outlays, and to induce or promote performance. In fact, however, performance-based budgeting and funding modes act as automata in place of governance and management. They stand in conflict with cultures within higher education which are designed to help improve performance, for instance evaluation (self-assessment and peer review) and accountability; they undermine transparency; and it is questionable to what extent they reach their purported ends.

Governance and Management Alternatives Performance-based budgeting or funding modes appear to not be very effective measures to foster sensible change and to direct institutions towards performance. There are better, tested, approaches around, found in current governance and management practices, but the incorporation of these approaches into a European framework would require a much more profound understanding not only of present higher education systems but also of the systemic aspects of possible future models. Effective reforms would have to rely on a much more open perception of — and debate on — various aspects which characterize European higher education. Issues include the following: the value of a diversified higher education system versus strong tendencies to normalize higher education; the value of education versus the value of degrees; the freedom of institutions to recruit their own students versus open access systems; education and research as separate but related factors versus education and research as lumped systems; budgetary systems within institutions versus budgetary systems of institutions; leadership versus administration.

Inertia and Challenges In spite of an understanding that higher education systems are at risk, and in spite of the observation that European higher education systems are far from regaining their once prominent place in the world of science and education, complacency within academia is widespread. Complacency and ill-directed ambitions are major stumbling blocks on the road to revamp higher education to serve students and society. Unless academia removes these, academic autonomy is bound to suffer. A new understanding is required regarding the focus of higher education and the respective roles of associated institutions and faculty.

Foreword

The last thing we need at the European level is co-ordination. What we want is pluralism, duplication, debate, and controversy. And we also need academic excellence [...]

Keith Pavitt (Pavitt, 2003; Lindner, 2003)

There is a difference between need and wants. Higher education needs to think more about society's needs rather than the academe's wants.

Joseph C. Burke (personal communication)

THE GIST OF THIS VOLUME has been pondered for some time now, and it will continue to occupy a prominent position in the higher education debate. The central question is how to govern, manage or fund higher education systems or institutions in order to assure or even raise the quality of higher education and research. This question is relevant everywhere, in all nations, but it appears particularly relevant within European countries. European universities were once the role models to emulate, but they appear to have been unable to regain a status which they lost after World War II. Some decades after that catastrophic period, European universities — with few exceptions — have lost their once prominent position within academia, and their prospect to regain such a status is hampered by factors which are strongly rooted in the respective higher education cultures.

In a changing world, proper adaptation is the key to success or survival. This is as true for biological or ecological systems as it is for the world of business or higher education. There can be no doubt that the world of higher education has dramatically changed in recent decades, but there are doubts regarding the appropriateness of adaptation strategies adopted by governments, higher education systems, or institutions. Improper adaptations of higher education have been decried for some time now by various scholars and politicians, and a certain awareness is developing regarding the slipping of the relative position of European and US science and higher education. The Italian government appears to long for a leading institute of technology (Tzermias, 2004, 19. Januar) to curb the emigration of scientists, to foster domestic technologies, and to enhance economic growth; these sentiments are shared by the European Union (Clery, 2006); the General Secretary of Germany's SPD, *Olaf Scholz*, generated consternation with his proposal to found elite-institutions (Krägenow, Jaklin, & Nink, 2004, January; SPD, 2004; Glotz, 2004); in Switzerland a debate is being intensified on how to fund higher education (Doerig, 2004; Weber, 2004) or research (Breu, 2004); and in the US alerts are being formulated regarding the average educational level of the future US workforce (Kelly, 2005) and its impact on US competitiveness (The National Summit on Competitiveness, 2005).

Funding crises in higher education have cropped up in many European nations during the past decades, but they have seldom been met with creativity. Frequently, employment freezes have been imposed by governments, as the sole measure to fight rising costs, with extraordinarily negative effects. Missing block grants only a few years ago and lacking managerial autonomy, universities were unable to implement necessary changes within the confines of a budget: they were practically immobilized, and adaptations that took place appeared to entrench inadequate organizational structures. In recent years, institutional — i.e., managerial — autonomy has gained ground to some extent, at least if one follows the rhetoric, but true institutional autonomy is still far from reality within the context of European higher education systems. The current tendencies in the field of performance funding appear to push further into the distance the horizon where institutions can act as mature, autonomous, and responsible agents.

Governance and management demand transparency of systems governed or managed. Transparency is based on data, models and analysis, and it is never absolute: we have to form an image of the systems acted upon (Boulding, 1961), and we have to calibrate and improve our images. Values play a role in governance and management, and values affect our images which guide our actions. For example, country reports on research productivity may or may not provide the information we need, and we may be misled by their findings. Country reports on research productivity which were published in the 1990s may have alarmed German observers regarding their own research system, but they have also contributed to a complacency with which Swiss observers assessed the situation in Switzerland (King, 2004). In various country reports and scientific fields, Switzerland is internationally ranked first or second among the leading science nations, and only recently more detailed studies have revealed what knowledgeable observers had presumed all along: namely, that a substantial research productivity gap exists which separates US research universities from the rest (CEST, 2002; Herbst, 2004b). Comparative bibliometric studies help to furnish a transparency which is vital for our higher education systems and vital for our respective societies. This is why they are undertaken. However, an implicit danger exists that the information provided is not just used to gain insight, and to govern and manage with greater profundity, but also to link funding to performance indicators, by funding formulæ. If one notices the popularity of performance funding, where the funding principle appears to be accepted in an axiomatic way, the danger I am talking about is clearly not seen by many. Performance funding is welcomed — even mandated — as an answer to the malaise of higher education systems, while a range of other options, sensible options from my point of view, remain practically unexplored. Furthermore, possible negative, deleterious effects of performance funding are being ignored. Reforms appear to be inconsistent: managerial decisions are being delegated down to the hierarchical level where the corresponding know-how is concentrated, and then performance funding systems are being implemented to reverse this process.

I have observed these tendencies since the late 1980s when I started my job as a university administrator, first with an open curiosity and later with growing concern. At the time, many of the instruments which are characteristic of modern institutions were not in place yet, and I exchanged observations and experiences with peers in neighboring countries or in the US. Clearly, European universities were not yet prepared to manage themselves. But government agencies were not in a position to manage institutions either, because they lacked the necessary information and insight. Course evaluations by students, which I had experienced as a young faculty member at a US university in the early 1970s, were just about to spread in Europe; course credit systems which were implemented in the US around the beginning of the 20th century — and which are vital for management purposes — have since been imposed by the Bologna process and are being implemented now, roughly 100 years after their creation by the Carnegie Foundation; comprehensive data management systems linking students', staff, and faculty records with financial or spatial information did not exist; academic planning was crude and only very loosely linked to budgeting.

Comparative analyses of higher education systems are vital. Only by comparing systems, only by benchmarking, can we understand our own institutions and carve out their strengths and weaknesses or identify their opportunities and threats[1]. My own involvement with comparative analysis started with such an attempt to compare institutions (McQueen, 1992). In the early 1990s an opportunity arose for the European Association of Institutional Research (EAIR), a professional organization of university administrators and researchers in the field of higher education, to hold its annual forum in Switzerland. In the summer of 1995 that conference took place at the Swiss Federal Institute of Technology (ETH Zürich)[2] under the heading of "Dynamics in Higher Education: Traditions Challenged by New Paradigms". A parallel event, taking advantage of the international experts present and geared specifically for a Swiss audience, was organized together with the *Gesellschaft für Hochschule und Forschung* (GHF)[3] and led to a separate publication with contributions on diversity in higher education, regional economic impact, entrepreneurial universities, governance and management, privatization tendencies, evaluations and assessments, professionalization of administrators, and research on tertiary education (Herbst, Latzel, & Lutz, 1997). The aim was to attune the Swiss audience to a broad range of issues which play a role in the attempts to reform tertiary education. A few years later a small team embarked on a comparative analysis of two leading research universities in an attempt to identify structural or cultural aspects which might be called upon to explain differences in research productivity (Herbst, Hugentobler, & Snover, 2002).

Unfortunately, broader solutions approaches to complex issues are seldom favored; instead, simple solutions are sought, such as performance-funding systems. In the present volume, an international audience is addressed, Europeans for the most part, but also others who are interested in comparative higher education. I have tried to recreate my early curiosity in order to retrace the logic of performance funding. When I began my research, I wondered where the re-reading of older documents and the exposure to new literature would lead me. The reader should know that though my review of materials has not affected my position on the subject matter that much, it has clearly helped me understand the situation better.

---

[1]SWOT-Analysis.

[2]Alternatively also abbreviated by the acronym ETHZ: "Eidgenössische Technische Hochschule Zürich".

[3]Disbanded in the meantime.

It is my hope that others can profit from this as well.

This book is based on a report, *Governance and Management of Research Universities*, commissioned by the *Centre d'études de la science et de la technologie* (CEST) in the summer of 2003 (Herbst, 2004a). François Da Pozzo, the now retired head of CEST, and Anne Roulin Perriard who headed CEST's scientometric section, clearly saw the need for a more comprehensive discussion of funding practices in higher education as they relate to CEST's own business: the observation and documentation of the world of science on the basis of scientometric indicators. Because performance-based budgeting and funding systems tend to rely on science metrics, however defined, they were concerned about a possible misuse of their own work and wanted to have the interplay between funding systems and science metrics elucidated. I am grateful for their permission to use that material in the present book.

Financing Public Universities differs in various respects from *Governance and Management of Research Universities*. A new chapter (Chapter 6: Inertia and Challenges) and a new appendix (Appendix C: The Atlantic Split) have been added, and the material of the original report has been updated and revised.

Drafts of the book at hand, or portions thereof, were given to a range of people in order to solicit comments or corrections. I am particularly thankful to the following for their critical and constructive reviews: Joseph C. Burke (The Nelson A. Rockefeller Institute of Government), Markus Christen (ETHZ), François Da Pozzo (CEST), Hanspeter Eichenberger (retired, IBM Research Laboratory and General Electric), Albert Fritschi (ETH-Board), Christoph Grolimund (ETH-Board), Joshua A. Herbst (ETHZ), Urs Hugentobler (ETHZ), János Kende (Michigan State University)[4], Dieter Imboden (President, Swiss National Science Foundation, and ETHZ), Gertrude Kreutzmann (retired, Geschäftsstelle des Deutschen Wissenschaftsrats)[5], José-Ginés Mora (Centre for Higher Education Management, Technical University of Valencia), Jakob Nüesch (President emeritus, ETHZ), Anne Roulin Perriard (CEST), Frank Schmidtlein (Department of Education Policy and Leadership, University of Maryland), Mantz Yorke (emeritus, Centre for Higher Education Development, Liverpool John Moores University), Alexander Zehnder (President, ETH-Board). I would also like to thank two anonymous referees for their detailed comments and sugges-

---

[4]János Kende, a survivor of Bergen-Belsen, a *mentsh* full of wit, *seykhl* and compassion, and a friend of mine since the 1950s, died September 26, 2006.

[5]Gertrude Kreutzmann, a wonderful colleague and friend, died May 30, 2006.

tions on how to improve the argument. Needless to say, any remaining errors or misinterpretations are mine alone. Lastly, I would like to thank Yael Shimoni and Edwin Beschler for their excellent editing[6].

Zürich (Switzerland), November 2006   Marcel Herbst

---

[6]This manuscript was produced with the LaTeX document preparation system, a number of GNU software tools, and the **R** statistics system.

Chapter 1

Introduction

My conclusion [. . .] is that a federal quest to understand or measure college costs essentially represents an ill-defined question for which there is no reasonable or useful answer.

David W. Breneman (Breneman, 2001; Cunningham, Wellman, Clinedinst, Merisotis, & Carroll, 2001)

HIGHER EDUCATION IS a service industry. Like other industries, it transforms resources into products, i.e., services. Were it to offer these services on the open market, it would do so at a price to recuperate the costs incurred and to produce a profit, at least in the longer run. A service provider which could not meet this objective eventually could not stay in business and would be pushed out of this market.

However, higher education institutions do not generally operate in the open market, and they do not price their services to cover their costs. This is particularly true for research universities, public or private alike, and there is no current visible which would want to change that. Educational institutions, and higher education institutions in particular, have a long history of operating outside the open market. They offer their services regularly far below the price levels necessary to cover costs, and they follow this policy out of conviction: to further educational attainment or to try to foster research for the benefit not only of the individuals concerned, but also for the society at large.

Indeed, this notion of public service is discernible at least since the inception of the modern university at the beginning or in the middle of the 19th century. It can be traced back to the French *Écoles polytechniques* and

1

the *Grandes écoles* of Napoleonic times, to Wilhelm von Humboldt's concept of the University of Berlin (1809), and to the Morrill Act (1862), which was instrumental in the formation of land-grant colleges in the US. The notion of public service was deeply embedded long before economists attempted to estimate rates of private or social returns on investments in the fields of education, and the notion remains valid to this day. While it has been always clear that individuals derive a private benefit from education, there are strong external effects involved, and social returns to education are considered sizable. Economic growth and prosperity are seen to be directly linked to educational achievement: higher education, as a "motor of economic development" (Gray, 1999), benefits even those who have never had the chance to attend a college or a university.

Because higher education services were not priced to cover their costs, and because tuition and fees cover only a fraction of the resources necessary to provide the service, other income streams have to be tapped. In the case of public institutions, there has been up to now a "social contract" in place and state funds have been allocated, in one way or another, to cover the difference. In addition, industry or philanthropy has supported research or advanced training. In the case of private institutions, missing state funds to cover teaching (Hebel, 2003) have been offset — or partially offset — by higher tuition and fees. Endowment income and proceeds from patents have provided funding sources.

Toward the end of this past century, however, the social contract which bound higher education institutions to their respective constituencies came under strain. A fiscal crisis developed in many countries which made it increasingly difficult to properly fund higher education (Commission on National Investment in Higher Education, 1997). This crisis, brought about by expanding obligations and conflicting demands, has the quality of many creeping processes which gradually transform life, environment, or societies, and we can count it among the problems which are here to stay, at least in the foreseeable future: it will form the base of — or drive — an ongoing debate on higher education. Three major reasons for this situation come to the fore:

- *Expanding higher education*: One of the main reasons for the fiscal crisis is the expanding higher education system. In Western nations, student populations have expanded — conservatively assessed — by factors of three to seven since World War II, partially because of population growth, but primarily because of higher participation rates. Ever higher proportions of relevant groups participate in tertiary education: women, ethnic minorities, and economically disadvantaged students find increasing access. In addition, life-long learning attitudes as well as further education attract older students. Various factors account for these growing student populations: private pay-offs to education; structural changes in the respective economies, primarily a reduced role of the secondary (manufacturing) sector and a greatly expanded tertiary (service) sector, with corresponding transformations of labor demand; and public policies to further educational or equal opportunities, or to strengthen the labor force in general and to reduce unemployment, welfare dependencies, or crime.

- *Competing priorities*: Expanding higher education systems are in need of resources: to employ growing populations of faculty and staff, to provide study grants or scholarships, to fund broader spectra of research areas, to build new teaching or research facilities, to preserve older capital investments, to stock libraries, or to furnish and upgrade complex infrastructures. Resources which flowed into higher education systems in recent decades have grown in absolute, but not necessarily in relative terms, and public service demands, in fields of health, welfare, et cetera, have competed with education. As a consequence, public investment priorities have shifted. The prospects for higher education funding are generally dim: costs of higher education often rise faster than inflation; and economic development and — implicitly — state revenues from taxes, spawned so to speak by education, are lagging behind because of the traditionally long periods which separate investments in education from subsequent economic prosperity.

- *Questions regarding efficacy*: Raising costs of tertiary education are accompanied by a public scrutiny on the efficacy of corresponding investments and by a general, even mounting, reluctance to allocate tax revenues to fully cover costs of public schools, or to subsidize private institutions[1]. This scrutiny takes various forms: investigations on the quality of education and research, quests regarding the reformation of governance and management of higher education systems,

---

[1]"[...] more attention needs to be given to ways to increase the trust and confidence among officials at all levels in higher education systems. When government seeks to examine quality, [...] it appears that they [...] are less concerned about the integrity and performance of the academic enterprise than [...] in seeking some other less politically appealing objectives such as budget reductions, further lessening trust and confidence between the two parties" (Schmidtlein, 2004, p. 20).

concerns with respect to efficiency of resource use or effectiveness of resource allocations, and discussions on funding regimes and funding levels.

While the fiscal crisis is evident to knowledgeable observers of higher education, and while the major contributing factors are generally known, there is still no consensus regarding the significance of the underlying causes. Participation rates in higher education vary from nation to nation, higher education systems differ in their structure, and it is open to debate at which level higher education systems should be run or publicly funded: too loose appear the ties which bind higher education to prosperity, too pressing are the demands of competing public programs, and too strong are vested interests of various pressure groups.

There is a common perception, or a common concern, that quality is slipping, both in teaching and research. There is also a talk of "slack in the system": higher education is not efficient or not effective enough, and value-for-money could be increased. There is a debate as to how to tighten the slack, with a focus on improved governance or management mechanisms, or new funding modes. Some argue that cost containment measures should be pursued more vigorously, and they point to increasing study times and low retention rates as indicators of inadequate efficiency. There are those who advocate higher tuition and fees because they reason that the benefits of higher education accrue primarily to the graduates themselves (Ziegele, Erhardt, & Müller-Böling, 1998) and that a higher financial commitment by students will reduce study duration and drop-out rates. Others warn that higher tuition and fees will turn out to be discriminatory in nature and that this measure will lower enrollment, general economic prosperity, and eventually state tax income, i.e., the very funding base on which higher education institutions depend. Still others place great hope in new technologies to reduce costs and to enhance teaching and research (Herbst & Schmitt, 2001; Hanft, 2001).

The present volume focuses on a range of these issues, but it views them from a funding or budgeting perspective. The aim is to trace the links which tie funding to other issues and to critically assess funding and budgeting as instruments of a management of change (Herbst, 1999) and goals achievement. The volume does not attempt to provide a country-by-country overview on funding mechanisms or funding levels, but tries to annotate, perhaps even to elucidate, various funding regimes and their ramifications. The book also refrains from giving specific advice: the readers will have to draw their own conclusions.

A first substantive chapter on "Mass Higher Education and Funding Bases" (Chapter 2) sketches the context: it concentrates on the fiscal crisis issue and its underlying causes and argumentative rationale, traces its development by a view on costs and funding, and raises quality issues which can be directly linked to funding and management. Higher education systems vary from nation to nation, and a broad range of corresponding missions, funding modes and funding levels coexist. While a more detailed review of the entire spectrum of higher education systems and funding would easily go beyond the scope of the present book, the chapter attempts nonetheless to provide a sketch of variations and an outline of system or funding principles based on representative examples.

The general theme of the volume has to be viewed in the context of an enlivened discussion on the role and function of government and public management, a discussion which started in this form in the middle of the 1980s and which affects, drives, and shapes government reforms and higher education governance and management in various nations (Barzelay, 2001; Brudney, Jr., & Rainey, 2000; Kettl, 2000; Pollitt & Bouckaert, 2000). Funding levels and funding regimes pose important questions in this context, particularly in a world with scarce resources, but we also have to be conscious of inappropriate forms of funding, of possible misuse — even abuses — of funding mechanisms. Hence, the second substantive chapter reviews the "Public Management Reform Debate" (Chapter 3) to provide a backdrop for the subsequent focus on higher education.

The past decades have shown that the funding of universities and colleges does not simply serve to financially support institutions or higher education systems. Resource flows, public as well as private, are increasingly used to influence the course of higher education: private philanthropy may provide funds to set up lab facilities or to erect new science buildings, government agencies tie their general support — or base funding — to bilateral agreements which specify the 'product' to be funded or the 'results' to be obtained, and industry might express interest in — and consequently finance — specific lines of research. While public funding mechanisms are the primary focus of this book, one has to be aware of the whole breadth of funding possibilities to properly assess specific funding modes. Furthermore, because funding modes are used, in part at least, in substitution of common governance and management activities, one has to be conscious of such substitution potential.

Public funding mechanisms which are not only contractually based, but tie funding to results obtained, appear to breed new forms of governance and may act as substitutes to management. In European higher education, and in university systems strongly shaped by European values, the separation of powers between government on the one hand and institutions — or institutional systems — on the other, was traditionally weak, or even blurred. Governmental agencies engaged in 'micro-management', in that they assumed functions which — in a different cultural context — are actually part of institutional management: they directly employed faculty or formed contractual arrangements with individuals concerning their work conditions, for instance, or they controlled the details of institutional budgets. The new thinking within European higher education during the past few years, frequently focused on institutional autonomy, tries to establish now a proper separation of powers: roles are clarified, buffer organizations set up, and contracts signed. The main topic of the book has significance in this particular context, and the chapter on "Performance-Based Budgeting or Funding" (see Chapter 4) attempts to illuminate and assess possible modes of operations of performance contracts in higher education.

Performance contracts are frequently advocated in lieu of other measures, old and new, tried and untried, and they are launched under various management labels. Because higher education systems differ in their history, structure and degree of development, a rich palette of experiences and management practices are available for analysis when assessing the merits of performance contracting or, in particular, performance-based budgeting or funding. Performance contracting is rarely the only sensible option available in higher education governance or management, and when designs of performance contracts are attempted — or before performance contracts are mandated — one ought to be conscious of the likely implications of such measures and of alternative courses of actions. Like all measures, performance contracts also have negative effects or consequences which have to be weighed against the expected positive ones — or against the negative or positive effects of alternative measures.

The chapter on "Alternative Governance and Management Modes" (see Chapter 5), hence, will juxtapose performance contracting — and performance-based budgeting or funding — with governance or management alternatives which fall outside the realm of performance contracting. It will focus on issues open to debate and will try to lay out the network of partially competing intervention and management measures: steps pertaining to the governance of institutional systems or individual institutions; management activities referring to differing layers within single institutions; accountability measures of institutions or institutional systems vis-à-vis governing boards, buffer organizations, governmental agencies, or the general public; and funding regimes and the corresponding funding rationale.

The last chapter, "Inertia and Challenges" (Chapter 6), serves as a conclusion: it attempts to summarize the main lines of critique which were assembled against performance-based funding; it evokes some major economic concepts which ought to be central in a future higher education debate; it does the same with some concepts of governance and management; and it tries to set the stage for future reflections regarding higher education. Because higher education is diverse, fragmented by the cultural histories of the various nations, it is often difficult to see the relevant issues, or the major concepts, worth focusing on. The chapter assembles foci which may not be central to the mainstream argument of the current debate, but which — I hope — will gain some attention in the future.

Finally, the volume contains technical appendices which provide background information (see Appendix A), clarify terms used (Appendix B), document research productivity (Appendix C), or illustrates funding systems referred to (Appendix D).

Chapter 2

Mass Higher Education and Funding Bases

An accurate picture of the current reality is just as important as a compelling picture of a desired future.

Peter M. Senge (Senge, 2000; Morey, Maybury, & Thuraisingham, 2000)

The future cannot be projected simply from present lines of development [...] the future must be imagined.

Harold Orlans (Orlans, 1967; Bell, 1967)

Before reflecting on higher education governance or management, it would be helpful to look at the current evolutionary trajectory of higher education itself. In order to guide processes, or in order to critically assess steering mechanisms, a notion of the process which is the subject of guidance is necessary. The aim here is not so much to sketch higher education as such, but to refer to primary driving forces of development as well as to major obstacles in the way of adjustment and change. In spite of the assessment that "many papers provide an over-supply of background and an undersupply of foreground" (Geoghegan & Ackoff, 1989), a picture of this context is helpful. A clear distinction between exogenous and endogenous development factors cannot be given, because higher education cannot easily be separated from the world surrounding it. Nonetheless, the present chapter shall focus on major forces, currents or impediments affecting higher education and its change over time: on mass higher education (Section 2.1) and associated funding crises

(Section 2.2), on the emergence and prospects of information & communication technologies (ICTs) and related globalization tendencies (Section 2.3), as well as on prospects of a general loss of quality (Section 2.4).

2.1   Mass Higher Education

Higher — or tertiary — education was once an elite phenomenon. Prior to World War II, higher education was identified first and foremost with university education, encompassing certainly the leading polytechnic institutions or institutes of technology, and perhaps some prestigious non-university type curricula in the fields of music or art. The less prestigious polytechnic institutions or professional schools were considered part of secondary education, at least in continental Europe. For example, in West Germany in 1960 still less than 5% of the relevant age groups attended institutions of tertiary education[1] (Bundesminister für Bildung und Wissenschaft, 1991, pp. 31f), and in countries surrounding Germany — in the UK, in The Netherlands or in Switzerland, for instance — the situation was quite similar.

After World War II, student numbers generally grew for a range of reasons (Clotfelter, Ehrenberg, Getz, & Siegfried, 1991; Herbst et al., 2002, pp. 91–92) that fed on each other: the rebuilding of post-war societies and subsequent economic growth, the rise of consumer economies, and a frequently virulent competition between Western nations and the Eastern Block. All these demanded educated work forces and led to a generous funding of higher education systems. Conversely, an increasingly educated population changed educational expectations and political agendas, which in turn fostered tertiary education and influenced participation rates. Higher education defined itself anew or was seen in a new light: portions of secondary education were redefined as tertiary education, not uniformly, but over time and at different speeds depending on the country.

In 1970 *Martin Trow* postulated substantive changes in the character of higher education systems once participation rates exceeded a threshold of 15%, and he foresaw further major changes should enrollment rates exceed 50% (Trow, 1970): the notion of 'mass higher education' was born. Basic to the concept of mass higher education is the notion that

- ever higher proportion of young adults will attend institutions of tertiary education, attracted by better income prospects of graduates or

---

[1]If one includes non-university level tertiary education, a total of slightly under 6% of the relevant age group (age 22 to 23) were enrolled.

driven into educational institutions by lessened occupational opportunities in blue color occupations;

- greater proportions of non-traditional students will attend institutions of higher learning, to complete studies that were interrupted because of parenthood, to pursue new professional directions, or to retool one's own education and training in the course of life-long learning (*l'éducation permanente*).

If ever higher proportions of the relevant age groups attend institutions of tertiary education, and if greater proportions of non-traditional, 'mature' students attend colleges and universities, student numbers swell, and the pressure toward diversity within tertiary education increases. Diversity in educational opportunities or lines of training is needed to address the specific profiles of a growing and increasingly heterogeneous student population.

However, diversity is also a matter of definition, or missions pursued. As the boundaries between secondary and tertiary education shifted, and as the efforts to integrate former lines of secondary education into tertiary education became an international trend, a redefinition of educational levels took place. This not only affected the education statistics; it also affected the perception of educational opportunities. This redefinition process is ongoing and has led to a range of solutions in different countries. In the UK, the former binary system of higher education has been abandoned, *Polytechnics* have been elevated to university status, and a unitary system has been formed. In Switzerland, a binary system was devised decades after the corresponding reforms in Germany, and *Technica* were integrated into higher education as *Fachhochschulen* only a few years ago[2]. Unitary, binary or trinary systems will constantly have to adapt to changing circumstances in various ways, but two aspects appear clear:

- Growth in higher education will slow down, in some countries earlier, in other's later. In the US, for example, forms of saturation are visible already.

---

[2]The process in Switzerland is ongoing, in the sense that a range of schools and curricula have yet to be integrated into *Fachhochschulen*. Furthermore, the forces which led to the abandonment of the binary system in the UK can now also be felt in Switzerland: both levels are to pursue teaching *and* research, and *Fachhochschulen* call themselves frequently (in English) 'Universities' of Applied Sciences instead of 'Colleges' of Applied Sciences. In Germany or Austria, for instance, the infatuation with titles led to the creation of the *Universitätsprofessor*. See in this respect the remarks later on (page 22) on the 'signaling effect'.

- Diversity of institutional missions and educational programs play an important role within respective strata of higher education. Permeability between strata has to be offered, and the 'hard-wired' linking of educational or professional programs and higher education strata needs to be broken. Certain educational and professional programs are only offered at one of the strata of higher education. While it might be clear that medical education is a prerogative of university education, it is unclear why industrial design, education or social work cannot be offered in some European countries at the university level[3].

Participation or Enrollment Rates. In the US, to provide a more detailed historical vision, participation rates in higher education were higher than in Europe for a number of reasons: the European dividing line between secondary and tertiary education followed slightly different notions; the US lacked developed apprentice systems that were prevalent in a range of European countries; and just before the end of World War II, initiatives were launched to strengthen research and to ease access to higher education through the so-called G.I. (or Veterans') Bill[4]. US higher education in the late 19th and early 20th century encompassed a tradition of college education, molded after the models of Oxford and Cambridge, and graduate education, emulating the German university. Part of what in Europe would fall under secondary education was falling under college education in the US: general or liberal education in colleges or universities, or the preparation for non-academic professions in vocational technical institutions or junior and community colleges.

In the US, high school completion rates increased from 51% in 1940 to 70% in 1960, and they have remained around this level ever since (Snyder & Hoffman, 2003, Table 103, p. 127). College enrollment of high school graduates increased from 45% in 1960 to 62% in 2001 (Snyder & Hoffman, 2003, Table 184, p. 223) and, hence, college participation rates must have reached a level of roughly 30% in 1960 and 43% around the turn of the millennium. Actually, the National Center for Education Statistics (NCES) reports slightly lower enrollment rates, namely 25.5% of the 18- to 24-year olds in degree-granting institutions in the year 1967 and 36.2% in the year 2001 (Snyder & Hoffman, 2003, Table 186, p. 225). From 1960 to 2000, the US

---

[3]See "The Founding and Funding of Disciplines" in this chapter, and in particular page 38.

[4]The Servicemen's Readjustment Act (Public Law 78-346), which is known as the G.I. Bill, was passed in 1944.

college population grew by 130%[5], but the actual growth took place during the decade of 1960–70, which was considered part of the 'golden age' of academia (Freeland, 1992): the growth in this period alone was 88%, while the growth during the subsequent three decades amounted to 22% (Snyder & Hoffman, 2003, Table 184, p. 223). To be sure, further enrollment in higher education was due to increasing numbers of non-standard, older students who returned to university and colleges in the course of an increasing awareness of life-long learning (*l'éducation permanente*): to 'retool' or to refocus themselves, to complete a degree after the children had grown up, for mid-career training (also often associated with unemployment or a change of professions).

In Germany, enrollment growth was even more pronounced in the post World War II era than in the US because of initially low enrollment rates. Between 1960 and 1990, university sector enrollment within the confines of the German Federal Republic tripled, and if we include the non-university sector within higher education, the growth factor was 2.7 (Bundesminister für Bildung und Wissenschaft, 1991, p. 31). In the decade of 1980–90, participation rates in tertiary education — i.e., universities, art schools, and *Fachhochschulen* — increased from 16% to close to 22%, and in the subsequent decade — i.e., the last decade of the past century, and within the Germany of today — to roughly 28% (Bundesminister für Bildung und Forschung, 2001, p. 154). In this past decade, growth leveled off. The now unified Germany has experienced even a negative enrollment growth of roughly 9% in spite of increasing participation rates, namely, because of smaller populations within the relevant age cohorts (OECD, 2003, Chart C2.2, p. 262).

In Switzerland, to provide another example, greater proportions are completing high school (or secondary school II): while in 1980 close to 11% of the relevant cohorts completed high school, at the turn of the century the numbers were 19% for the *Gymnasium* and 9% for the *Berufsmatur* (Fröhlicher-Güggi, 2002, p. 10). Roughly 30% of the relevant age groups enter an institution of higher education (Fröhlicher-Güggi, 2002, p. 15): 21% try to pursue a university education, and 10% enroll in a non-university type of tertiary education.

Binary Systems and Growth. In many European nations, a form of binary system is in place (see Table 2.1). Binary systems evolved through the grouping of non-university type institutions into a new higher education sector. Binary systems may have separate entry routes for students (such

---

[5]The college population is defined here by enrollment in the age bracket of the 16 to 24 year old.

Table 2.1: DISTRIBUTION OF STUDENT POPULATION: by Type of Higher
Education Institution (1996 head-count) (Huisman & Kaiser, 2001a, 2001b;
Klemperer, 2001)

COUNTRY (REGION):	university (%)	non-university (%)
Austria	98	2
Denmark	30	70
Finland	76	24
Flanders	38	62
France	58	42
Germany	76	24
Netherlands	37	63
Sweden	63	37
United Kingdom	100	0

as in The Netherlands, Denmark, or Switzerland). They exclude doctoral
studies in institutions other than universities, and they allow or even try
to foster applied research in their 'colleges of applied sciences' (except in
Denmark) (Huisman & Kaiser, 2001b, p. 26)[6]. The distribution of students
in university and non-university institutions varies from country to country, as Table 2.1 shows, and the figures are more indicative of the system
chosen than of the state of affairs in higher education. In the UK, a former
binary system was integrated into a unitary system. In unitary systems,
or in systems with a dominance of university education (i.e. in Austria),
common standards are difficult — if not impossible — to maintain, and
stratification or diversification paths will have to be pursued within the
respective higher education systems.

Enrollment growth is a function of population growth and enrollment
rates. Immediately following World War II, there was the so-called 'baby
boom', which was still visible a generation later. During the last quarter
of the past century, most Western nations experienced very low population
growth: they had birth rates which did not suffice to replicate the existing
population and immigration (often of adults) made up the difference. In

---

[6]The concept of (applied) research without access to doctoral (and post-doctoral) students appears inconsistent and will, in all likelihood, require a revision in the form of a
clear separation of teaching institutions from teaching-research — and doctorate granting
— institutions.

Table 2.2: GROWTH RATE OF STUDENT POPULATION: in % per an-
num, by Type of Institution, based on (Huisman & Kaiser, 2001b)
and Bundesamt für Statistik (`www.statistik.admin.ch/stat_ch/ber15/-`
`donbas_hsw/studbas_d.htm`).

COUNTRY (REGION):	Period	university (%)	non-university (%)
Austria	1990-98	1.7	n.a.
Austria	1994–98	n.a.	183.4
Denmark	1993-98	–2.4	7.4
Finland	1992–97	3.2	153.5
Flanders	1984–96	1.4	2.6
France	1995–98	–1.5	1.0
Germany	1990–98	0.2	2.0
Netherlands	1990–98	–1.4	2.1
Sweden	1987–98	5.1	n.a.
Switzerland	1997–03	2.7	44.1
United Kingdom	1992–96	4.8	n.a.
United Kingdom	1988–92	7.1	16.0

some countries at the end of the past century, growth in enrollment rates
was not enough to offset the shrinking cohorts, and some countries — e.g.,
Denmark, France, or The Netherlands — experienced a negative enrollment growth in the university sector (see Table 2.2). A certain saturation
may have been reached in many countries within the university sector, and
mass higher education has slowed down. Further growth can be expected
in the non-university sector (where it exists), and with the growth and ma-
turity of this sector, both the university and non-university sectors will be
able to redefine their missions and attract new students in accordance with
their clarified profiles.

2.2 Funding Crises

The funding crisis which is so common in higher education systems is due
to two primary factors: mass higher education, and the labor intensive
character of higher education. These two factors, accented by a backlog
of capital needed for the upkeep of — and new investments in — infrastructure, are responsible for rising costs in higher education. Furthermore,
state appropriations are declining, at least in relative terms, because of competing commitments (OECD, 2003, Chart B4.2, p. 225; Table B4.1, p. 227). It

is not surprising, then, that increasing costs and falling revenues are generating a discussion on new forms of funding higher education.

Tuition and Fees. In Europe where tuition and fees have played a relatively minor role in the funding of higher education, at least up to now, a discussion has come to the foreground with unusual force, and various proponents are demanding a reassessment of funding policies in general. In Germany, private universities (like that of Witten-Herdecke) and their funding modes are seen as models for public universities; in the UK, higher education and funding modes are being reassessed (Clarke, 2003); and in Switzerland proposals have been issued to raise tuition and fees (Arbeits-kreis Kapital und Wirtschaft, 2004; Stembeck, 2004; Weber, 2004). But the reassessment of the student body's role in financing European higher education is not a completely recent phenomenon, and there have been proposals which have gained credence and provided the basis for further discussions (Erhardt & Müller-Böling, 1998). The system proposed jointly by the *Stifterverband für die Deutsche Wissenschaft* and the *Centrum für Hochschulentwicklung* requires the following:

- To compensate for private returns resulting from tertiary education, students will have to pay tuition and fees.

- Equal opportunity demands that nobody should be excluded from access to higher education institutions due to 'objective' financial reasons. Subjective barriers should be minimized. The system of tuition and fees ought to be compatible with the general social agenda.

- The system has to make a substantial net-contribution to the funding of tertiary education, and in particular to its educational mission.

- The system ought to provide economic incentives for all concerned. In the case of students, the system ought to provide an incentive for performance. In the case of institutions, the system should provide an incentive to focus on educational demand and quality.

- Administrative costs associated with the implementation of a system should remain small. The system has to be feasible, and it requires broad political support.

Responding to the requirements listed, I shall start by taking a closer look at the third. What is a "substantial net-contribution" in this context? We know from the US experience that in the case of research universities tuition and fees contribute roughly 25% to 30% of the funds necessary to run an institution (Commission on Higher Education, 2002b, p. 104–106)[7], but scholarships and fellowships may amount to 10% to 15%, leaving a net gain of roughly 15%. In order to assess these figures and place them in the proper context, we ought to keep in mind that the US society has a long standing tradition of tuition and fees, but also a long standing tradition of philanthropy in higher education, which is practically absent in Europe. In the case of tuition and fees, middle-class families save early to send their children to college, and these savings are part of money management — not unlike pension schemes (Selingo, 2004). Furthermore, to enroll students from underprivileged backgrounds, various forms of financial assistance — in the form of grants, scholarships or loans — are offered. In order to introduce tuition and fees with the goal of having them make a substantial contribution to higher education institutions, we ought to be cognizant of co-requisites and possible side effects and implications.

Recently, the *Arbeitskreis of Kapital und Wirtschaft* proposed to increase current low level tuition and fees in Switzerland by a factor of four or five, to roughly Fr. 5,500.– per school-year. Is this substantial? If we presume that roughly half of that sum would flow out again in the form of financial assistance, the contribution to Swiss research universities would not exceed 3–5% of their annual budget[8]. In other words, we cannot expect 'substantial' contributions from this financial source, at least not at the envisaged level. If substantial contributions are considered, further increases of tuition and fees would have to be mandated. These increases could easily be warranted, because they simply "compensate for private returns resulting from tertiary education" (see the first requirement above). Furthermore, higher levels of tuition and fees would help students to focus on their studies and to perform better (fourth requirement).

The argument that higher education is primarily a private good, and that the beneficiaries of this good, the students, should pay for it, has become quite common. Such a stance is taken, for instance, by *Luc E. Weber* (Weber, 2004, p. 193):

> "[...] higher education is wrongly considered politically as a public good, which it is not. For a public economist, the two characteristics of a public good — that is [non-rival in consumption, and non-excludability] — are not met

---

[7]In the case of the University of South Carolina Medical School, tuition and fees amount to 4% of all revenues.

[8]In the case of the Swiss Federal Institute of Technology (ETHZ), the proposed contribution of tuition and fees would amount to roughly 3% of their annual budget (not including capital investments).

[...]. Therefore, there is no necessity to provide it for free, as long as access to all capable students from low-income backgrounds is made possible through targeted support, in particular grants and loans, and that due account is taken that the effort made by those studying has a positive impact even on those who do not (in technical terms, produces some external benefits)".

Weber describes a 'pure' as opposed to the more common 'impure' public good (and acknowledges the existence of external effects). Furthermore, he appears to negate the fact that some of the produce of higher education — and in particular of research universities — are indeed 'pure' public goods, namely knowledge[9].

The argument is amplified by the observation that higher income segments of the society profit more than others from the subsidies flowing into the higher education sector (LaRocque, 2003; Weber, 2004). This observation cannot be disputed, since in most societies students from better-off backgrounds are over-represented. But the argument negates the observation that education, and higher education, have strong positive, external effects (Bowen & Fincher, 1996). Not only do those profit from education who are directly involved, others profit as well. This is particularly true for higher education. Societies with a well educated work-force prosper. They are more inventive and adaptable, more politically balanced, and socially stable. The argument that higher education is primarily a private good also obfuscates the fact that private returns differ depending on course majors and future careers. Lawyers and M.D.'s might earn more later on in their careers than engineers or architects, and these in turn might earn more than social scientists or linguists. If we were to differentiate tuition and fees by disciplinary fields, and some institutions might want to pursue this avenue[10], economically less advantaged students would be doubly hit because they are generally more risk averse — and would therefore be less inclined to take on a loan[11]. This could lead to a further reduction of students from working class backgrounds in high tuition fields.

If higher education leads to higher personal income, taxes — and progressive tax rates — could be used to recoup the state investment necessary to fund higher education. An equity issue does not pose itself in the case of *Bill Gates* who has not completed his college education and whose taxes are

---

[9]One can think of knowledge as a private good, but not in an 'open' — i.e. modern, democratic — society.

[10]US universities generally do not differentiate their tuition and fees depending on course major.

[11]See: "Fear of Debt Deterring Would-be Students, Universities UK Survey Reveals" (06 December 2002), www.universitiesuk.ac.uk/mediareleases/show.asp?MR=330.

now used to fund higher education: Microsoft is unthinkable in a world other than ours. An equity issue does not pose itself in the cases of skilled or unskilled blue-color workers who have not attended universities, unless their own education was hampered by lack of educational opportunities or by economic barriers. If people earn high incomes, they earn this income not only because of their own proficiency, but also because other people — and former generations — have created wealth which can be transferred: there is a demand for goods and services as well as the ability to pay for them.

If higher education is seen primarily as a private good, and if tuition and fees are raised as a consequence of this stance, pressure will mount to reduce taxes. If tax income falls, public funding will become increasingly volatile and pressure will mount to increase tuition and fees: a vicious circle. No doubt, a good portion of our student population is in a position to pay higher tuition and fees. However, a good portion of the same population is not, and there may be not enough merit scholarships around to fund their education. Furthermore (and in contrast to the second requirement), the equity issue separates the average students coming from prosperous and less prosperous backgrounds: both may have no access to merit scholarships, but the first class is in a position to pay college tuition while the second class is not, or only under great strain[12]. There can be no doubt that higher tuition and fees would negatively affect the demand for higher education, and students from lower income groups in our society would be affected the most, to the detriment of their own intellectual growth and development of talent, and to the detriment of the society at large. If tuition and fees were significantly raised in continental Europe, students would look more closely at the quality of the education they are getting, and many would opt to attend institutions overseas[13].

---

[12]The argument that loans provide a solution for the needy is not really convincing, particularly in the case of students with the goal to pursue an academic career. Their education stretches over a prolonged period of time, covering doctoral and post-doctoral studies, and overlapping civil commitments such as marriage and parenthood. In these cases at least, loans are a tremendous burden, and perhaps not all students pursuing an academic career (eventually) will have access to merit scholarships. That is the reason why the US National Institute of Health (NIH) has started a loan repayment program; see: www.lrp.nih.gov/.

[13]Anecdotal evidence suggests that this is already the case today. Children from prosperous academic backgrounds — in Austria, Germany, or Switzerland — pursue not only their post-graduate education abroad, they enroll immediately at a reputable college in the US or the UK. This 'emigration' is generally not permanent, with social benefits accruing when the graduates return home. But it is an indication of weakness on the part of the home institutions, particularly if emigrating students outnumber immigrants. The argu-

Finally, tuition and fees are said to serve a pedagogic purpose (fourth requirement): higher tuition and fees should help students to focus on their studies and perform better. If a service is free of charge, or inexpensive, it may not be valued enough, thus leading to a lack of focus. In the case of European higher education systems which practice open access, at least for a broader substratum of a cohort[14], one can observe a certain prevalence of non-focused studies which are associated with frequent changes of study majors, prolonged study periods, and higher drop-out rates[15]. But there are other, more appropriate means to combat these deficiencies in the educational process, and before these other means are discussed and properly evaluated or tested, one should not focus on tuition and fees as a vehicle to help students to focus on their studies[16].

Private and Social Returns on Education. The position on tuition and fees is generally linked to one's perception of private and social returns on education. "Education pays" (Commission on Higher Education, 2002b, p. 43) is the common notion: as one climbs the educational ladder, earnings increase, at least in statistical terms. People with a Doctorate may earn 50% more than those who have completed their education with a Bachelor's Degree, and people with a professional degree may earn even more[17]. Male graduates of research universities may earn, depending on the country, between close to 40% (Norway) and 150% (Hungary) as much as those who

ment that higher tuition and fees would force institutions to look more closely at quality issues (fourth requirement) might contain some truth, but it is actually redundant. I would hope that institutions would look at quality issues regardless.

[14]Namely those who have graduated from high-school (i.e. *Gymnasium*).

[15]Changes of study majors happen in the US with some frequency too. This kind of flexibility in the system is, in my opinion, a good thing: it helps the student to find his or her field of interest, and it advances trans-disciplinary approaches. Unfocused studies cannot only be tied to a lack of motivation on the part of the student. It may also have something to do with rigid curricula and a lack of guidance.

[16]Clearly, many students complete their secondary school years nowadays without having developed a proper idea on what to study: they are unsure of themselves and their role in society, and they have not been exposed to many professions and academic activities within the spectrum of disciplines. The problem may be exacerbated by recent tendencies to 'live' predominantly within one's generation. Here, cooperation between secondary schools and universities should be intensified to combat information deficits. And within the higher education sector, active admission management and recruitment (i.e. no open access) and the proper implementation of credit systems (to administer part-time studies) might prove instrumental in bringing about more focused studies. *Mantz Yorke* reports "that nearly 40% of non-completing full-time students in six higher education institutions in NW England said that poor choice of study programme was a contributory factor in their departure" (personal communication). See in this respect also (Yorke, 1999).

[17]US Data from the Occupational Outlook Quarterly, Spring 2002.

have just completed upper secondary schools, and in the case of female graduates the relative advantage ranges from close to 20% (Italy) to over 100% (UK) (OECD, 2003, Chart A14.1, p. 157)[18]. From an individual point of view education pays if the additional years invested in education, i.e. the earnings foregone, are more than compensated by earnings later on during one's lifetime. And from an institutional point of view differences in pay are warranted on the basis of differences in expected productivity which can be tied to education, or wage differences simply reflect the supply and demand for various occupations.

If one looks at the case of the (average) individual, economists use costs and revenue streams to compute the private return on education, or the internal rate of return on the private investment. Educational investments on the part of a prospective student would be justified, for instance, as long as the internal rate of return on the investment exceeds the expected rate of return procured by a common alternative investment. And if the internal rate of return on private educational investment exceeds market rates (after taxes), there is space, as we have seen above, to raise tuition and fees. This argument is basically correct, as far as it goes, but it does not touch significant factors affecting private and social investments in higher education, primarily:

- differences in investment propensities and risk aversion separating students of disparate economic backgrounds, and

- external effects, positive as well as negative, which are associated with education.

While the relationship between education and economic growth has become a central focus of economic research during the past half century (Griliches, 2000, pp. 33–44), many issues remain under-researched, and the scope for interpretation remains large.

Apart from the private return on education, social returns on education as well as external effects, externalities, as the economist calls them, play a

---

[18]The relative advantage of university graduates over upper secondary school leavers is not always higher for males: in the cases of Canada, Ireland, Switzerland, Korea, Australia, Belgium and Norway females have a greater advantage. However, "[...] earning differentials between males and females with the same educational attainment remain substantial [...] Some of the gap in earnings between males and females may be explained by different choices of career and occupation, differences in the amount of time that males and females spend in the labor force, and the particularly high incidence of part-time work among females (OECD, 2003, p. 159).

role. Two forms of externalities require attention, namely the 'ability bias' and the 'signaling effect'. With regard to the former effect, *Zvi Griliches* (Griliches, 2000, p. 38) asks:

> To what extent [do] observed income differentials exaggerate the contribution of schooling because of positive correlation between native ability and the levels of schooling obtained by different groups in the population? There were conflicting views on this in the early to mid-1960s, and it is still an issue that has not been fully settled.

Education and educational levels attained generally reflect abilities: people with greater innate abilities have a tendency to reach higher levels of education. If one correlates earnings with education, one may not know whether the relation is causal or spurious, unless one controls for ability levels. Studies using twin samples focused on this topic and *Griliches* concludes that, "[i]f anything, the schooling coefficient is underestimated within the standard ordinary least squares (OLS) earnings equation framework". A recent study attempting to control for ability (Bonjour, Cherkas, Haskel, Hawkes, & Spector, 2002) used identical (female) UK twins to make these tests[19]. It came to the conclusion that if one excludes ability bias, education matters and the private return on education (for women) amounts to close to 8%. These results were similar to those of another study (Dearden, 1998), which obtained estimates for the private return on education for UK women. After controlling for ability and family background, the return also amounted to roughly 8%.

The second externality I listed affecting private and social returns to education is the 'signaling effect' (Spence, 1974). If wages are tied to educational levels obtained, and if educational levels are only loosely correlated with ability, innate or acquired, a signaling effect is in place. The loose correlation between education and proficiency may have a number of roots:

- people learn outside educational institutions, "on the job", as the saying goes, and they may acquire a professional proficiency far beyond what their initial training would suggest;

- economically less advantaged students may not have had the opportunity — or the mentorship — to invest in the kind and level of education which matched their talents[20];

---

[19]The study also controlled for other factors, such as birth-weight, smoking, and family characteristics.

[20]"[...] evidence for the United States suggests the payoff to investments in education are higher for more disadvantaged individuals" (Krueger & Lindahl, 2001).

- learning on how to learn should be a prime focus of higher education, and in particular of doctoral studies, but we cannot assume on an a priori basis that people with higher levels of education have greater insight or perform better[21].

In systems where signaling effects are common, able individuals may earn less and are less likely to be promoted than individuals of lesser talent and abilities but more formal training, to the detriment also of the society at large. Anecdotal evidence suggests that signaling effects are somewhat frequent, at least in Europe, and they may even provide a primary motivation to pursue an educational program. Signaling effects flourish whenever academic degrees — or positions — are taken as a cipher for (academic) accomplishment and understood as entitlement[22].

Apart from the private return on education, the social return on education can be analyzed from the perspective of two different definitions: one which defines social return in narrow terms, and a second with a broader meaning. The narrower definition takes account of productivity gains tied to the investment in education from all sources, and it includes the corresponding costs that are relevant, i.e., not only those which accrue to the student herself, but also those of the other actors or stakeholders. The broader definition of social returns is much more difficult to measure. It generally tries to take account of "noneconomic benefits [associated with the investment in education], such as lower crime, better health, more social cohesion and more informed and effective citizens" (OECD, 2003, pp. 162–163). Furthermore, it attempts to include social benefits attributed to the increased productivity due to higher education which are not fully accounted for by wages. Generally, such social benefits are attributed to various agglomeration economies which reflect education and associated innovation, but also

---

[21]We may make these conclusions on a statistical basis, otherwise formal education would be ineffective and perhaps pointless. But if we place too much emphasis on formal credentials, we may oversee the talent of people who pursued, or had to pursue, unconventional career paths.

[22]In a former report (Herbst et al., 2002) and a subsequent paper (Herbst, 2004b), the negative impact of inordinate hierarchies in higher education institutions was addressed, a theme which is linked to the signaling effect. While excessive hierarchies and signaling effects are common, their negative impact is rarely addressed, as if both were natural — unalterable — ingredients of our industrial societies. In a recent interview, *Bruno Staffelbach*, a Professor of Business at the University of Zürich, and a one-star General in the new Swiss Army, remarked — perhaps in jest (Mühlethaler, 2004): "Die Armee und die Universität unterscheiden sich nicht so stark. Auch die akademische Welt ist sehr hierarchisch [...]" ("The army and the University are not that different. The academic world, too, is strongly hierarchically structured [...]"; my translation).

Table 2.3: PRIVATE INTERNAL RATES OF RETURN AND SOCIAL RATES OF RETURN TO TERTIARY EDUCATION (IN %): by Country, and Males (M) and Females (F) (1999–2000) (OECD, 2003, Tables A14.3 and A14.4, p. 167)

	private return		social return	
	M	F	M	F
COUNTRY:	(%)	(%)	(%)	(%)
Canada	8.1	9.4	6.8	7.9
Denmark	13.9	10.1	6.3	4.2
France	12.2	11.7	13.2	13.1
Germany	9.0	8.3	6.5	6.9
Italy	6.5	n.a.	7.0	n.a.
Japan	7.5	6.7	6.7	5.7
Netherlands	12.0	12.3	10.0	6.3
Sweden	11.4	10.8	7.5	5.7
United Kingdom	17.3	15.2	15.2	13.6
United States	14.9	14.7	13.7	12.3

business cultures and legal structures. (Lampe, 1988; Fujita, Krugman, & Venables, 2001; Fujita & Thisse, 2002; Grübler, 1998; Saxenian, 1994)

Because of the measurement problems mentioned above, OECD figures on social returns on education reflect the narrow definition. Social returns (in this narrow sense) are generally slightly lower than private returns (see Table 2.3), with exceptions[23], but they are above risk-free real interest rates. The rates, private as well as social, differ from country to country. High rates of returns, such as those in the United Kingdom, appear to be associated with shorter study periods, and conversely, lower rates, such as those in Germany, seem to reflect the comparably long study durations. OECD estimates that "if the average length of tertiary studies were to be shortened by one year without compromising quality, the internal rate of return for males in the countries under review would increase by 1 to 5 percentage points, if all other factors were held constant" (OECD, 2003, p. 161).

The observer also notes (in Table 2.2) some significant differences between private and social rates of return, such as those referring to Denmark or Sweden. These higher differentials may be due to labor shortages

---

[23]OECD lists France and Italy among the countries with higher social than private returns (Table 2.2).

for university graduates in general, driving up, perhaps only temporarily, their earnings; or it may be a labor shortage for particularly able and motivated individuals. In the case of singular professions, we may have professions characterized by higher contributions to the economy, but with lower private returns on education, and vice versa. Engineers and lawyers are prime examples for this phenomenon, with engineers generally making a larger — and to some extent indirect — contribution to economic growth, and lawyers reaping the greater private rewards for their direct contribution (Murphy, Shleifer, & Vishny, 1991).

Reviewing the literature, including various meta-analyses (Barro, 2001; Bowles, Gintis, & Osborne, 2001; Krueger & Lindahl, 2001; Bils & Klenow, 2000; Hanushek & Kimko, 2000), I come to the conclusion that the economic profession is far from presenting a clear picture on the relationship between education and growth. The issues studied are far too complex, and the diversities separating the various countries too great, to come up — up to now, one has to add — with a simple theory or model which would catch the various aspects that affect the relationship under investigation. But the studies, irrespective of methodological approaches and data bases used, provide us with a heightened awareness concerning the interplay which governs the relationship between education and economic growth. In a strict sense, schooling may not simply drive growth, growth may also drive schooling (Bils & Klenow, 2000): education is seen as a motor of economic development; and conversely, growth affects constant changes in economic sectors and employment structures, with corresponding changes in higher education and life-long learning. "Education", as *Frederick Harbison* and *Charles Myers* suggest metaphorically, "is both the seed and the flower of economic development" (Harbison & Myers, 1965, p. xi)[24]. These two aspects cannot be easily separated, and the two together form an interactive system which shapes our respective cultures and economies.

If one wants to capture the economic merit of education and assess the social returns on higher education, in its broader sense, one has to focus on the systemic aspects just sketched. Economic science appears to not yet be ready to make such an assessment in non-ambiguous, quantitative terms, but certain partial results emerge nevertheless (Krueger & Lindahl, 2001):

- First, one has to recognize that education, and higher education, generally have a long latency to take effect. While the outcome of changes in education over shorter periods of only a few years is frequently imperceptible, and while we know that certain changes require decades

---

[24]Cited after (Krueger & Lindahl, 2001, p. 1131).

to take effect, impacts over periods of 10 to 20 years can generally be
seen.

- Second, available evidence suggests that "the [social] payoff to investments in education are higher for more disadvantaged individuals"
  (Krueger & Lindahl, 2001, p. 1107). While such a general statement
  has its primary validity regarding primary and secondary education,
  it retains its validity with regard to tertiary education.

- Third, studies based on individual-level data on education and income do not allow us to conclude that social returns to schooling exceed private returns. In order to address social returns, a broader
  framework of analysis becomes necessary. Macro-economic models
  indicate that if the relationship between economic growth and schooling is followed over decades, large returns on educational investments have already been measured, "equal to three or four times the
  private return to schooling estimated within most countries" (Krueger
  & Lindahl, 2001, p. 1120).

2.3   Virtual Tendencies

In recent years, hope was expressed that technological development, and
specifically the new virtual tendencies within higher education, would lead
a way out of the funding crisis. The hope is based on a notion of higher
education as an industry which could follow a path from labor intensive to
capital intensive production.

But higher education, viewed as an industry, does not appear to follow
the common path of industrial development. Industrial development came
into being by exploiting natural resources which were unevenly distributed
over the globe, and the subsequent industrial bases developed at the locations where natural resources were harnessed. Early industries were labor intensive, but in the course of industrial development, machinery —
or capital, as the economists would say — was substituted for labor and
industries became increasingly capital intensive. Industries for which the
substitution of capital for labor proved less economically feasible moved to
places where labor was cheaper and, by doing so, provided an economic
growth incentive for developing nations. Developed nations have since
transformed themselves into post-industrial societies with a focus on service functions, and they have passed the threshold of a new knowledge
era.

While higher education is bound to play a dominant role in the formation of future knowledge societies, it has not followed the pattern of other industries, at least not up to now. Although higher education has become much more capital intensive, capital has been used as a co-requisite of — and not as a substitute for — labor. The labor intensiveness of higher education has remained rather stable over the past half century, at least in the successful research universities, and where the labor input was reduced, generally a drop in the quality of instruction or research resulted (Weber, 2004, p. 180). Following *William Baumol*, colleges and universities work in a way resembling string quartets (Massy, 1996, p. 52), in that their means of production are those of times past. For the lovers of baroque music as well as for everybody else, *Baumol's* view should not be read primarily as a critique but as a simple statement of fact. Tendencies to substitute capital for labor or to make use of economies of scale in higher education have emerged in the past, of course, but their impact was imperceptible because the freed resources were immediately absorbed in an expanding enterprise. The common use of textbooks in colleges may serve as an example whereby less time is required in the preparation of course materials and possible scripts, but the efficiency gains are instantly reinvested to increase the quality of instruction or the amount of research activities[25].

With the continuing spread and development of information & communication technologies (ICTs) new possibilities are emerging to increase the productivity of higher education and to substitute capital for labor. The new possibilities frequently run under the label of the 'virtual university' (Robins & Webster, 2003) or the 'virtual campus' (Herbst & Schmitt, 2001), but it is unclear to what extent these new developments are real substitutes for existing activities and to what extent ICTs will change the very core of the colleges and research universities as we know them. More likely, the virtual university will expand into uncharted territories and new market segments and will provide services on top of those provided by the existing institutions. It is difficult to assess the future, even over a relatively short time period of 30–35 years (Bell, 1967) or if only technology is to be assessed (Kahn & Wiener, 1967)[26], but my feeling is that the virtual univer-

---

[25]The use of textbooks is not as widespread in Europe as it is in the US. This is partially a language issue, in that appropriate textbooks in a given language are not always available, but frequently also a cultural issue: faculty may prefer to use their own scripts.

[26]Looking at earlier forecasts can be an instructive "back to the future" exercise. Of the 100 technical innovations *Herman Kahn* and *Anthony J. Wiener* cite in (Kahn & Wiener, 1967, pp. 711–716), many — at least three quarters — have come to fruition; others, perhaps fortunately, have not.

sity debate exhibits some parallels to a discussion which was prominent in the 1970s and the 80s and which was feeding on the hope that communication could serve as a substitute for urban and interregional commuting and transportation. Only sophistry would claim that communication technologies have reduced and acted as substitutes of transportation. In fact, both systems expanded significantly, and while we can detect, in particular cases, forms of substitution, it is more likely that the spread of communication technologies has been instrumental in accelerating transportation growth.

Martin Trow (Trow, 2003b) identifies five defining characteristics of ICT which "are likely to survive changes in the technology itself". The first of these characteristics is the speed by which ICTs develop, affecting not only disposition and planning but also the underlying decision-making or legal structures (National Research Council, 2000). The second is a tendency to "weaken and blur institutional and intellectual boundaries of all kinds": between pure and applied research, between non-profit and profit seeking affairs, between teaching and research, between disciplines, between localized and global work. The third refers to a renewed and extended democratization of higher education; the fourth to widely varying impacts on disciplines, academic subjects and levels of education; and the fifth characteristic refers to different ways with which ICTs reach students of varying abilities and motivation. If we were to delve into these characteristics and explore some details, we would quickly see the enormous potential for change, both within existing institutions as well as regarding new providers or agents of higher education.

In the context of the current debate on the impact of ICTs in higher education, distance-education stands in the foreground. In the US, for instance, 56% of all higher education institutions — or even 89% of all public 4-year-institutions — offer distance-education courses (The Editor, 2003, p. 14), but all indicators point to the fact that we are observing an experimental scene[27]. Various technologies are used in support of distance-education[28], some of which pass probably as self-study guides and cannot properly count as representing the 'new' technologies. However, it is clear that there is potential in the field of knowledge or skill transfer, particularly at the propædeutic or vocational levels. Entire new student populations can be

---

[27]The figures cited refer to the academic year 2000–01. In that year, over 125,000 different courses were offered, with an average enrollment of 24 students per course!

[28]Two-way video with two-way audio, one-way video with two-way audio, one-way prerecorded video, internet (with live-interaction, or without live-interaction), CD-ROMs, et cetera.

addressed, particularly people who lack easy geographic access to higher education institutions[29] or retirees trying to keep abreast with the new information technologies[30]. In the course of teaching alliances which bind together two or more institutions, one course may serve all the institutions; in the context of shared library resources, students of differing institutions have access to the same pools of information; and in the research field, researchers in different institutions or nations may have joint access to shared laboratory or experimental data.

Having made this statement, I do not wish to discount the strong impact of virtual tendencies on higher education or research; nor do I claim that virtual tendencies will not transform higher education. They will compete with traditional modes of teaching and research[31], and virtual institutions or institutional branches will compete with 'brick-and-mortar' institutions. Virtual tendencies in higher education will expand with the general expansion of ICT, but they will not, in all likelihood, change the core values of higher education nor the general setup of research universities. As *Neil L. Rudenstine* remarks: "No one should believe that electronic communication can be — or should be — a substitute for direct human contact" (Rudenstine, 2001, p. 124)[32]. And further [p. 121]:

> In most cases [...] the new technology acts primarily as a powerful supplement to — and reinforcement of — the major methods that faculty and students have discovered, over the course of a very long period of time, to be unusually effective forms of teaching and learning in higher education.

---

[29]People living in low density areas, for instance, such as in Canada or Australia.

[30]This market, in Germany or Switzerland for instance, is relegated to the *Volkshochschulen* or the new *Seniorenuniversitäten*.

[31]It is clear that in the research fields, virtual tendencies will have a great impact. More and more data repositories will be created, giving researchers and scholars all over the world access to documents or experimental data to analyze. In addition, communication in the research fields will be eased to the point where we barely can see differences in local and virtual communication. These data repositories and communication options will help inter-institutional and international collaborations; they will help in the mobility of faculty, students and staff; but they will not act as a substitute for well-grounded local institutions. One should also note that the eased access to — and the spreading of — information does not simplify the research, and it doesn't make it less expensive.

[32]Still, *Guy Neave* refers to a dangerous tendency to "unbundle" teaching, learning, and research: "The separation of knowledge transmitted from the social experience incorporated in 'grouped' learning is not just a breakpoint in the history of pedagogy. It also raises a wider-ranging question, that of social cohesion, solidarity and community awareness in the Knowledge Society itself, just as it raises the question of which community and how defined such a socio-technical construct should serve". See (Neave, 2002; de Boer & others, 2002).

But most importantly in the context of the theme of the present volume, virtual tendencies will greatly affect governance and management of higher education systems, and conversely, properly governed and managed systems of higher education will be better prepared to take on the challenges of the still embryonic information & communication technologies (see Chapters 5 and 6).

2.4   The Quality Slide

While the hope for a salvation of higher education through virtual tendencies must be discounted, higher education has to fight a drop in quality: mass higher education, coupled with restricted resources, is likely to be accompanied by a reduction in the quality of education — and by implication, also of research:

- Broader spectra of students have been attending universities, some of whom are unprepared, academically or even emotionally, to pursue courses of their choice;

- research universities may have catered to the 'wrong' student populations, in the sense that there has been a mismatch between students' aspirations and institutional expectations, at least partially, and university — or higher education — systems seem to have been lacking the diversity necessary to cater properly to the diversified student population;

- because higher education institutions — and in particular universities — have been under-financed and because their mission has been set poorly, quality of education and research have been stagnating or even tumbling.

Therefore, as higher portions of the relevant cohorts enter tertiary education, more resources have to be allocated, or efficiency gains have to materialize to offset insufficient resources. In the past, societies were generally in a position to increase the GDP portion that they allocated to higher education, in part because increased funding in the field of higher education spawned economic growth. But major efficiency gains, at least those resulting from a possible shift to more capital intensive educational systems, do not appear to be on the horizon, particularly if one looks at research universities. With universal access around the corner in a range of nations, the growth of tertiary education will slow or level off, but costs will have a tendency to rise further, partially because of the labor intensiveness of higher education and partially because traditional higher education will take on new missions, such as lifelong learning (*l'éducation permanente*). And finally, rising costs in higher education will continue to compete with other worthy causes on the public agenda.

Achievement in Primary and Secondary Schools. I shall digress for a moment and address the issue of quality in the context of pre-tertiary education. Quality in higher education is a difficult concept to measure or to assess. There are primarily two reasons which account for this difficulty: the non-standard nature of higher education, and the continuing expansion of higher education. In contrast, primary and secondary schools (of level I) are much more standardized for comparative purposes and they have, in our hemispheres at least, not been expanding any more[33]. It might, hence, be instructive to look at the factors which affect scholastic achievement at the pre-tertiary level first.

Achievements of primary or secondary school students are much better researched than at the tertiary level (OECD, 2001; Mullis et al., 2001; Burton & Ramist, 2001),   giving rise to further studies on pupils' attainment levels (Akerlof & Kranton, 2002; Haveman & Wolfe, 1995). But in spite of the fact that the attainments of pupils are measured by a range of standard tests, it has proven difficult to establish a link tying achievement to resources. In a very detailed review of the literature, *Anna Vignoles et al.* (Vignoles, Levacic, Walker, Machin, & Reynolds, 2000) assessed the matter by looking at the various methodologies employed[34] as well as at various inputs possibly affecting pupils' achievement[35]. The authors demonstrate that it is very difficult to establish the input-output link: "The most serious problem in literature as a whole", they write, "is the potential endogeneity of educational quality" (Vignoles et al., 2000, p. 4). If family characteristics have an impact on achievement of pupils, and if characteristics of schools correlate with characteristics of families whose children attend these schools, "some of the apparent gain from additional school quality will in fact be a 'return' to pupils' socio-economic background". Conversely, if educational departments operate compensatory programs

---

[33]Practically all children attend these grades of schools.

[34]Regression models (value added models, simultaneous equation models, randomized experiments); production frontier models (stochastic frontier regression, data envelopment analysis).

[35]Expenditure per pupil, class size or teacher-pupil ratio, teacher characteristics (experience, education, salaries).

for weak learners in poorer areas, and "if the link between socio-economic characteristics and funding is not fully controlled for, a model will tend to generate a spurious negative correlation between school resources and achievement" [p. 5].

Indeed, family — or cultural — characteristics of pupils and students appear to play a major part in explaining their performance (Akerlof & Kranton, 2002). There are at least two aspects to keep in mind in this context: (i) the self-image of pupils and students as they fit into the culture of the school or college; and (ii) the norms and expectations of the institution with regard to measurement of educational progress. At least since *James S. Coleman* (Coleman, 1961), it has been amply demonstrated that if the self-image of pupil and student clash with the norms and expectations of the institution, educational progress will be curtailed. Schools have a tendency to use a self-referential system in that they classify their children as promising or weak learners depending on the grades these children receive. But grades are not only a matter of cognitive ability; grades are affected strongly by motivational factors, such as emotions or peer culture[36]. Furthermore, schools may use inappropriate — or ill-conceived — learning and grading norms, particularly in the case of minority pupils or children of immigrants. As *George A. Akerlof* and *Rachel E. Kranton* state: "Anthropological studies show how school routines and curricula can convey to [minority] students that there is something 'wrong' with them and their background" (Akerlof & Kranton, 2002, p. 1192). Feedback such as these messages reinforce learning deficiencies.

When confronted with the scantiness of results linking institutional input factors to scholastic achievement, we have to keep in mind the relative homogeneity of primary and secondary schools, at least in comparison to institutions of higher education. Curricular orientation is similar and while teacher-pupil ratios may differ from school to school and from period to period, they do not differ greatly: in schools not plagued by disciplinary problems, teacher-pupil ratios can easily be higher than in others and still reach educational targets. Differences in the results of the recent PISA assessment for many nations cannot be — and are not — explained on the basis of differing resource inputs (OECD, 2001). Not even elite schools, such as The Bronx High School of Science[37], differ greatly in their structural setup from other institutions. Elite schools primarily differ from other schools because

---

[36]Peer culture, as a counter-culture, may keep pupils from focusing on educational achievement.

[37]See: www.bxscience.edu.

they cater to fine pupils whose culture and ambitions match those of the school. Clearly, elite schools make — or should make — fine students better. But such a goal should be the mission of any school, namely to improve the scholastic or skills achievement of those enrolled[38].

I have ventured briefly into foreign territory to show that in the case of pre-tertiary education, the link between resources and educational achievement is not that significant. Other factors, not resource-based, appear to play a much more dominant role, factors which will have to be researched and experimented with in order to gain a deeper understanding of the mechanism involved in educational improvement. The setting of uniform and clear performance standards cannot serve as a substitute for such a deeper understanding, particularly when the schools are instructed to focus on meeting these standards — to the detriment of other educational or pedagogic goals[39]. The non-resource based factors which affect pre-tertiary education affect tertiary education — as we shall see — as well, and the possible solutions or remedies in higher education are not that dissimilar from those of pre-tertiary education.

Achievement in Tertiary Education. In contrast to primary and secondary education where vital resource inputs appear not to vary that much, resources for tertiary education do vary and the variations appear to affect educational achievement and research production. While there is no easy way to assess achievement in higher education directly[40], there is indirect evidence that quality is slipping in European research universities.

- First and foremost, European research output, as measured by standard bibliometric methods or by major prizes, is not on a par with that of the US (Da Pozzo & Roulin Perriard, 2003; CEST, 2002; Herbst, 2004b; Herbst et al., 2002; van Vught, 2004): there is an 'Atlantic split' (see Appendix C).

- Student-faculty ratios increased. In Germany, for instance, student-faculty ratios[41] at universities and art colleges increased from 47.5:1

---

[38]Perhaps the most significant factor explaining student achievement is the quality of teachers.

[39]The side effect of the turmoil caused by the PISA studies in various countries might be the following: the setting of ever stricter standards of achievement leave teachers fewer degrees of freedom to pursue a broader notion of education.

[40]In the US, the Graduate Record Exam (GRE) scores of college students are available and can be correlated with the Standard Aptitude Test (SAT) scores or matched with institutions, but in Europe no corresponding data appear to be available.

[41]Student-faculty ratios are defined as the quotient of the number of students enrolled,

in 1960 (Bundesminister für Bildung und Wissenschaft, 1991) to 54.7:1
in the year 2000 (Bundesminister für Bildung und Forschung, 2002).
While this increase might not amount to much, one ought to keep in
mind that corresponding student-faculty ratios at US research institutions vary around 10:1 to 25:1 (Herbst et al., 2002, Table 4.1 on p.
40)[42].

While one can observe a certain tendency to recognize this Atlantic split, if
only reluctantly (Richter, 2003), there are few proper clues as to why such a
gap might exist: too varied seem the European higher education systems,
too varied their funding regimes (Clark, 2004b). Still, funding levels and
funding regimes are frequently quoted when lamenting dismal research
performance. In the case of Germany, it is correctly being noted that universities are underfunded, basic research is frequently concentrated in specialized research institutes — such as those of the Max-Planck-Gesellschaft
(MPG) —, and that doubts are justified regarding the effectiveness of this
'division of labor' (Herbst et al., 2002, Table 7.1 on p. 89):

> "[The] lacking differentiation [within German higher education] impedes not
> only the formation of critical masses in research, it impedes particularly the
> optimal development of the next scientific generation [...] An aggravating
> fact is that substantial portions of basic research are being conducted outside
> of universities. Hence, young scholars are more excluded from the top centers
> of research rather than led up to, and this in a country where the unity of
> teaching and research is invoked at every occasion" (my translation) (Richter,
> 2003)[43].

But even the generously funded institutes of the MPG do not appear to
research very effectively and are dominated by institutions with smaller

---

divided by the faculty of professorial rank. An explanation for this definition is given in
(Herbst et al., 2002, pp. 39–42).

[42]European readers may claim that student-faculty ratios of European institutions should
not be compared to those of US institutions (because of differing morphologies or personnel structures characterizing the two university cultures). Such a stance is ill-founded. The
differences are not merely definitional and have great impact on the teaching-learning environment within institutions. The matter is taken up on the following pages. For a more
detailed discussion, see in particular (Herbst et al., 2002, Chapters 7 and 8).

[43]"[Die] fehlende Differenzierbarkeit [im deutschen Hochschulwesen] behindert nicht
nur die Herausbildung kritischer Forschungsmassen, sie behindert insbesondere die op-
timale Förderung des wissenschaftlichen Nachwuchses [...] Erschwerend kommt hinzu,
dass ein gewichtiger Teil der Grundlagenforschung außeruniversitär betrieben wird. Der
Nachwuchs wird dadurch von der Spitzenforschung eher ausgeschlossen, als an sie
herangeführt, und dies in einem Land, in dem bei jeder Gelegenheit die Einheit von
Forschung und Lehre beschworen wird".

research budgets (Richter, 2003; Kahn, 1996). Interestingly enough, few studies exist which investigate research environments in an international, comparative context and which tie research productivity issues to the structural setup, or more precisely, to the 'morphology' of institutions (see Section 6.2). Institutional morphology is a concept of *Pierre Bourdieu* (Bourdieu, 1988 (1984)) and — implicitly — of *Joseph Ben-David* (Ben-David, 1991)[44] that can be captured by indicators such as student-faculty or staff-faculty ratios. The sparsity of such studies implies that perhaps institutional productivity is not seen as being linked to institutional morphology. A more likely reason for the sparsity of such investigations could be that cross-cultural, international studies on the history and sociology of higher education have simply been lacking in recent years, in spite of efforts to compare higher education systems.

Achievement in higher education clearly cannot be assessed simply by looking at the research achievement. This is naturally so if we look at institutions which have no research focus, which are dedicated toward teaching. If we look at institutions with such teaching foci, if we look at the non-university sector of higher education, we observe no great morphological differences which would separate institutions in one Western country from another. However, if one focuses on the university sector, morphological differences are often pronounced: student-faculty and staff-faculty ratios tend to be higher at European institutions than at comparatively funded US institutions. A range of implications flow from these differences: class sizes tend to be larger in Europe than in the US, particularly during the early years of study; lecture courses dominate true seminars; knowledge transfer is still more important than active learning; teaching loads of faculty are generally higher, and administrative duties more time-consuming; dropout rates of students tend to be higher, study durations longer, and graduates are older; advising and mentorship is underdeveloped and the social distance between students and faculty — and frequently also between staff and faculty — is too large[45].

---

[44] *Bourdieu* introduced, to my knowledge, the term in our context, but *Ben-David*'s investigations, carried out earlier, focus on the thesis which links morphology to the research productivity of institutions.

[45] A recent review of Harvard's curriculum is critical of the faculty-student distance. The university should be known "not only as an institution in which students can sit in lecture halls"; rather, it should be experienced as a place where students interact with professors "in seminar and small class settings". According to *William C. Kirby*, Dean of the Faculty of Arts and Sciences, Harvard should appoint more professors (among other measures to further faculty-student interactions). See (Bartlett, 2004).

If we look at the morphological setup of institutions over time, if we look at indicators such as student-faculty or staff-faculty ratios, we observe no really pronounced changes in the US over the last century; in particular, student-faculty ratios did not generally grow. Stanford University may serve as an example. In the period between 1900 and 1960, Stanford's student-faculty ratio varied between 14.8:1 (1910) and 20.7:1 (1950)[46]. Subsequently, student-faculty ratios ranged from 10.0:1 (in the year 1990) to 11.1:1 (1970). In contrast, for instance, the Swiss Federal Institute of Technology in Zurich (ETHZ) had a student-faculty ratio of 15.2 in 1900 (Bergier & Tobler, 1980). During the period of 1955 and 1980 the student-faculty ratio ranged from 22.4:1 (1975) to 31.8:1 (1960), and in subsequent years from 34.8:1 (2000) to 40.0:1 (1990); today (i.e. 2005), the corresponding ratio is 36.4:1[47]. Other continental European research universities are characterized by less attractive indicators (Herbst et al., 2002, Table 4.1, p. 40); *Robert McC. Adams* calls them "unmanageable" (Adams, 2002, p. 11)[48].

Low student-faculty ratios are indicative of US research universities, but their origin lies in an early teaching focus of US colleges which was retained in today's research-oriented institutions. Student-faculty ratios have not grown in recent decades in spite of great financial pressures, and in contrast to the European scene. This strong teaching orientation of US institutions, once perhaps pursued because of a possible poor preparation of high school graduates and held onto after the birth of mass higher education, was instrumental for securing low student-faculty — and by implication also low staff-faculty — ratios. And these, in turn, appear to have provided the basis for what we might call the 'Atlantic split' in research productivity (see Appendix C).

The Founding and Funding of Disciplines. Looking at the investment situation as it presents itself for any institution, economic rationale would suggest that investment should go where it can generate the highest return. In an equilibrium — or optimum — situation, all institutional investment options would be characterized by equal marginal rates of return. If we adopt this rationale to assess the distribution of resources to the various disciplinary sectors, professional schools, or educational opportunities within an institution of higher education, resource flows should be directed in such a way as to equalize the rates of return on investment[49]. We have

---

[46]See: www.stanford.edu/home/stanford/facts/chron.html.

[47]See: http://www.fc.ethz.ch/facts.

[48]*Adams* refers to an average student-faculty ratio in Germany of 59:1.

[49]Or, maximize utility subject to resource constraints.

briefly covered the subject matter regarding private or social returns to education in Section 2.2, and we are conscious of the fact that the expected returns on educational investments are difficult to assess. But in spite of these difficulties or shortcomings, it appears that different educational opportunities are associated with widely differing private or social rates of return and that it would be worthwhile to assess the intra-institutional distribution of funds on the basis of this general economic rationale[50].

The investment rationale referred to above is quite alien to European higher education, in part because of its open admission policy, and in part because of conservative notions regarding which academic disciplines or educational programs should be offered at the university level. The spectrum of programs or disciplines pursued within Swiss universities, for instance, has remained quite stable, in spite of some changes which have taken place over time. If educational programs are reasonably restricted in number, the open admission policy will have the effect that students will have to choose among the disciplinary fields offered. Some fields then attract many students while other fields are characterized by a low demand. Administrators and politicians apparently assume that students flock to certain fields not only because they are attractive to the students who have chosen to pursue this line of study, but also because of the private return graduates can expect. Furthermore, if the economic returns for graduates change, educational demands will change in accordance with changes in the remuneration of graduates: for fields with low remuneration, demand will drop, and the lower supply of professionals with this orientation will have the effect of stabilizing or helping to raise wages again; conversely, fields characterized by high remuneration will generate further demand, which will then finally be associated with an oversupply of associated professionals and a down-adjustment on the wage scale. Hence, there is no need to worry about disciplinary distributions of student populations, because the system regulates itself. Furthermore, because of this self-regulation, disciplines, fields and educational programs can — and should — be funded in terms of associated student numbers or number of graduates (see Chapter 4).

"But is it true?" (Wildavsky, 1997). Is it really sensible to assume that we are confronted here with a reasonably proper self-regulating system? To begin to answer this question we might note at the outset that Euro-

---

[50] An analogous problem presents itself, at least in theory, regarding the inter-institutional distribution of funds. Because this is a much more delicate — and difficult — matter in practice, we shall not cover it here: measurement and equity problems may be so severe as to be prohibitive.

pean, Humboldtian higher education systems define disciplinary foci far more conservatively than US systems: new disciplinary orientations are frequently difficult to pursue and the founding of new university departments is often an ordeal. If we compare US universities with peer institutions in Germany, Austria or Switzerland, we observe that the number of departments or courses of study offered at US institutions is easily double that offered here. US research universities cover a broader spectrum of science or professions, and they cover this spectrum in greater detail (see Table A.3). When demand for particular lines of study at US institutions grows, student numbers are curtailed by the availability of resources, by sensible limits on the size of departments, and by active admission management. If demand exceeds supply at a given institution, quality can be raised, and excess demand can be funneled into new fields of study or directed toward other institutions. The founding of new fields or new departments will generate new demand, which in turn is handled in like fashion. In this way, US research universities have managed to increasingly improve their academic status and their international research prowess.

In contrast to this, continental European institutions tend to be very conservative regarding the founding of disciplines or departments and regarding the perception of what is properly included at the university level of education. New disciplines frequently take hold in Europe years — even decades — after corresponding departments in the US have been established. For example, in the case of information technologies and computer sciences, a new department was opposed because it was argued that information technologies and computer sciences were proper parts of established fields, namely mathematics and electrical engineering, and that there was no need to pursue something administratively new (Zehnder, 2001). In the case of environmental sciences, to present another example, the argument was that existing fields of biology and chemistry would already cover all that was purportedly addressed by environmental sciences (Koller & Imboden, 2001). Some fields are — or were — excluded from European or Swiss universities because they lack or lacked supposedly 'scientific' merit: nursing, social work, landscape architecture, design (industrial, interior, graphic, media), et cetera, fields that are generally relegated to the second tier of higher education, the *Fachhochschulen*. Other fields, such as education, are still confined to special schools, i.e. *Pädagogische Hochschulen*, and not made part of the universities proper.

The conservative stance regarding disciplinary or departmental orientation and the notion of a self-regulating system are all the more perplexing in light of fields which are often overcrowded — such as psychology[51] — or are characterized by a restricted demand for labor[52]. Study courses where the number of graduates continually exceed labor demand indicate a demand for lines of studies where the supply spectrum of higher education institutions is not broad enough. Here, new lines of courses should be implemented which cater to the talents and aspirations of the students enrolled in the respective courses and which serve the needs of society[53]. Economically speaking, graduates in courses where supply exceeds demand in the labor market have a reduced private as well as a reduced social return on investment[54]. Institutional resources, hence, are sub-optimally invested and redirecting resources to other lines of educational programs might help to equalize the marginal rates of returns on investment, provided sensible new programs are chosen, or — to put it differently — governmental charters and governing boards allow institutions to choose new programs. Two further examples are given here:

- The redirection of institutional resources is a policy theme of great importance. The fact that the Swiss Federal Institute of Technology in Lausanne (EPFL) was able to integrate the life sciences into a former engineering school, for instance, has great merit. Today's overlapping of engineering and natural sciences is very significant, and a school focusing on engineering alone could not expect to do frontier research or teaching. The integration of the life sciences into EPFL

---

[51]At the University of Zürich of today (i.e. 2005/06), for instance, some 2,000 students study psychology. See: www.imc.unizh.ch/stud/fk/fpf_a.php.

[52]At the Federal Institute of Technology in Zürich (ETHZ), architecture has been a program of high demand, with an enrollment of circa 1,600 students a few years ago and a current enrollment of roughly 1,300 students (see: http://www.fc.ethz.ch/facts/studierende/zeitreihen/stud/Studtotalle1990_2005.pdf). In spite of the fact that the program produces more graduates than can be absorbed by the market, a committee rejected a proposal a few years ago to launch a study course in landscape architecture on the premise that landscape architecture does not meet the standards of university education. Landscape architecture is not inherently different from architecture itself, a fact that prompted Harvard University to start offering a corresponding program at the end of the 19th century. Today, ETHZ offers an individualized post-graduate course in landscape architecture for a planned enrollment of 8–16 students.

[53]To provide an example of the University of Zürich once again, a new course in the field of media sciences (*Publizistik*) was recently implemented, with scant resources, which attracts now (i.e. 2005/06) almost 1,000 students (i.e. far too many; see: www.imc.unizh.ch/stud/fk/fpf_a.php). The great attraction this new study line enjoys is indicative of a need for a far broader choice of study options.

[54]The general argument here is that graduates have pursued a *studium generale*, so to speak, and they will manage to infiltrate other professions or lines of employment.

was perhaps a matter of survival, at least at the level of a leading
Institute of Technology.

- A similar — but perhaps less dramatic — case can be made regarding
  the full integration of the social sciences and the humanities into the
  realm of the Swiss Federal Institutes of Technologies (which is prohibited by Federal mandate), an integration which was demanded
  for the field of economics more than a decade ago by *Jürg Niehans*.
  Since World War II, economies have shifted their foci and universities
  — and Institutes of Technologies — have had to adapt. Today's Western economies employ roughly two thirds of their labor in the tertiary
  (i.e. service) sector, and it is clearly short-sighted — and damaging —
  to prohibit Institutes of Technologies to offer new programs, particularly in those social sciences where structural analyses and mathematical models play a constructive role[55]. A problem orientation of
  a modern technical institution demands the inclusion of the social
  sciences and the humanities since most problems of today are man-
  made: they cannot be addressed in purely engineering and natural
  sciences terms[56].

---

[55]ETHZ has recognized this fact for some time now. In 1994, for instance, the RiskLab was
formed (together with Credit Suisse (CS), Swiss Re and Union Bank of Switzerland (UBS)),
aiming, in particular, for the "promotion of the scientific competence and methodology in
the general area of integrated risk management, [and] of fundamental and pre-competitive
applied research [in the finance industry]" (see: www.risklab.ch/AboutRiskLab.html).

[56]In 1997 the *Planungskommission* of ETHZ demanded a new focus for the institution as a
whole, encompassing a triad of broad fields: (i) natural sciences, (ii) engineering, and (iii)
social sciences and humanities (ETHZ, 1997).

Chapter 3

Public Management Reform Debate

> *Knowledge about knowledge has a peculiar multiplier or leverage effect on the growth of knowledge itself. The more we know about learning and the transmission of knowledge, and the more we know about the processes by which knowledge advances at the frontiers, the more efficient will be the use of resources, both in education and in research.*
>
> *Kenneth E. Boulding (Boulding, 1968)*

I
N ORDER TO ASSESS emerging currents in higher education management and governance, a focus on the general public management discourse — and the implicit cultural change — will set the stage for a subsequent discussion on performance-based budgeting or funding measures in higher education (see Chapter 4). We cannot review this discourse in great detail here, but a range of topics should be touched on: movements as they developed during the past two decades to reform government and public administration, the particular foci of this reform, and lastly the question regarding the political versus the academic orientation of this reform.

3.1 Impetus of Reform

The debate on government and its role is old, perhaps as old as civilization, but during the recent decades we have witnessed a surge in this debate, fostered in part by the ideological schism separating East and West during the most part of the 20th century. "Governments are not famous for efficiency" writes *Mancur Olson* (Olson, 1973, pp. 355f) in the early 1970s, "yet", he continues

> "it remains true that the reasons for exceptional inefficiency that is alleged to occur in the public sector have not been codified, nor incorporated into the body of economic theory, nor even stated in a sufficiently clear and general fashion to bring this matter (important as it is) into elementary textbooks".

A dozen years later, after the demise of the Soviet Union and its allies, a resurgence of a debate transpired which tried to refocus Western societies and to redefine public and private spheres. Government and government operations were criticized still, as *Lawrence R. Jones* and *Donald F. Kettl* observe (Jones & Kettl, 2003), alleging that they

> "[…] are inefficient, ineffective, too large, too costly, overly bureaucratic, overburdened by unnecessary rules, unresponsive to public wants and needs, secretive, undemocratic, invasive into the private rights of citizens, self-serving, and failing in the provision of either the quantity or quality of services deserved by the taxpaying public".

As *Jones* and *Kettl* note, "[f]iscal stress has also plagued many governments and has increased the cry for less costly or less expensive government, for greater efficiency, and for increased responsiveness". The time, apparently, was ripe for a new reform movement.

Reinventing Government. New Zealand is generally given credit for being one of the first countries to "reinvent government" (Osborne & Gaebler, 1993; Boston, Dalziel, & St John, 1999), starting the corresponding activities around 1984 (Evans, Grimes, Wilkinson, & Teece, December 1996). "Any understanding of the [reform movement]", write *Jones* and *Kettl*, "must begin there". In New Zealand, public management reforms came to the foreground because national economic performance was lacking, because inflation ran high, because new and increasingly competitive markets emerged within the Pacific Rim, and because it was felt that the subsidized and overly regulated economy was not up to its task. By 1988, accrual accounting (Freeman & Shoulders, 1999) and output contracting arrangements were implemented, while subsequent reforms extended way into the 1990s and affected higher education (Ministry of Education, 1997) as well as public management reforms in general (Schedler & Reichard, 1998; Kettl, 2000, 2002). By the end of the past century, new management modes in the field of higher education were on the agenda in a range of Western nations (Bauer, Askling, Marton, & Marton, 1999; Henkel & Little, 1999; Braun & Merrien, 1999; Bleiklie, Høstaker, & Vabø, 2000; Kogan & Hanney, 2000; Committee on Science, Engineering, and Public Policy, 2001a).

New Zealand, a small country of roughly 4 million inhabitants, had a long tradition as a welfare economy, going back to the 1920s — or even to the outgoing 19th century[1]. While prior to World War II New Zealand's per capita gross national product (GDP) was still roughly on a par with that of the US, by the mid-1970s this measure was down to roughly half of that of the US[2]. The following decade saw a further downturn in the economy which culminated in 1984 in a foreign exchange and constitutional crisis. Subsequent to this crisis, "New Zealand embarked on what evolved into one of the most comprehensive programs of economic reforms of any OECD country in recent decades" (Evans et al., December 1996, p. 1860). Current account and government fiscal balances became less negative — or even positive — in subsequent years, but consumer prices started to climb, at least during the first few years of reform, and by the mid-1990s, unemployment rates were still higher than a decade before[3].

One of the characteristics of New Zealand's reform, which is still in process, is that — since its inception — it has been maintained by all its governments. Initiated by a Labour Government that won elections in June of 1984, a broad agenda of reforms was pursued which continued to be supported by all subsequent governments: the National Government which took power in 1990, and the two coalition governments which have held office since 1996 (after establishing a proportional representational system in the parliament). It is difficult to assess the extent to which the reforms were — and are — successful, and such assessments are clearly outside the scope of this book. Important to note, however, is the persistence with which reform efforts were carried forward and the echo the reforms of this small nation found in other countries. New Zealand's reform efforts became models for reforms elsewhere, particularly in Europe, less I presume because the reform ideas were novel, but rather because New Zealand's economy had to travel a particularly long route to recovery. Reforms in the

---

[1]In 1898, the Old Age Pension Act was passed, in 1911 benefits were extended to widows, the Family Allowances Act was passed in 1926, and in 1938 "a comprehensive system of social security was implemented by the Labour Government" (Evans et al., December 1996, pp. 1858–1860).

[2]As of 2001, this figure decreased to 37%; see: www.stats.govt.nz/.

[3]As of 2001, unemployment rates (of 5.3%) are roughly half of what they were in the early 1990s, but they are still higher than in the mid 1980s, for instance. See: www.stats.govt.nz/.

fields of monetary or fiscal policies appear not to have made a lasting imprint on reforms elsewhere, perhaps because New Zealand was perceived here not to play a spearheading role. But regarding the re-framing of government and its role, it appears, New Zealand is given credit for its efforts to redesign the welfare state (Boston et al., 1999).

The Spreading of Reforms. The reforms — or better: reform movements — which stand in the foreground here run under different labels: New Public Management (NPM) (Barzelay, 2001) appears to be a kind of generic term, National Performance Review (NPR) was the term used under the Clinton-Gore administration, and the current US administration under G. W. Bush links all their corresponding documents to the Government Performance and Results Act (GPRA) (Committee on Science, Engineering, and Public Policy, 2001b, Appendix F, pp. 167–188). Different political agendas have embraced the reforms. "Whereas the New Zealand reforms were launched from the left, the British reforms grew from the right with Prime Minister Margaret Thatcher's neo-conservative venture to shrink the size of the state. In 1982 Thatcher launched the government's Financial Management Initiative" (Kettl, 2000, p. 13). The current UK government has a Next Steps initiative (Cabinet Office, 1999), and the reforms in Switzerland run under the label of *Wirkungsorientierte Verwaltung*. Reforms have eventually spread to many nations and regions around the globe: to Australia, Hong Kong, and the Scandinavian countries. They have spread in the sense that changes in public management were made with particular reference to the reform movement. "Reform-watching in public management" write *Christopher Pollitt* and *Geert Bouckaert*, "can be a sobering pastime. The gaps between rhetoric and action, and between views from the top and experiences at the grassroots, are frequently so wide as to provoke skepticism or — according to some — cynicism" (Pollitt & Bouckaert, 2000, p. 188f). We shall see whether this pessimistic view has some merit.

3.2   Reform Ideas Assessed

Models, not in the sense of iconic replicas or mathematical representations of phenomena or processes, but in the sense of conceptual ideals, are associated with implicit dangers. Ideals need to be operationalized in order to serve their function as guiding principles, and if we want to judge the merit of the model or the quality of the ideal, we ought to look at the way the ideal is translated and given form (Newell, 1969; Aronowsky, 1969; Herbst, 1970, 1999). This practice is common in the history of political thought where ideas are assessed, in part, in terms of the regimes they spawned or influenced. But the practice is not that widespread: if we were to judge the merit of architectural innovations by the quality of epigonic works, for instance, the history of architecture — or the critical reception of architecture — might take on a different look.

Hence, in order to assess reform ideas in the field of public management, we should not only look at the ideas as such but also at how these ideas are implemented. There are differences between general principles and concrete plans and programs, and while there might be a consensus regarding the general principles, there may be differing views regarding the ways these principles are executed[4]. Evaluation and performance assessments are some of the basic tenets of the public management reform movement, and we shall apply these — in a very tentative way — to the reform movement itself.

State versus Private Ownership. To begin our review of governance and management measures in the public domain, we will start with a short reflection on state versus private ownership (Shleifer, 1998). Common modes of thinking once reserved market industries for private ownership. In contrast, other industries (where stronger market imperfections, such as monopoly power or externalities were evident) were reserved for state ownership. The position of the dividing line between what belongs to the state and what does not has not always been agreed upon. Various schools of economic thought have assumed different positions on this issue. Recent decades have witnessed a shift in thinking, brought about in part by advanced contracting theories and accelerated perhaps by the collapse of the Iron Curtain. Until recently, government-owned enterprises in key industries — such as steel, energy or telecommunication — were common in a range of Western nations. The newer doctrines generally see no need for state ownership in these industries and, consequently, many of the key industries have been privatized in recent years.

The privatization of government operations touches two major classes: operations which are released from government control, and operations which are not:

---

[4]To illustrate this point, I hope the reader will forgive me if I cite from a paper which I wrote as a younger person at the height of the Vietnam conflict (Herbst, 1970): "It is always the outcome of a structuring process which matters. We may pursue such ill-defined objectives as 'peace', but ultimately strive for well-defined objectives such as 'reduce the enemy supply by x%', or 'defoliate y acres of forest of enemy territory'. Looking at the well-defined objectives, we often wonder whether it was really 'peace' we wanted to achieve". See also footnote 11 on page 49.

- The first class encompasses former state industries, such as steel for instance, which now function like any other firm in the market economy.

- The second class refers to operations which are being sourced-out. Here, the government ceases to perform the operation in-house, so to speak, but delegates it to a private agent who takes on the responsibility for the operation on behalf of the government.

In recent years, many formerly governmental services have been sourced-out, among them engineering or architectural works, administrative or social services, or garbage collection. Contracts — and principal-agent models (Holstrom, 1983; Boyer & Kihlstorm, 1983) — provide the theoretical bases for such activities. The question which has to be posed in this context is whether the "mode of provision matter[s] even when the government pays" (Shleifer, 1998, p. 136).

The common notion today is that the mode of providing these services does matter. Private enterprises are seen as more cost-effective because they are not encumbered by various bureaucratic rules and regulations, and because they are profit oriented. According to this view, outsourcing pays because the same service is being offered, only at reduced costs. However, the current discourse does not offer clear boundaries between which activities are those of the state and which activities are not, and it is frequently a matter of political judgment where the boundaries are drawn regarding the provision of government services: various nations follow differing strategies. In certain cases it may not matter which services are being offered by the state and which are contracted out, because there is no intrinsic reason why government agencies cannot operate at similar levels of efficiency as private firms, particularly when quality or security concerns stand in the foreground[5]. However, there are clear cases where contracting-out opportunities have their limits, as *Andrei Shleifer* observes, namely where "the government cannot fully anticipate, describe, stipulate, regulate and enforce exactly what it wants" (Shleifer, 1998, p. 137). If contracting-out occurs in spite of these limitations, i.e., if contracts take account of only a subset of relevant factors,

> "[...] cost reductions for which private suppliers have stronger incentives have potentially deleterious effects on the non-contractible qualit[ies]. [...] In

[5]National railroads may serve as an example here. Privatization may have severe negative effects on the culture and operation of the enterprise, as the recent history — in the UK, for instance — shows.

such situations, strong incentives may lead to inefficient outcomes [...] Ironically, the government sometimes becomes the efficient producer precisely because its employees are not motivated to find ways of holding costs down" [p. 138].

While *Andrei Shleifer* posits that "in most of the situations where cost reductions have adverse consequences for non-contractible quality, private ownership is still superior" [p. 139]. He is specifically referring to the private non-profit organization to take care of situations characterized by non-contractual qualities.

There is no need to delve further into questions on state versus private ownership, a discussion which is central to the economic sciences, but peripheral in the context of the present volume which does not attempt to focus on private higher education, at least not in a normative way[6]. However, if the focus is on public higher education, questions of governance and management will have to be addressed, and if the principles of public management reform (and governance and management modes) are influenced by the state versus private ownership debate, aspects of this debate have relevance in the present context[7].

General Principles. Let us look at the general principles — and the various agendas — of a reform movement which is frequently referred to as New Public Management (Barzelay, 2001). *Christopher Pollitt* and *Geert Bouckaert* attempt to describe what the reforms are about (Pollitt & Bouckaert, 2000, p. 17): "[...] public management reforms [consist] of deliberate changes to the structures and processes of public sector organizations with the objective of getting them (in some sense) to run better". Public sector organizations do

---

[6]This volume is written from a Swiss — or European — perspective where private higher education institutions play a marginal role. This does not imply a rejection of the idea of private, non-profit, institutions. In my assessment, private institutions of higher education could only leave their status of marginality in Europe if a few well-endowed, well-managed institutions enter the scene. I judge the necessary initial endowment for a research university to be around € 6–10 billion. Only with an endowment of such magnitude would it be possible to set a mark, be truly competitive internationally, and to overcome the practically non-existing culture of private non-profit institutions in Europe. The endowment mentioned appears large, but commitments by a few dedicated philanthropists could make it possible.

[7]Endowments, as mentioned above, do not only have relevance in the context of private universities. Some years ago, the Swiss National Bank decided to sell some gold reserves in the amount of over € 11 billion. The case is still pending. There was never a public debate on the creation of an endowment to fund higher education or research. When taking office in 2004 as President of the ETH-Board, Alexander Zehnder had informal talks with politicians regarding the creation of such a fund, but was told that his idea came too late to influence the parliamentary debate (personal communication).

things: they administer, but more importantly in our context, they plan or manage processes. They are also occupied with certain tasks, or leave tasks for others to perform. The reform is now not focused, in *Pollitt's* and *Bouckaert's* view, on administration, management or planning directly, but rather at the meta-level of organizations by which processes are affected indirectly. These indirect, meta-level activities have always been a subject of the policy sciences. It is the deliberate change-orientation of public management reform and its political will, its 'mission' so to speak, that set it apart from the academically oriented policy sciences.

Focusing on the agenda of reform issues, we observe a very wide spectrum of measures addressed. *Lewis Evans*, for instance, refers to the following (Evans et al., December 1996, p. 1859): measures pertaining to the financial market, such as the removal of interest rate and foreign exchange controls, the floating of the exchange rate; measures pertaining to the goods market, such as the removal of price and rent freezes, of agricultural subsidies, of export assistance, of import licenses, of tariffs, et cetera; measures pertaining to monetary policy; measures pertaining to the reform of trading organizations, such as privatizations; measures pertaining to the reform of government departments, such as the introduction of private sector employment conditions, of output contracting arrangements, of information systems, of accrual accounting; measures with regard to various taxation reforms; measures which aim at budget reforms, focusing on a reduction of government expenditures, cuts in welfare, a shift to 'user pays'; measures dealing with the health system and health insurance; measures which focus on a de-regulation of the labor market by lifting wage freezes; measures which address the division of power between central and local government, or which redraw the boundaries of jurisdictions; and measures which address the political system or the representational system of government: a broad spectrum of measures, indeed.

Donald E. Kettl, focusing not on measures but on the major foci — or foundations — of what he calls "the global public management revolution", lists the following six principal orientations (Kettl, 2000): a

- focus on productivity or, viewed from a different angle, on efficiency of government operations; an

- orientation toward marketization, i.e., the replacement of "traditional bureaucratic command-and-control mechanisms with market strategies" [p. 2]; a

- service orientation, designed to make government more responsive to the needs of its constituency, instead of lining out government programs which reflect the interests of the service providers; a

- dedicated move toward the decentralization of power and the placing of decision-making authority near the location where courses of actions have to take place; a

- separation of roles with respect to the initiation or contracting of services, and the service provision; and lastly

- the affirmation of government's accountability, the constant pursuit of accountability measures, and the pursuit of result-driven systems.

At this level, a doctrine seems to be forming to provide a guiding principle for decision-making.

If we look at the first principal orientation of public management reform, we are not confronted with anything new. The focus on productivity or efficiency of government operations has a very long tradition, dating back at least to World War II and the subsequent major developments in economics (Moss, 1973), political science, and operations research. The list of fine books which have addressed issues of productivity or efficiency of government operations can easily fill a large library. Developments in such fields as mathematical programming, game theory, cost-benefit analysis and project evaluation, planning-programming and budgeting systems (PPBS)[8], management by objectives (MBO)[9], zero-based budgeting (ZBB)[10], total quality management (TQM), et cetera, may have a dusty aura. But some of these fields are still at the center of development, and some fields — such as PPBS — have been abandoned because of inherent deficiencies, which appear in the process of being duplicated by the public management reform movement (Grove, 1973)[11]. All the fields together attest to the fact that productivity and efficiency have always mattered.

---

[8]The Government Performance and Results Act (GPRA) of 1993 can be traced back to the Program, Planning, Budgeting System (PPBS), established during the US administration of President Lyndon B. Johnson and Secretary of Defense, Robert McNamara.

[9]This focus during the mid 1970s can be linked to the US administration of President Gerald F. Ford.

[10]The reference is here to the US presidency of Jimmy Carter.

[11]One of the aberrations of PPBS *Ernest W. Grove* refers to (Grove, 1973, p. 394) was the infamous US practice during the Vietnam war of measuring 'progress' in terms of 'body counts' of Vietcong fighters. He then generalizes his critique [p. 395]: "This [US practice] is quite typical of the way the PPB system has worked since it was forcibly and inflexibly foisted on all government departments in 1965. The result was a triumph of technique over purpose, and a tremendous burgeoning of new jobs and unnecessary work. It is impossi-

The orientation toward marketization is a newer — and clearly more controversial — subject matter which appears to lie at the center of the reform movement and which I addressed, in part, in the context of the short discussion on state versus private ownership. Markets, where they exist and work, are a wonderful thing, but markets — functioning markets — do not exist everywhere and they do not provide the solutions to everything. Marketization strategies can provide a seemingly clear path to efficiency or effectiveness. However, such strategies can also be misguided: performance of operations may have nothing to do with marketization strategies. *James Q. Wilson* cites case after case where the performance of operations were unrelated to market forces (Wilson, 1989). "Bureaucrat-bashing", he observes, is not the answer and, referring to *Charles Wolf* (Wolf, 1993), "both markets and governments have their imperfections; many things we might want to do collectively require us to choose between unsatisfactory alternatives". But to do better, he suggests, "we have to deregulate the government" (Wilson, 1989, p. 368–369).

The service orientation of the reform movement is the third focus on *Kettl's* list. Service orientation is a very important issue with regard to government operations. Public services, in spite of their name, do not always provide the quality of service that they should. But it would be foolish to deny the service orientation of government in general: indeed, service orientation stands at the very core of democratic governments, and always has. Private enterprise, on the contrary, does not have a general service orientation: indeed, private firms have a sales orientation, or a market-share orientation, or a return-on-equity orientation, and they pursue their service orientation only as a means for other ends. Government service and bureaucracy have flawed images, fed by common anecdotal evidence regarding lazy, pompous, or otherwise ineffectual — or non-serving — public officials. But deficient government service is not intrinsic: it need not be there, and the long standing service debate within government attests to the fact that there are many able and proud officials, teachers, and administrators trying to serve their respective constituencies.

The fourth issue *Kettl* mentions refers to a decentralization of power. Here, we may have to make a distinction between the macro and the micro levels. At the macro level, decentralization may mean shifting power within a government, perhaps on the basis of redefined boundaries of min-

---

ble to disagree with the basic principles underlying the PPB system; the problem arises in their practical application, as all kinds of cooked-up statistics, fudged or invented data, and other necessary subterfuges are likely to arise when basically sound principles are indiscriminately applied to all areas of government activity".

istries or agencies. It may also mean shifting power from central to local government, or from government to public institutions (such as higher education) and giving them more autonomy to pursue their own agenda. At the micro level, it may mean giving departments or individual groupings within governmental agencies a protective — autonomous — status to shield them better from outside interventions, which may turn out to be politically motivated, and which may interfere with the very mission of the department or grouping under consideration. "In general", *Wilson* writes (Wilson, 1989, p. 372), "authority should be placed at the lowest level at which all essential elements of information are available". But decentralization may not always be the proper strategy: in certain cases one may want to centralize decisions which formerly were decentralized, perhaps in order to ease coordination or to ensure a comprehensive view[12]. In federal systems, the centralization–decentralization dichotomy has always loomed in the foreground of the political agenda, and it would be wrong to assume that decentralization should serve as a general prescription.

The fifth principle calls for a separation of roles concerning the policy function of service provision and the actual service-delivery. Contracting and principal-agent theories, which originated within economics some decades ago, were transplanted into the public management debate around the mid-1980s, and these were instrumental for an increased tendency to source-out services. I have already commented on contracting-out activities above, in the context of a brief discussion on state versus private ownership (see p. 45). Contracting-out reduces the size of government agencies. This in itself, however, is not enough to justify such practice. Frequently, quality of service delivery can be improved and the associated costs reduced, provided the service is of a standard nature and there are many agents available who can deliver this service. If the service is of a standard nature, government is in a position to specify contractual arrangements with potential agents, and contractual arrangements eventually can be supervised, monitored, and assessed. Contracting-out, however, is associated with potential — and well-known — dangers of corruption (von Maravic, Patrick and Christoph Reichard, 2003). *Mancur Olson* has pointed out, to-

---

[12]In Switzerland, strong local interests influencing land-use planning and zoning, for instance, prevented a more orderly, less expansive and better serviceable (by public transportation) regional development, as foreseen by the Swiss federal authorities in the 1970s in their comprehensive development plans and their concept of 'decentralized concentration'. The processes of sub-urbanization have since reached Alpine regions (such as the Engadine valley) and are slowly destroying environments of great natural beauty and architectural heritage.

gether with others, "the need to be wary of the influence of organizations representing inputs used in government on the allocations chosen by the political and administrative processes" (Olson, 1973, p. 383). If the dangers are not those of outright corruption, others loom around the corner. In the contracting of engineering services, for example, there is an implicit pressure toward implementation. While one advantage of planning lies in the evaluation of a wide spectrum of alternatives, the sequence of studies — pre-feasibility study, feasibility study, project studies up to final implementation — has a tendency to always favor the next step of investigation. If collusion develops between engineering firms and governmental agencies, investigations are quickly biased or corrupted — to the detriment of the general public. In those cases, however, where the services under consideration are of a non-standard nature, contracting-out is a much more delicate business[13].

The last of *Kettl's* principles refers to accountability measures and to result-driven systems. This principle touches perhaps the core of the reform efforts, particularly if viewed from a perspective which focuses on higher education. Accountability, as such, is undisputed. Democratic governments are accountable to their constituency and governmental agencies should be transparent — and be made transparent. Hence, reports and analyses which portray the respective institutions in a transparent manner are mandatory. The same applies regarding higher education systems and institutions.

The principle appears to become problematic if specific accountability measures are mandated. It is also clearly problematic if accountability measures are directly tied to specific incentive or funding schemes to induce or to provoke change. When this is the case, systems adapt, trying to meet the accountability measures mandated, and in doing so they may deviate from their own path of goals and mission achievement[14]. Or, as *Kettl* mentions,

---

[13]Military procurement programs might fall into this category, or higher education for that matter.

[14]The following anecdote illustrates the case: An Indian provincial government, trying to control the proliferation in the snake population, set out on a program to pay the peasants for any cobra they would turn in, only to find out later that the peasants embarked on cobra breeding programs (von Maravic, Patrick and Christoph Reichard, 2003, p. 121). Another anecdote is mentioned by *Olson*: "There is the classic case of the early Soviet nail factory in which quotas were set in terms of 'weight' of nails produced. In response to this implicit incentive a small number of very large nails was produced. When an attempt was made to correct this obvious distortion by measuring output in terms of the 'number' of nails, quotas were met and Stakhanovite awards were won by producing a large number of very small nails" (Olson, 1973, p. 387f).

referring to the reform in New Zealand and to *Allen Schick's* interpretation of that reform (Schick, 1996):

> "[...] managers tended to rely on a 'checklist' mentality of meeting narrow output goals without necessarily fulfilling the broader purpose, and [that] the new competition model imposed its own compliance costs [...] The problem [becomes] especially serious 'when unspecified matters escape accountability' [i.e. a reference to *Schick*], especially issues not anticipated in management contracts, for which clear responsibilities cannot be defined in advance or for which outputs cannot clearly be measured after the fact" (Kettl, 2002, p. 94).

We have furthermore, in the context of contracting-out, referred to the possibilities of unethical behavior. Mandated accountability measures which are tied to funding may have a similar effect, in that agencies might try to fudge figures[15]. *Kishore Gawande* and *Timothy Wheeler*, referring to the work of *Heckman, Heinrich* and *Smith* (Heckman, Heinrich, & Smith, 1997), mention "that bureaucrats can 'game' the performance standards system, since they have the discretionary power to maximize their private returns, in an attempt to maximize a center's measured performance" (Gawande & Wheeler, 1999). Obviously, there is ample space for unethical behavior associated with performance funding, requiring additional — not fewer — bureaucracies to check and fight these tendencies. I shall cover performance-based budgeting or funding in some detail later on (see Chapter 4), and shall try to assess their appropriateness in the context of higher education.

3.3 Performance Reporting

Institutions generally have a mission to pursue, and they have, or they require, resources to pursue this mission. The mission has to be translated into more specific goals and targets to be reached, and measures and programs have to be devised — and resources budgeted and allocated — to reach these aims. Activities with these aims in mind are normally grouped

---

[15]A recent scandal in higher education in The Netherlands, whereby Dutch institutions fudged their student enrollment, corroborates this. The Dutch Court of Audit notes that "the Ministry of Education had failed to supervise the investigated sectors of education properly. Departments within the Ministry have paid too little attention to the risk of misuse and improper use, despite receiving signs that irregularities were occurring". In her response, the Minister of Education "postulated that the audit had never been intended to ascertain the scale of the irregularities and claimed that this was in fact the task of the Court of Audit. The self-cleansing audit was allegedly only partially intended to chart and evaluate the extent to which institutions could manipulate funding regulations". See: (Algemene Rekenkamer, 2003).

under such headings as strategy formation or planning, and the documents which deal with such activities are called mission statements, strategy papers, or plans. Strategies or plans cannot be simply implemented because institutions operate, naturally, in an environment characterized by insufficient information on what the future will bring and what other actors will do. Hence, goals achievement will have to be monitored: institutions need to see whether they are on track in the pursuance of their goals, they need to evaluate the effectiveness of measures taken, and they may have to modify or change their mission, goals or plans if they find themselves in a situation which warrants these changes.

To engage in such activities is a time and resource consuming — but necessary — endeavor. Many people within an organization or a university will have to be called upon to participate, at various levels. Quality improvement groups may operate on a continuing basis, in order to improve current practices or procedures; standing committees may pay attention to more strategically oriented questions which require vigilance; ad hoc committees address particular problems; planning or budgeting offices work out plans or budgets within a framework of formalized consultation; college alumni-offices may survey graduates regarding their career; et cetera. All these groups and administrative offices prepare reports, memoranda or documents of various kinds, some of which are of a more general nature and can be used to enhance the intra-organizational communication, and some are aimed specifically to serve accountability vis-à-vis steering or funding agencies, or vis-à-vis the general public. Looking a bit more deeply into the archives of today's major universities, one is indeed surprised by the wealth of information which these archives — accessible online — make available to the public.

In light of this, we may ask how performance reporting, a central aspect of the public management reform, fits into pursuing institutional objectives. Performance monitoring, it should be clear, is an integral part of any improvement or planning activity, and so is to report on the results of the monitoring activity. Good planning practice of the past was unthinkable without monitoring or performance measurement, as unthinkable as driving an automobile without looking where the car is heading and without steering to keep the vehicle on course or out of trouble. Performance monitoring, as part of a planning activity, is a task of those who plan. But it is also a research activity of wide scope by scholars, stakeholders and observers of systems monitored. Professional organizations and topical journals exist to enhance communication among those affected and to exchange ideas and experiences. The literature on agencies of various kinds, or on systems of agencies or institutions, is immense, and a good portion of this literature focuses on matters of performance. Schools and school systems are assessed regarding their effectiveness in pursuing their mission, and so are hospitals or health insurance systems, institutions of higher education, et cetera. A great deal can — and should — be learned from this kind of research to improve existing practices and modes of operation.

However, performance reporting does not appear to be concerned simply with performance monitoring and the subsequent reporting of the findings. Performance reporting is a formalized approach whereby bureaucratic units — i.e. agencies or institutions — report on their performance with respect to contractually predefined performance targets[16]. We shall have the opportunity to look into performance reporting with regard to specific cases within higher education later on, but for the time being I would like to direct a spotlight on this practice by quickly looking at such an exercise as demanded by the US Government Performance and Results Act (GPRA)[17].

Review of Agency Reports. The gist of the GPRA is summarized as follows (United States General Accounting Office, 2001a, p. 5): "Under GPRA, annual performance plans are to clearly inform the Congress and the public of (i) the annual performance goals for agencies' major programs and activities, (ii) the measures that will be used to gauge performance, (iii) the strategies and resources required to achieve the performance goals, and (iv) the procedures that will be used to verify and validate performance information [...] Annual performance reports are to [...] report on the degree to which performance goals are met" (United States General Accounting Office, 2001a, p. 5). The essence of GPRA is sound — but trivial — and reads like any prescription for planning: identify the goals (or outcomes) to be pursued in your plan, operationalize these goals, list the courses of actions and resources required to achieve these goals, note the measures required by which to assess goals achievement and, finally, report on goals achievement and deviations. As of 2002, two dozen agencies issued plans and reports, from the Department of Agriculture, to the Treasury, to NASA, to the Social Security Administration[18]. Each plan lists outcomes to be pursued, which in turn are further operationalized by performance objectives

---

[16]Their definition is part of performance contracts, *Leistungsaufträge* or *Leistungsverein-barungen*, et cetera, which focus on the principal-agent relationship.

[17]In support of GPRA, a Program Assessment Rating Tool (PART) has been created. See: www.whitehouse.gov/omb/part/.

[18]See: www.gao.gov.

and indicators to measure progress toward achieving a particular outcome. I shall comment briefly on five of the plans, in order to give an impression:

- *National Science Foundation* (United States General Accounting Office, 2000e, 2001e): The NSF focuses on two key outcomes: (1) that "research funding awards lead to discoveries at and across the frontier of science and engineering", and (2) that research grants are administered "efficiently and effectively". Regarding the first outcome, "NFS judged its performance as successful" (United States General Accounting Office, 2001e, p. 5); and the same applies regarding the second outcome[19].

- *Department of Education* (United States General Accounting Office, 2000a, 2001a): Six outcomes are listed: (1) that "students reach challenging academic standards that prepare them for responsible citizenship, further learning, and productive employment", (2) that "children receive a solid foundation for learning", (3) that "greater public school choice [is] available to students and families", (4) that schools are "strong, safe, disciplined, and drug-free", (5) that "less fraud, waste, mismanagement, and error in student financial assistance programs" take place, and (6) that "students have access to high-quality postsecondary education and lifelong learning". With regard to the first outcome, "little progress" was attested[20]. Regarding the second outcome, the assessment was the same, partially because of lack of data to report on annually. The achievement with regard to the third outcome was more favorably reviewed, because of the pursuance of charter schools[21]. Regarding the fourth outcome, the use of unsuitable proxi-measures was decried, and with regard to the fifth out-

---

[19]It is noteworthy how 'efficiency' and 'effectiveness' is understood in this context: "NSF exceeded by 21 percent one of the management performance goals — to receive at least 60 percent of full grant proposal submissions electronically through a new computer system called FastLane. NSF also exceeded by 5 percent another management goal that at least 90 percent of its funds will be allocated to projects reviewed by appropriate peers external to NSF and selected through a merit-based competitive process. NSF continued to miss one of its investment process goals — to process 70 percent of proposals within 6 months of receipt — dropping from 58 to 54 percent in fiscal year 2000" (United States General Accounting Office, 2001e, p. 56).

[20]"The interim report contained seven objectives and 35 indicators for this outcome; however, fiscal year 2000 data were only available for nine [of the 35] indicators. In analyzing these nine indicators, we found that Education has made little progress toward achieving this outcome" (United States General Accounting Office, 2001a, p. 3).

[21]The target for the year 2002 was 3,000 charter schools. The program was reported to be on track.

come, the goals or objectives to address this outcome were seen as lacking. Finally, the meeting of the final outcome was judged to be "mixed".

- *Environmental Protection Agency* (United States General Accounting Office, 2000c, 2001c): Four key outcomes stand in the foreground: (1) safe and healthy air in every community, (2) safe water for drinking, recreation, and agriculture (3) clean-up of hazardous waste sites, and (4) making sure that "food supplies are free from unsafe pesticide residues". With regard to the first two outcomes, the EPA is judged to pursue a proper program, in spite of problems with data and measurement. Regarding the third outcome, the assessment is more reserved: "Of the six agreements targeted for completion in fiscal year 2000, only two were completed" (United States General Accounting Office, 2001c, p. 3). Lastly, regarding the fourth outcome, EPA's "reported strategies appear clear and reasonable".

- *Department of Transportation* (United States General Accounting Office, 2000b, 2001b): The DOT pursues four key outcomes: (1) "fewer transportation-related accidents, death, injuries and property losses", (2) "reduced flight delays through air traffic control modernization", then (3) "less highway congestion and improved highway pavement condition", and (4) "reduced availability and/or use of illegal drugs". Regarding the first outcome, "DOT reported mixed success in achieving its aviation, rail, and transit safety goals" (United States General Accounting Office, 2001b, p. 2). Regarding the second outcome improvements require a longer time frame because circa "70 percent of flight delays were due to bad weather" and technologies which address this problem will become effective only in years to come. With regard to the third outcome, DOT "met its goal to improve pavement conditions" and "exceeded its goal to install intelligent transportation systems in [...] metropolitan areas"; however, it "did not meet its goal to reduce highway delays". Lastly, the fourth outcome is pursued by a "multi-agency strategy to reduce the supply of illicit drugs entering the United States" but, unfortunately, DOT was unable to report an improvement in seizure rates for cocaine, et cetera.

- *Department of Health and Human Services* (United States General Accounting Office, 2000d, 2001d): HHS lists six key outcomes: (1) "less fraud, waste, and error in Medicare and Medicaid", (2) "high quality nursing home services", (3) "[self-sufficiency] of poor and disadvantaged families and individuals", (4) "improved prevention of

infectious diseases, including vaccine-preventable diseases", (5) "reduced use of illegal drugs", and (6) "prompt access to safe and effective medical drugs and devices [by the public]". With regard to
the first outcome, the reviewers note that the Health Care Financing
Administration (HCFA) is not in compliance with the Federal Financial Management Improvement Act, mainly "because it lacks a fully
integrated financial management system" (United States General Accounting Office, 2001d, p. 9). Regarding the second outcome, HCFA
is not seen to give proper recognition to the Nursing Home Oversight
Improvement Program. With regard to the third measure, "the Administration for Children and Families (ACF) reported that it lacked
fiscal year 2000 performance data for 18 of the 26 measures associated
with programs whose performance is critical in reaching this key outcome". "Mixed progress" is reported toward the fourth measure, i.e.
"towards achieving the 15 infectious disease prevention goals associated with this outcome". Concerning the fifth outcome, problems
were associated with "collecting data for about half of its 80 goals",
but the Substance Abuse & Mental Health Services Administration
(SAMHSA) reports that "it met or exceeded its targets for nearly 90%
of the goals for which it had data". And lastly, with regard to the
sixth outcome, the Federal Drug Administration (FDA) "reported results for 17 out of 19 goals [...] and reported that it met or exceeded
14 goals, did not meet 3 goals, and lacked outcome data for 2 goals".

What are we to make of this? A first comment may relate to the outcomes
used and how they were assessed. Let us take case by case.

With regard to the NSF, the reaching of the two goals is somehow trivial. In the case of the Department of Education, the six outcomes assessed
cover rather well the entire spectrum of issues to be addressed, although
not all outcomes can be seen to occupy the same hierarchical level: the
first, the second, and the sixth are clearly to be seen at a higher level than
the third, the fourth, and the fifth. The Department's progress was assessed
less than enthusiastically, in spite of the fact that no other nation, and no
other Department of Education, researches education at comparable depth.

With regard to the Environmental Protection Agency (EPA), a systems
argument may have to be invoked. Factors which affect the quality of air,
water and land are not under the influence of EPA. Emissions from trans-
port or heating affect air quality, and here the Departments of Transportation or Energy are involved; water quality is affected by a range of factors
of which one, pesticides, falls under the jurisdiction of the Department of

Agriculture. EPA stands at the forefront as a monitoring agency and cannot easily be held accountable for air or water quality.

In the case of the Department of Transportation, four 'outcomes' are used to assess the work of the department, the first three of which address means of service delivery, not outcomes in a stricter sense, while the fourth appears to belong subsumed under the first. Not addressed are the aims of transportation, and not addressed are vital points in transportation and land-use planning, such as modal split (e.g., urban metro versus automobile, rail versus flight traffic, transportation versus communication), or zoning and sub-urbanization in relation to transportation modes.

Regarding the Department of Health and Human Services, we observe again that means of service, not outcomes, stand in the foreground: four of the six areas of investigations refer to means of service delivery. Public health is not addressed as such, only two sub-categories: infectious diseases, and use of illegal drugs; neither is a major focus discernible regarding rising cost levels within the health system and how to curb these.

If one looks at a Next Steps Report by the UK Cabinet Office, to take a European example, one learns "details of performance against 1,265 key targets which were set by 136 Agencies plus 2 of the 4 Departments operating on Next Steps lines [. . .] Overall, Agencies met 75.7% of their targets, in line with last year" (Cabinet Office, 1999, p. 5)[22]. The report self-critically remarks that "whether or not an agency meets a particular target reflects both the level at which the target is set and the performance of the agency". Service improvement is a further issue: "Where direct comparisons can be made with the previous year, performance exceeded that achieved in 1996–97 against 52% of targets"[23].

All the activities referred to above are exercises which are mandated politically. They follow a scheme of performance-based reporting — if you will — which try to measure goals achievement, measures which are methodologically flawed: they are not suited to assess complex, interrelated phenomena which are characteristic of our modern societies, and they are not suited to assess the merits of an organization or to identify strength and weaknesses of governmental units.

---

[22]The corresponding figures for previous years are as follows: 1993–94: 80.0%; 1994–95: 83.0%; 1995–96: 75.0%.

[23]I.e. performance was better in 52% of the cases; in 14% it was worse, and in 34% of the case about the same.

3.4   Political vs. Academic Orientation

To assess the public management reform movement is a daunting endeavor and clearly outside the scope of this volume. A range of books are around, however, with this aim in mind (Jones, Schedler, & Wade, 1997; Boston et al., 1999; Kettl, 2000; Brudney et al., 2000; Pollitt & Bouckaert, 2000; Barzelay, 2001; Kettl, 2002). In spite of my reservations regarding a well founded assessment — or critique — of the reform movement, a few general observations might be admissible. More specific reform proposals as they pertain to higher education shall then be addressed in the subsequent chapters.

General Observations. The first observation pertains to the speed with which the reform movement has spread. For anybody who is accustomed to the slow movement of change, in government in general and in higher education in particular, the reform movement has spread rapidly[24]. *Donald F. Kettl* observes (Kettl, 2000, p. 5): "The reform movement has spread like a wildfire, often without careful analysis of the results they have produced or the preconditions for success". *Jones* and *Kettl* reiterate this observation two or three years later (Jones & Kettl, 2003, p. 9):

> "[...] the new public management reforms spread around the world with an energy and simultaneity never seen before with any kind of management reform [...] Never before have so many governments tried such similar things in such a short order".

My own hunch is that the reform movement had a stronger impact on societies where modern management and planning approaches were lacking in development, where bureaucracies were still entrenched in their traditional modes of operation, where change was difficult to bring about, and where the reflective positions and natural immunity against management fads was least developed.

The second observation is that the reforms affected widely differing — mainly democratic — governments, quite irrespective of their particular profiles and problem structures. In a sense, the reforms took on the form of 'package deals', and they were propagated and branded as such.

---

[24]To indicate that change management is a difficult task, I included in the MIT-ETHZ report (Herbst et al., 2002) a quote from *Per Nyborg* (Nyborg, 2000): "Changing a university is like moving a graveyard — it is extremely difficult and you don't get much internal support". Subsequently I found an earlier remark by *Wilson* (Wilson, 1989, p. 368) which *Nyborg* may have used: "[c]hanging [a bureaucratic] culture is like moving a cemetery: it is always difficult and some believe it is sacrilegious".

No individual reform measures were standing in the foreground, selected for particular national conditions or specific public services. Rather, those 'deals' became an almost amorphous prescription of general guiding principles — or a fancy cocktail of some of the more modern fiscal measures, combined with newer management concepts imported from private industry. Because of its amorphous nature, it is very difficult to critically evaluate the reform movement: most reform measures subsumed under the reform label make sense in a particular context. The reform as a brand was so strong that it itself became the very driving force of change, rather than the problems that needed to be solved: the solution itself was omnipresent.

My third observation refers to the political versus the academic orientation of the reform. It is clear that the reform movement grew out of political necessities as perceived by political parties, governments, and their associated advisers (Osborne & Gaebler, 1993; Gore, 1993, 1996). It is also clear that the reform relied on a broad range of management concepts which have evolved during the past half century, and it covers subject matters which span many disciplines, from economics, to political science, to law, to management and sociology. As such, the reform movement has a political orientation, and the particular packaging of diverse ideas, its doctrine, made it appealing. But the speed with which reforms were initiated and adopted cannot be explained by the power play of political parties, nor by the succession rate of governments — or the problems faced in the particular contexts, for that matter. The speed with which reforms spread probably has to do with both the acceptance the reform found in academic circles and the eagerness with which reforms were embraced — perhaps even used — by members of the university community (Abbott, 2001), particularly in Europe[25].

The Tides of Reform. In all the exuberance regarding performance-reporting and the current reforms in public management, one easily forgets that previous generations have done their work as well. Goals, targets and priorities have been set before, and prior developments were reviewed (Schultze, Hamilton, & Schick, 1970; Council of Economic Advisors, 1971). Some of the best minds have helped to shape public investment policy (Dorfman, 1965; Congress of the United States, Joint Economic Committee, 1969; Moss, 1973). Before the Balanced Scorecard concept was developed (Kaplan & Norton, 1996), there were people studying multi-criterion decision-making (Keeney & Raiffa, 1976; Starr & Zeleny, 1977) or decision

---

[25]Academicians frequently play a prominent part in government but, with the exception of the recent public management movement, they rarely belong to one school of thought.

and value theory (Arrow, 1963 (1951); Fishburn, 1964, 1973). Year after year, scholars and students alike tried to understand, improve and apply economics, planning, law, political science and quantitative analysis in order to improve public service and decision making (Gawande & Wheeler, 1999). What I am trying to say is the following: all fields develop continually, more or less; particular fields may stagnate for a time, but stagnation in many fields cannot be observed in our era.

Finally, reform is not necessarily tied to development or improvement, in spite of its common meaning; the term also refers to restoration or repair. In a wider sense, reform is an ongoing process initiated by whoever aims to re-form. *Paul C. Light* describes tides of reform, an ebb and flow of movements, which continuously shape the profile and character of public administration (Light, 1997). He distinguishes four ideal-types of reform: (i) 'scientific management', with a focus on discernible management principles and a reliance on structure, rules, and chains of command; (ii) 'liberation management' with a focus on performance and a reliance on targets and evaluations; (iii) 'war on waste', with a focus on efficiency and a reliance on audits, inspections, and investigations; and (iv) 'watchful eye', with a focus on fairness and a reliance on information, accountability measures, the media, and 'whistle-blowing'. Most policies or programs today will have ingredients of all four of the ideal-types mentioned, and even more commonly, differing administrations will emphasize one or the other aspect of reform.

Light is concerned with a range of problems associated with reforms and he calls for "better analysis and greater experimentation". The problem with 'bureaucratic naturalism', as he calls it, is that the

> "[...] tides of reform create *cumulative*, not isolated, effects [...] the tides of management reform appear always to produce accretion, whether in the form of paperwork, rules, or administrative thickening — that is, more layers of management and more managers at each layer" [p. 117].

The second problem he locates in a tendency to pursue comprehensive, government-wide reforms which cannot easily be targeted toward particular agencies or problems and which may, hence, produce mismatches between problem situations on the one hand and reform approaches on the other[26]. The third problem he sees in the fact that reform approaches fre-

---

[26]"It may be", *Light* writes (Light, 1997, p. 221), "that tight hierarchies and specialization are particularly appropriate for certain kinds of high-volume processing agencies, such as the Social Security Administration or the Internal Revenue Service, but inappropriate for knowledge-producing agencies like the National Institute of Health or NASA's Jet Propul-

quently create contradictory effects when combined or sequenced. Particularly 'liberation management', his reform class most closely matching the current tendencies within public management and comprehensive — government wide — in scope, he sees as

> "[…] self-consciously disdainful of […] of compromises with structural machinery. It tends to view itself more as a social movement for rescuing government than as a mere engine of tinkering with the structure of the past" (Light, 1997, p. 222).

Lastly, a fourth problem he perceives in the apparent accelerating rate of reforms.

In view of such constant attempts to reform, to improve, to renew, or to adapt, current reform efforts ought to be promulgated with a sense of modesty and be received with a sense of perspective. The adjective "New" in the concept of NPM may conjure the notion that a true paradigm shift is at work, replacing 'old' thinking. But this is not the case. Complex societal problems cannot easily be solved, and it should be clear that it is quite questionable to approach a wide spectrum of disparate problems with the same approach, the same doctrine.

---

sion Laboratory. It may also be that employee teams and empowerment are much more suitable for such highly professionalized workforces as air traffic controllers or custom inspectors but a poor fit for agencies which long histories of internal division or high vulnerability to fraud, waste, and abuse".

Chapter 4

Performance-Based Budgeting or Funding

> *Ironically, by focusing on performing for someone else's approval, corporations create the very conditions that predestine them to mediocre performance.*
>
> *Peter M. Senge (Senge, 2000)*

A DISCUSSION ON performance-based allocation of resources in higher education will have to clarify a number of issues. First, we need to have a clearer notion of what the concept stands for, how it relates to what we might call more generally indicator-based — or formula driven — allocation of resources, and whether it is important to distinguish between budgeting and funding (Section 4.1). Second, we need to distinguish the levels of resource allocation[1] and the forms of funding. In this context, it will be important to clarify the relative magnitude of resources which are allocated on the basis of performance criteria (Section 4.2). Third, we should present illustrative examples regarding the practice of performance-based resource allocation in various countries and higher education systems, and should assess various ramifications (Section 4.3).

4.1   Indicator-Based Resource Allocation

Performance-based allocation of resources have to be seen in the more general context of indicator-based resource allocations. In the public sphere

---

[1]As a function of the resource flows: from the state to institutional systems, from institutional systems to institutions, and finally within the institutions themselves.

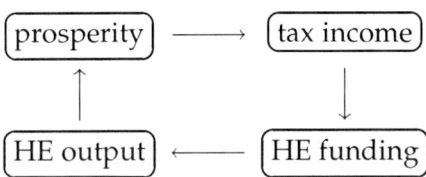

Figure 4.1: ECONOMIC IMPACT CYCLE OF HIGHER EDUCATION.

at least, resources are allocated in terms of perceived — relative — needs, resource allocation is constrained by the availability of resources, and these in turn are dependent on fiscal policies and regulations. A comprehensive view of this cycle — fiscal policies and revenues (tax income), budgeting of public program needs (higher education funding), resource allocation within specific sectors and programs and generation of output in education and research (HE output), and the tracing of economic impact and the assessment of economic growth and fiscal revenue prospects (prosperity) — is a complex macro-economic endeavor clearly outside the scope of this publication (see Figure 4.1). Suffice it to say here that the assessment of program needs, in the public sphere of democratic societies and in relative terms, has always been information or indicator based. There is no way to perceive program needs other than to review information or program indicators, and while most public resource allocation processes of the past were not formula driven, they always took into consideration pertinent information.

A certain confusion is evident regarding the definition of performance indicators. *Martin Cave, Stephen Hanney* and *Maurice Kogan* contribute the following definition (Cave, Hanney, & Kogan, 1991, p. 24):

> "[…] we define a performance indicator as an authoritative measure — usually in quantitative form — of an attribute of the activity of a higher education institution. The measure may be either ordinal or cardinal, absolute or comparative. It includes both the mechanical applications of formulæ (where the latter are imbued with value or interpretative judgments) and such informal and subjective procedures as peer evaluations or reputational rankings".

This definition appears misleading and too broad: misleading, because it seeks to include "absolute" measures, and too broad, because it subsumes all indicators under the label of performance indicators[2].

---

[2] Another aspect is touched by *Mantz Yorke*: "That the initial expectations regarding performance indicators have not been fulfilled is revealed in the work of *Cave et al.* In the

First, we ought to note that not all data can be used as indicators: data used in this way have to be 'indicative', to 'point out', to 'hint' or to 'suggest' (Little, Fowler, Coulson, & Onions, 1967 (1933)). "Absolute measures" are not indicative as such, unless they are used in a comparative context and are combined with other measures. Indicators are normalized in one way or another: as ratios of two sets of data (e.g. student-faculty ratios), as percentages of target achievement, saturation or exploitation (e.g. age participation rates, drop-out rates), as reference points on an interval scale (e.g. research performance ratings), or as relative positions among a set of positions (e.g. research performance rankings).

Second, *Cave et al.* call indicators "performance indicators" whenever they are used to address activities of higher education systems or institutions. This appears clearly too encompassing. Even a clause which would tie performance indicators to the assessment of performance aspects would not suffice because most discourses regarding higher education touch, in one way or another, performance aspects. In reference to the US context, *Cave et al.* themselves note the questionable value of defining 'performance indicator' in too broad terms and, referring to *Herbert H. Kells* (Kells, 1986), they state (Cave et al., 1991, p. 58):

> "He points out that although quantitative data are collected in the USA they are not akin to Western European [performance indicators] because they are used to inform peer review and to assist internal management and formative self-assessment rather than related to governmental goals and published in league tables that might influence funding decisions".

In other words, *Herb Kells* reserves the term 'performance indicator' for the situation where indicators are tied to the allocation of resources, i.e. to performance-based funding or budgeting, irrespective of whether or not indicators are performance indicators in a strict sense[3]. In the context of the present volume, we shall rely on *Kells'* notion of the term.

A second confusion arises in relation to 'performance-based' vs. 'indicator-based' allocation of resources. It should be clear that the latter — generic term — can serve to encompass the former (but not the other way around), and that the term 'indicator-based' can be used synonymously

---

second edition of their book on performance indicators *Cave et al.* [p. 24] defined an indicator (rather blandly, it has to be said) as 'an authoritative measure — usually in quantitative form — of an attribute of the activity of a higher education institution'. The definition in the third edition is similar, but has one notable omission — the word 'authoritative' " (Yorke, 1998).

[3]In the strict sense, a performance indicator relates output to input.

with 'formula-based' or 'formula-driven'. Formula-based resource allocation mechanism might tie funds to input measures, for instance when resources are distributed according to the number of students enrolled. Performance-based funding, in contrast, would attempt to link resource allocation to performance-indicators or output-measures[4]. Furthermore, while *Joseph C. Burke* distinguishes performance funding from performance budgeting (see p. 70), in the sense that he ascribes to the two terms different foci and contents, I prefer to not make this distinction (other than to retain the time-order of the terms, namely that budgeting takes place before funding).

4.2   Block Grants vs. Line-Item Budgeting

In order to arrive at a clearer notion of performance-based resource allocation, we shall focus first on resources flowing from the government to higher education systems or to individual institutions, provided these are financed directly by the state. Here, we shall have to distinguish two basic funding modes:

- block grants, where the power to allocate funds is handed over to the funded institution; and

- line-item budgeting systems, where the power to allocate funds rests with the funding agency (Massy, 1996).

Block grants[5] allocate a specified sum of funds, ideally without a great deal of strings attached, at least as long as the institution is pursuing a course which is not conflicting with the institutional mission: funds are basically 'unrestricted' and can be used for whatever purposes the recipient agency or institution deems relevant. Specifically, funds can be transferred from one budget category to another, and from one year to the next. In more restricted cases, the budget is still subdivided into broad budget categories, and the transfer of funds from one budget category to another will have to be approved by the funding agency. In contrast to block grants, when line-item budgeting systems are put into effect, the funding agency retains the

---

[4]While one can clearly separate performance funding from indicator-based (or formula-based) resource allocation, the distinction in the literature is not that easy because (i) both resource allocation modes are often used simultaneously (and for the same motives) and (ii) authors frequently fail to recognize this distinction.

[5]In the current German — or Swiss-German — discussion, the term is translated as *Globalbudget*.

power of resource allocation[6]: no transfers between budget categories and no inter-annual financial carry-over are feasible.

Historically, line-item budgeting systems (with the power of resource allocation retained by the funding agency) appeared to play no significant role within the US regarding the state funding of institutions[7]. From the very outset, US institutions had to scramble for funds and early on they developed broader funding bases than their European peer institutions. State institutions would receive block grant appropriations from their state for instruction and self-supported research, but they would also receive directly earmarked — i.e. restricted — resources from government or industry to fund research or specific projects, and they collected tuition and fees from students. In addition, institutions benefited directly from philanthropy and indirectly from governmental grants and loans given to students. Today's public universities receive less than half of their income from their respective state[8].

The US tradition of block grant state appropriations and broad institutional budgeting bases is in clear contrast to the European situation where block grant systems are a relatively recent phenomenon, implemented in a few countries and partially implemented in others. While US public higher education never had to shift from governmental line-item control to block grants, European — and also many outer-European — systems were called upon to make this transition[9]. In contrast to the US situation, however, where institutional autonomy has a long history and is comparatively well developed, managerial autonomy and block grants in Europe are not simply granted but tied to elaborate funding systems: institutional autonomy is granted by the state, but only within narrow margins of state control. While European — Humboldtian — institutions experienced autonomy in the context of *Lehr- und Forschungsfreiheit*, their managerial autonomy was

---

[6]Line-item systems are characteristic of budgeting modes of the *Kameralistik*.

[7]However, line-item budgeting did — and to some extent even do — play a role in the internal allocation of resources of US institutions.

[8]See (The Editor, 2003, p. 24) or Tables D.4 and D.5.

[9]Both *Joe Burke* and *Frank Schmidtlein* point to the fact that block grants may have a line-item budgeting base (not as detailed as that in Europe). For instance, "over half of the [US] states require that institutional budgets be prepared listing [...] 'objects of expenditure' [...]" (*Schmidtlein*, personal communication). Furthermore, "the controls states place on transfer of funds between 'line-items' after the budget has been approved by the state vary considerably, with some states requiring approval of transfers between some of the line-items and others giving the institution considerable flexibility in reallocating funds among line-items. Around a third of the states employ budget formulas to calculate the amount of funds [needed] for public institutions [and appropriate a percentage of these funding targets]".

traditionally restricted: *Kantone* and *Länder*, for instance, retained strong control over matters pertaining to resource allocation, curriculum development, degree courses, and even faculty appointments. Faculty and rector's offices didn't have to 'bother' with the broader aspects of running an institution and they could devote themselves to the strictly academic aspects of higher education. Such systems appealed not only to Europeans but also to US scholars (Flexner, 1930; Kerr, 1994).

A byproduct of globalization is a certain alignment of higher education cultures or particular aspects thereof: the current Bologna process (Bollag, 2001; Edwards, 1999) can be seen in this light. There are European tendencies to emulate particular aspects of US higher education, and rightly so, but there are also tendencies which point in the opposite direction: US higher eduction appears to integrate notions and concepts which originated elsewhere, in Australasia or in Europe, for instance[10]. Performance budgeting has to be seen as part of a new cultural change and adaptation process which affects different systems differently: European or Australasian systems with a tradition of direct government control and associated line-item budgeting are affected much more strongly than US systems, with block grant appropriations and powerful institutional leadership.

The US Experience. Let us look at the North American experience first. Experiments with performance funding in the states of Tennessee, Connecticut and Hawaii date back to the 1970s and 1980s (Burke, Joseph C. and Associates, 2002). Learning — and performance — became a research focus in the 1980s (Astin, 1985, 1993), and the subsequent focus on performance budgeting or funding in higher education was influenced by general management reforms (Peters & Waterman, 1988 (1982); Hammer & Champy, 1993), by the reform movement which affected government in the early 1990s (Osborne & Gaebler, 1993), and — naturally — by the fiscal and financial crises which affected funding states and higher education systems (see Chapter 2).

Joseph C. Burke distinguishes performance funding from performance budgeting — and from performance reporting (Burke, Joseph C. and Associates, 2002, p. 21f):

---

[10]The exchange of ideas and the mutual influencing among differing cultures is, of course, natural and old and can be traced throughout the entire history of higher education. In particular, the early US research university profited a great deal from Humboldtian — or German — ideals (Schwinges, 2001; Flexner, 1930) while during the later years, i.e. during the post World War II era, the US research university played the dominant role (Graham & Diamond, 1997; Geiger, 1993; Freeland, 1992).

Table 4.1: US USE OF PERFORMANCE INDICATORS: Number of States practicing the measure, by year (1997–02) (Burke & Minassians, 2002).

MEASURE:	1997	1998	1999	2000	2001	2002
Performance Funding	10	13	16	17	19	18
Performance Budgeting	16	21	23	28	27	26
Performance Reporting	n.a.	n.a.	n.a.	30	39	44

"*Performance funding* ties tightly specific resources to institutional results on
each of the designated indicators. The tie is automatic and formulaic. If a
campus achieves a set target on a designated indicator, it receives a specific
amount of performance money for that measure. Performance funding focuses on the distribution phase of the budget process.

Performance budgeting allows governors and legislators, or coordinating or
system boards, to consider campus performance on the indicators collectively
as merely one factor in determining the total allocation for a public college or
university. The link is loose and discretionary. This approach usually concentrates on budget preparation and slights — even ignores — budget distribution."

According to *Burke*'s assessment, within the period 1997–2002, performance funding in colleges and universities has expanded (see Table 4.1):
from 10 (of 50) states in 1997 to 18 in the year 2002. In the case of performance budgeting, *Burke* counts 16 states in 1997 and 26 states — i.e. more
than 50% of all states — in the year 2002. Furthermore, 50% of the states
practicing performance funding also practice performance budgeting (year
2002), and 23% of all the states with performance budgeting systems in
place also practice performance funding. But the situation is not such that
states practicing performance funding form a subset of states with performance budgeting in place, and these in turn would form a subset of states
practicing performance reporting (intersections percentages are found in
Table 4.2).

The picture thus painted can easily be misleading. In the case of performance funding and in the construction of performance formulæ, states
include varying numbers of indicators, perhaps only a single indicator,
for instance, the percentage of minority students among those enrolled,
or the percentage of women faculty[11]. If few indicators are included in

---

[11]*Burke* notes in this respect: "Performance indicators identify areas of anticipated
achievement. [Their number] run from as few as one in Connecticut to as many as 37 in
South Carolina's original plan, with most programs using around ten" (Burke, Joseph C.
and Associates, 2002, p. 26f). See also Appendix D.2.

Table 4.2: US Use of Performance Indicators: Relative share of performance measures (year 2002) (Burke & Minassians, 2002).

Measure:	PF	PB	PR
Performance Funding (PF)	–	50%	94%
Performance Budgeting (PB)	23%	–	88%
Performance Reporting (PR)	36%	52%	–

the funding rationale, and if the approach is not comprehensive[12], performance funding is a way to add "incentive bonuses for institutions that meet or exceed state- and self-defined goals" (Carnevale, Johnson, & Edwards, 1998) and is not that much different from project funding[13]. Performance funding, in *Burke*'s assessment, has a limited impact even when applied: it affects only roughly 0.5% to 6% of the state's general fund support and averages around 2%. And performance budgeting, as *Burke* defines the term, is linked to performance reporting and appears to mandate a form of funding which takes information — and performance indicators — into consideration. However, performance rewards are frequently added to the base budgets of the institutions and, "by earning modest rewards every year, [colleges] can bring about substantial cumulative growth in budgets over time" (Schmidt, 2002a)[14].

The most common indicators which states take into consideration are the following (Burke, Joseph C. and Associates, 2002, p. 10, pp. 229–233):

- *input indicators*: admission standards and measures (quality of incoming class);

- *process indicators*: freshmen and minority retention, graduation rates, faculty workload, student satisfaction studies (satisfaction of alumni), remediation activities (and success rates), number of accredited programs (quality of instructional programs), evidence of elimination of programs, classroom and lab utilization rates;

---

[12]Comprehensive approaches affect the whole budget of an institution in its entirety. European concepts work that way. See in this regard, for instance, Appendix D.1.

[13]Specific institutional projects are funded by the state depending on whether certain criteria have been met.

[14]Whether this rationale makes sense is another matter: it smacks, to use a term popularized by *Robert Zemsky* and *William F. Massy*, of the "academic ratchet effect" (Massy, 1996, pp. 81–85). If public funds are limited (for one reason or another), and if state institutions improve performance (because of performance funding), steadily increased funding cannot be feasible.

- *output indicators*: transfer rates, degrees awarded, sponsored research funds, national ranking among US research universities (based on publication counts);

- *outcome indicators*: placement data on graduates, pass rates on licensing programs, satisfaction of employers, national ranking among US research universities (based on citations).

But it is unclear just how these indicators are grouped to assess institutional performance, because indicators alone cannot easily grasp the systemic aspects of an institution. It is not institutional performance that appears to stay in the foreground, but specific goals or targets (Schmidt, 1996). *Burke* reports that performance funding, budgeting, or reporting was judged as having an impact on the improved performance of public colleges and universities (Burke & Minassians, 2002, pp. 17–21): in the year 2002, 50% of the states reported that performance funding affected institutional improvement at least 'moderately', 46% reported that performance budgeting had at least a 'moderate' effect on institutional performance, and 48% stated that performance reporting had at least a 'moderate' effect on the improvement of performance.

    In Appendix D.2, I cover a particular US funding system, that of the State of South Carolina. The funding system of South Carolina has gained some notoriety because it purported to allocate 100% of the state funds on the basis of a performance funding concept, a novelty in the US. The early euphoria, at least among the state legislators, appears to have dissipated. As *Catherine Watt* and her associates, in reviewing performance funding and quality enhancement in the state of South Carolina, conclude (Watt, Lancaster, Gilbert, & Higerd, 2004):

> "As of Fall 2003, the performance funding system in South Carolina is all but dead. The system has lost the support of the institutions, and it has also lost the support of several leading state legislators. The staff of the Commission on Higher Education has requested assistance in drafting a new programme that responds to the demands for accountability without tying results to allocated dollars. However, after significant cuts that leave funding at the mid-90s level, both legislators and institutional leaders seem hesitant to alter a system without funds to support it. Performance funding for several states appears on the way out as a management fad; other priorities supersede outcomes when there is no money with which to reward performance".

Apparently, institutions were lured into supporting performance funding on the promise to reward performance[15]. When it became clear that 'per-

---

[15] A similar tendency can be observed in Europe.

formance' is not that easy to measure and to reward, particularly not in a mechanistic way, the optimistic — if not opportunistic — support for performance funding on the part of the higher education institutions vanished.

The UK Experience. In the UK, to give another example, performance funding was initiated with the Research Selectivity Exercise (RSE) in 1986 (later to be termed the Research Assessment Exercise (RAE)). Up to the early 1980s, funding was administered by the University Grants Committee (UGC). With the onset of mass higher education, and facing unprecedented budget cuts, the UGC paved the way to a new assessment of the higher education landscape and to a new way to allocate — and concentrate — resources.

Since then, the RAE has run though five cycles. Performance funding and the RAE were "designed to drive core funding by rewarding high achievers in a system with a spread of performance, so academics worked even harder to achieve excellence because higher grades led to better resourcing" (Adams, 2002). Performance funding and the RAE were to play a critical role in the distribution of scarce resources. There was a tendency to allocate fewer and fewer funds on a per student basis, and this was coupled with the aim to embrace an ever wider student population within higher education. Since 1989/90, annual (public) funding per student dropped from close to £8,000 to roughly £4,600 today (2002/03). The newest plans within the UK call for an enrollment (or participation) rate of 50%, and they demand substantial additional funding of circa 80% (Crewe, 2004).

To put this situation in context, we ought to recognize that of the £12.8 billion total income of UK's higher education sector (in the year 1999/2000), some 60% stem from the UK public sector and only circa 40% were grants of Funding Councils (see Table 4.3). Nonetheless, the reduction of public funding during the past decade, and the corresponding weakening of higher education, stands in contrast to the positive economic role of higher education. Higher education is viewed as an industry with an exemplary output or employment multiplier effect (see also Section 2.2): calculations by *Kelly* et al. (Kelly, Marsh, & McNicoll, 2002), based on input-output analysis, indicate that higher education institutions fare much better than many established industries[16]. During the same decade, UK research performance progressed[17], but it is difficult to tell whether research performance improved because of the policy change of the RAE. Research output

---

[16]Such as banking & finance, computing services, legal activities, oil processing & nuclear fuel, agriculture, advertising.

[17]Along the lines "do more with less".

Table 4.3: ESTIMATES FOR THE PATTERN OF UK HIGHER EDUCATION IN-
COME, BY SOURCE AND PURPOSE, in % of Total, Year 1999/2000, based on
(Kelly et al., 2002, p. 11).

SOURCE:	Private Sector	Public Sector	Rest of EU	Other Overseas	Total Income
Funding Council Grants	0	40.3	0	0	40.3
Academic Fees & Support Grants	6.0	9.8	0.7	5.7	22.2
Research Grants & Contracts	5.4	8.7	1.3	0.7	16.1
Other Services	2.9	1.4	0.7	0.3	5.3
General Operating Income	10.2	3.1	0.2	0.4	13.9
Endowment & Interest	2.2	0	0	0	2.2
Total Income	26.7	63.3	2.9	7.1	100.0

or performance, as measured, had been on the upswing for a number of
nations: improved research and office infrastructures are responsible for
an increased output, and the generally enlarged worldwide research base
is responsible for a heightened reception or impact of good research.

The RAE is an evaluative scheme on which to base the funding of research (see Appendix D.1, and particularly the paragraph on "quality-related research funding" on page 192). This evaluative scheme stands in
contrast to the descriptive approach chosen by the US National Research
Council (NRC) to assess research-doctorate programs (National Research
Council, 1995)[18]. The detailed report of the NRC aims to (National Research Council, 1995, p. 28):

- Assist students and advisers in matching students' career goals with
  the facilities and opportunities available in relevant research-doctorate
  programs;
- inform the practical judgment of university administrators, national
  and state-level policymakers, and managers of public and private funding agencies; and
- provide a large, recent data base that can be used by scholars who focus
  their work on characteristics and its associated research enterprise.

In other words, the aim of the NRC is to inform the various constituents or
stakeholders of the higher education landscape and to provide a vast data-
base in support of higher education research. This aim may be subsumed

---

[18]Originally designed to be issued roughly once in a decade. The first report by the NRC
was issued in 1982 and the second in 1995. The next report is expected to be published in
2007.

under a broad concept of accountability, but it is fair to say that the approach of the NRC preceded the current wave of accountability concerns[19]. In contrast to the NRC, the approach of the RAE is not primarily to inform, but to provide a rationale to allocate resources. These resources are aimed at the top performing departments, and they provide implicitly for some stability of resource allocation (Shattock, 2003), but it appears questionable whether the concentration of funds on well-performing departments alone is sound: performance does not appear to improve with size, once a threshold of a critical mass is passed (Adams & Smith, 2003), and research performance is more a matter of individuals or teams, not of departments (Trow, 1996).

Apart from the RAE, and apart from performance funding, the Higher Education Funding Council of England (HEFCE), for instance, distributes funds for teaching and learning formula-based — and basically according to the number of students enrolled, i.e. indicator-based or formula-driven (Appendix D.1). While research funding aims to concentrate its resources on a subset of well performing departments, and while research funding aims to pursue a policy to keep alive a few vital research universities[20], funds for teaching and learning are basically spread over all institutions. The distribution of funds is driven by program demands and does not make provisions for various levels of programs (within the university sector).

4.3   Assessment of Funding Regimes

The examples mentioned above point to the fact that a wide spectrum of assessment and funding cultures coexist[21]. Following, we shall attempt to trace the implications of funding regimes and shall concentrate on: (i) resources which flow to higher education systems or institutions (and not

---

[19]It is of interest to note here that an agency that is not 'accountable' in a strict sense for higher education institutions provides such a detailed and extensive picture of research-doctorate programs. The picture covers 3,634 separate doctorate programs in 274 universities, involving 41 research fields (or departmental orientations).

[20]Successfully, I should add. British universities are among the best in Europe, and among the very few non-US institutions that show up on the roster of the 50 best research universities world-wide. See (CEST, 2002).

[21]A range of nations influenced or molded by the Humboldtian tradition, of which the Netherlands and Sweden serve as examples, have responded to mass higher education and the funding crisis by quiet reforms. These reforms often evoke the language of performance funding, but the measures themselves point to systems which ought to be characterized as indicator-based or formula-driven (Huisman, 2001; Fritzell, 1998).

to students in the forms of grants, loans, or fellowships); and on (ii) aspects which characterize higher education funding systems on both sides of the Atlantic.

US versus European Approaches. In the US, performance assessment affects primarily the educational mission of colleges and universities, because research is funded in great measure through federal research funding agencies or through industry. Furthermore, US performance funding effects only a relatively minor portion — perhaps only 1% — of the institutional budgets[22], provided performance funding is implemented at all. This stands in contrast to the form of performance funding as practiced in the UK, for instance, where 100% of funds directed for educational purposes are distributed formula-based and substantial portions of research funds performance-based.

Apart from noticing that performance funding affects separate portions and domains of appropriations in the field of higher education, we also notice that different sets of indicators are called upon to describe performance characteristics of institutions. Because institutional performance is, by the very nature of higher education and research universities, a multi-dimensional matter, many well-defined indicators would have to be called upon to characterize an institution. Furthermore, input, process, output or outcome indicators used to characterize the performance of an institution or a higher education system are not necessarily, by themselves and in a strict sense, performance indicators. In spite of this, we notice that performance funding systems may use only very few indicators, perhaps even a single indicator, on the basis of which funds are allocated. In the US case, indicators are primarily used to promote — and fund — a particular cause, almost in the sense of project funding, whereas in the UK case a few indicators are functionally related to define — comprehensively — state appropriations (see Table 4.4 and Appendix D.1).

This duality of funding systems implies a disassociation from established funding modes and a choice of opposing directions which may — or may not — lead to a possible future alignment of funding cultures:

- In many European countries, funding systems are used to transfer decision controls from state agencies to buffer organizations and eventually to institutions, and to shift from line-item budgeting (under the control of the state) to block grants (under the control of the in-

---

[22]See in this respect the discussion on pp. 70f.

Table 4.4: CHARACTERISTICS OF FUNDING MODELS (formula driven or performance-based): The US versus the European Case.

CHARACTERISTIC:	US Model	European Model
Subject Matter	education only	education & research
Broadness of Focus	single targets	comprehensive approach
Budget Portion Affected	small segment	all public appropriations
Funding Form	incentive-based	formula-based
Original Funding Mode	block-grants	line-item approach
Change Direction	toward line-item approach	toward block grants

stitution). In this respect we may talk of a European model[23] which concentrates on a comprehensive, formula-based approach to funding.

- In the US model — and in contrast to the European model — performance funding is used to back up from a purely block grant allocation of resources and to give the state a direct influence on specific institutional aspects, similar to those under line-item budgeting systems. The US model concentrates on a target-oriented and incentive-based form of performance funding.

The two funding approaches appear to be in the process of entrenchment: they are trying to hold their place and are spreading within their respective systems of higher education. In spite of their relative success, however, critics voice their reservations, and there appears to be little prospect for a genuine rapprochement of systems which are in the process of development on both sides of the Atlantic.

Funding and Governance. One of the early models of a comparative — international — analysis within higher education was offered by *Burton R. Clark*. He proposed to analyze higher education within a coordinate system of three poles: the academia, the state, and the market (Clark, 1983, p. 143). This tri-polar system proved very influential and has provided a framework of analysis to this day (Braun & Merrien, 1999; McNay, 1999; Sporn & Aeberli, 2004; Weber, 1999). *Henry Etzkowitz* and *Loet Leydesdorff* have subsequently expanded *Bob Clark*'s model under the concept of "a triple

---

[23]Under the "European model" one can subsume also higher education systems shaped by European culture, such as those of Australia and New Zealand.

helix of university-industry-government relations" (Etzkowitz & Leydes-dorff, 2001 (1997); Etzkowitz, 1999). All three axes of such a tri-polar system are frequently addressed: the state-market axis which generally provides a backdrop for a discussion on public services, and which I covered in Chapter 3; the academia-state axis which is in the foreground in the context of the present report; and the academia-market axis which actually addresses two intertwined issues: university-industry relations and regional economic impact of higher education institutions (Lampe, 1988; Saxenian, 1994), as well as looking at higher education as an industry operating within an educational market (Clark, 1998). It is important to keep in mind that any discussion on the interrelationship between state and academia must take into consideration normative notions. Indeed, any discussion about the choice of funding modes and associated control mechanisms (which are based on a given separation of powers) must consider normative notions of how to position higher education within an educational market.

As we implied above, funding modes are tied to governance: depending on the funding system in place, different forms of governance are being practiced or, better formulated yet, depending on the system of governance chosen, corresponding funding systems will have to follow (see Table 4.5). The changes in funding modes we observe in the US and in Europe are in fact changes in governance. While European institutions were bound to some form of academic freedom in the past, at least during periods of democratic rule, managerial — as opposed to academic — control of most continental institutions remained curtailed. The recent European shift in governance toward institutional autonomy is driven by the vision of a re-formulated social contract which binds higher education and society together (Henkel & Little, 1999), which would allow universities to play a more pro-active, entrepreneurial role (Clark, 1998, 2004b), and which could assign universities a more encompassing mission (Gray, 1999).

The move of European higher education systems toward managerial autonomy has strings attached: institutional autonomy appears to be offered with one hand — and taken back with the other. The strings pertain not to a possible contractual arrangement between government and institutions concerning goals to pursue and missions to shoulder. Such an arrangement would delegate to higher education institutions the task of pursuing goals and missions and, as public institutions, to pursue them as effectively as possible. In return, government, through some appropriately chosen buffer organizations or boards, would see to it that institutions could operate in an environment suited to the pursuance of the chosen goals and missions[24]. In reality, however, governments would not simply oversee the operations of institutions under their jurisdiction, would not simply focus on contractual arrangements regarding institutional goals and missions. Governments started to focus on institutional 'performance' — on *Leistungsvereinbarungen* and *Leistungsaufträge* in the German language context — and, to operationalize the concept, defined performance targets to be met [25]. By doing so, the original intention of moving managerial control from government agencies to institutions is partially being reversed: managerial controls are transferred, but with strings attached.

The move of European higher education systems toward managerial autonomy is judged to be necessary by many, but the question remains whether performance funding systems should be counted as proper measures to pursue this venture: much more simple means which respect a separation of powers appear necessary. In countries with European-inspired higher education management systems, performance funding systems take hold because of a perceived market failure: higher education 'products' appear not specific enough because institutions lack diversity to enrich the supply side of higher education (Trow, 1979; Gans, 1979; Clark, 1997; Trow, 1997) and, as a consequence, the demand for higher education services is not structured and focused enough. Instead of trying to foster a more natural and healthy competition among higher education institutions by letting them develop their own profiles, and instead of creating 'price' differentials by giving the power to institutions to select their own student population, a quasi-market behavior is artificially created. This is done in an attempt to lure institutions closer to positions deemed preferable by authorities: in the name of the efficient use of resources, coordinative measures are put into effect which, in a different context, would violate anti-trust laws because they are basically designed to retain an academic oligarchy. Instead of fostering institutional leadership and management, performance funding systems are implemented to constrain institutional autonomy and to transfer decision-making powers which were handed over to institutions

---

[24]*Frank H.T. Rhodes* subsumes this under the concept of the nurturing, fiduciary function: "[...] the trustee is more than an overseer; he or she is a fiduciary, a guardian, a protector, not only of the performance and accountability of institutions, but also of the institution itself and of the standards and values it embodies". See: (Rhodes, 2004) in (Weber & Duderstadt, 2004b).

[25]Buffer organizations or boards appear to exhibit a clear preference to oversee the operations of institutions under their jurisdiction, and they are prone to micro-management. They see this as their main *raison d'être*. Performance funding in the context of performance contracts — *Leistungsvereinbarungen* and *Leistungsaufträge* — helps them to pursue this preference.

Table 4.5: FUNDING MODES AND GOVERNANCE: The US versus the European Case.

CHARACTERISTIC:	US Model	European Model
Original Funding Mode	block grants	line-item approach
Original Locus of Power	institution	ministry or buffer organization
Change Direction	toward government	toward institutions

back again to governmental supervising bodies or boards.

In contrast to European higher education, the US has traditionally retained a diversified and rather autonomous higher education system which developed quite naturally (Trow, 2003a) and which appeared to provide the foundation for its dominance today (Altbach, Gumport, & Johnstone, 2001; Herbst, 2004b). The primacy of institutional autonomy is being softened now by the introduction of performance funding measures. These measures were introduced primarily, in spite of particular performance goals (see Table 4.6), for political reasons: to demonstrate governmental strength and focus on efficiency in the face of mounting public concerns regarding rising costs of education, and to address particular constituencies and pressure groups. The impact of and enthusiasm for performance funding measures, as I have shown, has remained limited. The coming years shall tell whether we will observe an expansion of performance funding within the US, in substance as well as geographically. If higher education systems find ways to adapt to change by means other than performance systems, as I presume they will, the core values of US higher education governance and management, as we know them, will survive: performance funding will remain a fringe phenomenon and there will be increasing pressures on European higher education systems to look across the Atlantic.

Expectations Associated with Performance Funding. As mentioned, performance-based funding systems appear to be becoming entrenched, at least in Europe, but the link between the aims pursued through performance funding and the results obtained appears tenuous. As *Peter Schmidt* observes (Schmidt, 2002b):

> "[...] few of the performance-based financing systems have yielded either of the benefits that higher-education leaders had hoped they would bring: clear improvements in education, and an increase in state support for public colleges that have proved themselves [...] So far, most of the systems have produced paperwork and controversy".

Proponents or sympathizers of performance-based budgeting or funding argue that "[l]inking performance to appropriations gives policy makers and customers a clearer sense of how the public's investment in education is being used" (Carnevale et al., 1998), but these aims can also be pursued — and much better, presumably — with mandated accountability measures, such as proper and open reporting.

Performance-funding appears to have its own momentum: "[...] college officials really have no choice in the matter", writes *Schmidt*: "performance-based financing is going to be imposed on their institutions, regardless of how they feel". He cites an associate of the National Center for Higher Education Management Systems: "The question of whether it [i.e. performance-funding] works is irrelevant" and, given the popularity of such funding modes with legislators, performance-based financing systems "are not going away. They are simply going to remain part of the landscape". While these assessments refer to the development in the US, they appear to touch a more general mood (Cave et al., 1991).

Performance-funding systems in higher education are being pursued for the same reasons as public management reforms (see Chapter 3): to increase productivity, to foster competition, to "fund for results", to increase service orientation, to separate client-agent roles, and to further accountability. In addition, we may add a further goal, namely to distribute funds equitably among institutions within the same jurisdiction. These aims are broad-based, reasonable, and worth pursuing. The aims are not contended by many, I presume, but the means are. The contentions are, basically, that performance funding systems are not that suited to pursue the stated aims, that there are other — and tested — means available to pursue a performance orientation (see Chapter 5), and that performance-funding systems are not only ineffectual in pursuing their aims but directly harmful in their effects. In particular, a range of issues are being raised in connection with performance funding which we shall briefly address:

- the reliance on simple indicators or formulæ to pursue funding foci;

- the impact of performance funding on the intra-institutional allocation of resources;

- competition and the equitable distribution of resources;

- maladaptation and fraud.

Indicators, Formulæ and Funding Foci. Comparative analyses and benchmarking are necessary to assess where institutions or systems stand, but comparisons need to be done in a sensible way. In a comparative setting it is frequently shortsighted to compare indicators without assessing the broader context. It may even be meaningless to compare indicators of a particular class. To illustrate this point, I shall give three examples:

- grant programs which are linked to graduation rates;
- the use of student satisfaction statistics; and
- the comparison of sets of indicators.

Regarding the first point I shall refer to a plan of the US Department of Education to create a grant program which is designed to reward educational institutions "for retaining students and graduating them on time" (Burd, 2003). The general aim of the program appears reasonable: if students are retained, they will graduate (eventually); and if study periods are reduced, graduates will enter the labor market earlier and with higher credentials, allowing them to earn higher salaries.

State agencies might follow similar agendas, for example in Pennsylvania, where a "$6-million grant program [was created] to reward institutions that graduate at least 40 percent of their in-state [undergraduate] students within four years". But the effect was "that last year [i.e. 2002], when the first grants were awarded in Pennsylvania, not one public college in the state was among the 65 institutions on the list [receiving grants]". Public colleges have lower retention and graduation rates in comparison to private institutions, not necessarily because they are deficient, but because they cater to a different student population. They have larger proportions of non-traditional — and older — students who work in support of their part-time studies, or students who enroll in particular courses to enrich their education or to add new skills. "Public officials warn", *Stephen Burd* reports (Burd, 2003), that

> "[…] a shift in federal policy that would reward colleges for their success in retaining and graduating students would encourage institutions to shut their doors to students who need their services most".

The proposed federal program — and the implemented state program — is designed to improve the quality of student-aid programs, but it also aims at improving educational efficiency or effectiveness, for the benefit of the economy. The criteria by which the quality of student-aid programs are being assessed are neither obvious nor transparent, and it is very questionable whether efficiency or effectiveness of educational services are affected through such programs: in the US, where course credit systems are in place, students require services from the university in direct proportion to the credit hours taken, and they graduate when the required credits are accumulated.

The second example refers to student satisfaction statistics which are frequently used in the comparative assessment of institutions and the publication of league tables[26]. Inter-institutional and inter-disciplinary student satisfaction statistics cannot be compared because student responses at the various institutions or programs cannot be viewed as random samples from the same student population (and, hence, the scales of the respective assessment cannot be considered 'standardized'). We can observe, for example, that students from excellent institutions are less satisfied with their institution (or with their educational programs) than their peers from less prestigious institutions. This single fact alone does not suffice to make a judgment or rank the institutions: students at an excellent research university may be more discriminating and critical, while students of lesser-ranked institutions may be more grateful for receiving an education. In other words, student satisfaction statistics when used to compare institutions say little about the quality of an institution or a program, and the ranking of institutions along these performance measures is meaningless[27].

I will draw from *Jill Johnes* and *Jim Taylor* (Johnes & Taylor, 1990, pp. 173–180) to illustrate the third example, and remark again on the problems that can arise when comparing indicators. *Johnes* and *Taylor* report on a comparative ranking of 43 universities of the UK where five performance-indicators provide the basis for a ranking: the non-completion rate of students (i.e. dropout-rate); the percentage of graduates obtaining an honors-degree; the percentage of graduates obtaining permanent employment; the

---

[26]Student satisfaction statistics are frequently used by magazine surveys (like those of US News & World Report, Der Spiegel, Facts, India Today, et cetera), and magazine surveys appear to have gained a certain reputation in recent years.

[27]This is not to say that student satisfaction statistics have no meaning in single institutional course assessments, however. Indeed, there they have great meaning. First and foremost, they give faculty members insight on how courses are perceived by students and provide valuable information on how courses can be improved. And secondly, they may provide comparative information (regarding different classes of the same course) and clues for a comparative assessment of faculty (regarding different instructors of the same course) because here survey samples can more properly be regarded as belonging to the same population. But in an inter-institutional setting, student satisfaction surveys are very difficult to implement properly and their results are frequently questionable.

percentage of graduates proceeding to further education or training; and the average research rating obtained by each university. The five indicators appear well chosen, i.e. properly related to assess performance of (research) universities. Among the 43 institutions, we find Oxford and Cambridge listed as having the best research ratings (ranks 1 and 2, respectively), but if we look at other indicators, we see no natural correlation: regarding the percentage of graduates proceeding to further education or training, Oxford has rank 42 (of 43), and with regard to the percentage of graduates obtaining permanent employment, Cambridge is found in rank 41. Conversely, City University is listed as having the best employability of its graduates (rank 1), but has a research rating of rank 42. Furthermore, regarding honors-degrees, City University finds itself in rank 8, while Cambridge has rank 15 and Oxford rank 39.

How is this possible? First, the set of indicators chosen appears not that wisely selected, after all. Institutions pursue different missions, and because of their different orientation they cannot be easily compared with the same criteria in mind. If Oxford scores relatively low on further education or training, it might just be an indication that the education these graduates have received suffices for many. When Cambridge and Oxford score relatively low regarding honors-degrees, it presumably just means that both institutions have exacting standards. When Cambridge scores low regarding permanent employment, it might mean that graduates pursue non-permanent academic or research jobs. One the other hand, City University ranks low in the research assessment exercise but appears to do an excellent job in preparing their graduates for jobs demanded by the economy. Should one assess, on the basis of such comparisons, the "performance" of institutions and tie its funding to performance measures?

Intra-Institutional Allocation of Resources. "Performance-funding", as *Joseph C. Burke* assesses it in the US context, "focuses on institutional performance [and] should stimulate increased interest in institutional achievements as opposed to individual activities of professors and professionals" (Burke, Joseph C. and Associates, 2002, p. 271). But, *Burke* observes, performance funding "has only a minimal impact on most of the goals often set in performance-funding plans" (Burke, Joseph C. and Terry A. Lessard, 2002, p. 73). Also programs "have little impact below the levels of presidents and vice-presidents" (Burke, Joseph C. and Associates, 2002, p. 271). His own surveys in five states indicate that, on a score of 1 to 5 (with 1 denoting "very high impact" and 5 denoting "no effect"), performance funding measures score no better than 3.2 (and have mainly a "moderate" or a "minimal

Table 4.6: Impact of Performance Funding on Campus Goals
(Burke, Joseph C. and Terry A. Lessard, 2002, p. 74)

Campus Goal:	Score
Mission Focus	3.2
Administrative Efficiency	3.5
Quality & Quantity of Student Learning	3.6
Faculty Performance	3.7
Inter-Institutional Cooperation	3.9
Faculty-Student Interaction	3.9
Research Funding	4.0
Graduates' Job Placement	4.1
Graduates' Continuing their Education	4.1

impact"; see Table 4.6). Performance-funding effects are somehow shielded from faculty and staff, and performance-funding measures, consequently, do not trickle down enough to affect intra-institutional resource allocation.

While *Burke* documents the weak impact of performance funding on institutional management, we ought to keep in mind that if the impact were significant, it would imply a reduction of institutional autonomy and a corresponding shift of power from the institutions to funding bodies and governmental agencies (see Table 4.4). Ineffective performance funding measures and resistance on the part of the institutions combine to keep the effect of performance funding within bounds. The implicit clash between government agencies and higher education systems or institutions is the result of a growing rift between the two and associated attempts to redefine the roles of government agencies and institutions within the US in recent decades.

Within Europe, the aim of performance funding seems to be: to impinge on institutional management, to coerce. This aim is also an expression of lacking trust regarding academia. This lack of trust is not entirely unfounded. Academia has a centuries-old tradition of self-government and faculty have been given privileges which are defended and not easily reinterpreted or changed. The perception of the faculty as a conservative body is prevalent almost everywhere, but there are clear differences in the form of self-governance, particularly if one contrasts faculty and institutional governance cultures on both sides of the Atlantic. The contrasting picture as painted some years ago (Herbst et al., 2002, p. 104) (see Table 4.7) may have softened a bit by a converging movement of both US and European cultures, but the major contours of both cultures are still distinctively dis-

Table 4.7: GOVERNANCE, PLANNING AND MANAGEMENT INFLUENCE, by Policy Level and Culture (US vs. European), based on (van Vught, 1997).

POLICY LEVEL	Institutions:	
	US	European
State Government	low	high
Presidency (Rektorat), School, Department	high	low
Faculty Member	low	high

cernible. Self-government in Europe does not extend enough into the management of institutions, and this in turn fosters tendencies on the part of buffer organizations or boards to mistake management for governance.

Indeed, institutional management issues not properly covered by academic self-government can be seen as one reason why performance funding has gained ground; the other, of course, is lack of trust[28]. A gaping void in the academic self-government of many European institutions has yet to be filled, and this void pertains most prominently to the resource allocation mechanism within institutions (Massy, 2003). US institutions started earlier to reform their internal resource allocation modes (Hopkins, 1981; Massy, 1990, 1996), moving from line-item budgeting to more appropriate modes and, in doing so, decentralized resource allocation within their institutions (Whalen, 1991). It is perhaps instructive to note that performance-funding systems appear to be most attractive where the internal resource allocation mechanisms are least developed: in Europe, or in higher education systems strongly shaped by European culture (see Table 4.8).

It is clear why internal resource allocation mechanisms lack development in Europe: there was no use for it before because government agencies were practically distributing funds directly down to each individual faculty member[29]. US institutions were much better prepared than their European peers to make the transition from centralized, internal line-item budgeting, to decentralized "responsibility center budgeting", in particular because they had course credit systems in place, which are gradually making their inroads in the European context as well (Whalen, 1991). In Europe, apparently, a top-down mandate from the European Rectors' Con-

---

[28]*Frank H.T. Rhodes* writes: "Unless universities show more responsibility in self-regulation, it seems increasingly likely that increased external regulations may be imposed." See: (Rhodes, 2004, p. 8), as well as the quote by *Martin Trow* on p. 91.

[29]Until recently, we may claim in jest, a typical Rector's office just had a yearly budget to pay for various banquets.

Table 4.8: PERFORMANCE FUNDING AND INTERNAL FUNDING MODES, by
Higher Education Culture (US vs. European).

	Culture:	
CHARACTERISTIC	US	European
performance funding doctrine	marginal	significant
internal resource allocation	decentralized	centralized
academic self-government	developed	under-developed

ference (ERC) proved helpful to introduce a form of such course credit system, the European Credit Transfer System (ECTS). While the ECTS is being
introduced now, the term itself suggests an inordinate focus on credit transfer, from one institution to another: European and Swiss institutions have
yet to discover course credit systems as helpful — even vital — for their internal course management, resource allocation, and space management[30]
mechanisms. Unless proper course credit systems are implemented, and
unless exams are tied to course credits, no proper accounting and management of educational resources can be implemented.

Modern internal resource allocation systems are directly tied to performance funding: if the former are lacking, the latter is seen as a necessity;
and conversely, if the latter is being fought, the former will have to be implemented. If modern internal resource allocation or budgeting systems
are absent, institutions have a tendency to spend all their money without being able to free and reallocate resources internally in order to fund
new ventures. *William F Massy* and *Robert Zemsky* describe two classes of
"cost diseases" (Massy, 1990): the "administrative lattice" and the "academic ratchet" (Massy, 1996, pp. 80–85) (Herbst et al., 2002, pp. 158f). The
administrative lattice refers to the "proliferation and entrenchment of administrative staff" at universities:

> "Like a healthy vine, the growth of support staff often leads to more growth
> as professionals seek to expand their areas; yet another possible result is that
> professionals may perform tasks to a better degree — and consequently, at a
> higher cost — than an institution requires" (Massy, 1996, p. 81).

The "function lust", as *Massy* calls the tendency to perfect services and to
provide the required resources, is not an indication of ineptitude on the
part of administrators but more an indication of a lack of perspective — or

---

[30]The assignment of courses to lecture halls and seminar rooms, including longer-term
space management and planning.

an indication of a biased assessment of marginal utilities. The "academic ratchet", on the other hand,

> "[...] denotes the specific process that causes [...] output creep [...] and describes the steady, irreversible shift of faculty allegiance away from the goals of a given institution, towards those of an academic specialty [...] The increasing outputs or primary gainers from the ratchet are research, publications, professional services (consulting), and curriculum specialization. Diminishing outputs or the primary losers include teaching quality, advising, mentoring, tutoring, and curriculum structure" (Massy, 1996, p. 81).

Massy and *Zemsky* call this process "academic ratchet", because strong pressures are brought to bear toward funding particular lines of research, or particular faculty, and once a certain level of funding is perceived as 'normal', more pressure is exercised; a reversal of such processes, even if good arguments would speak for it, is frequently very difficult.

University administrators accustomed to management know that the two processes, the "administrative lattice" and the "academic ratchet", exert very strong internal budgetary pressures, and if institutions cannot fight these pressures from within and are unable to free resources to fund new projects or a reorientation, they are immobilized and perceived — quite rightly so — as resisting change. If this perception gains ground, for whatever reasons, pressures will mount to intervene from the outside. This intervention may also be prophylactic, in the sense that an a priori arrangement is being introduced to steer from the outside, via performance funding for example, the internal resource allocation before any evidence develops that institutions are unable to properly manage a new autonomy.

Internal and External Accountability. Higher education systems, public and private alike, operate outside the open market, and they do not price their services to cover their costs (see Chapter 1)[31]. In open markets, consumers have a broad spectrum of competing products to choose from, and product suppliers compete on the basis of price and quality. In the field of higher education, in contrast, competition appears to be curtailed, to the detriment of institutional cost-efficiency and quality. Because of this, performance funding systems are advocated and introduced in the public sphere as quasi-market instruments to rectify the purported deficiency of higher education systems.

---

[31]The exceptions are 'for-profit' institutions, such as the University of Phoenix, which focus generally on the skills-market. There are, to my knowledge, no research universities worldwide which operate as for-profit institutions.

Table 4.9: Usages of Accountability Measures, by Modes (Trow, 1996).

	internal	external
financial & legal	USAGE 1: management	USAGE 2: audit
academic	USAGE 3: quality control, evaluation & planning	USAGE 4: governance

The rationale of performance funding is that funds should flow to institutions where performance is manifest: 'performing' institutions should receive more income than lesser performing institutions, which would provide performers with a competitive edge and would stimulate less-performing institutions to perform. Output should be rewarded, not input. But if some institutions receive more funds than others, they can improve quality in teaching and research, and thus secure or raise their position and reputation. Input would drive output. In fact, the general rule is that well-funded systems perform better, at least within the same class of institutions. Performance funding may not stimulate performance more than funding as such and is probably not doing what it is purported to do. That is: it does not serve as a substitute for market forces and, as I shall try to illustrate below, it appears less effective in fostering performance than in cementing existing structures.

Martin Trow places performance funding in the general context of accountability (Trow, 1996). He distinguishes four modes: internal and external; and financial or legal, and academic. According to these four modes, we can distinguish four usages of accountability measures (see Table 4.9): to provide internal management with the necessary information to assess financial situations and legal compliances (Usage 1); to provide matching information to government and external stakeholders (Usage 2); to monitor quality internally and to support academic planning (Usage 3); and to provide information to the government and to funding bodies regarding academic programs and mission achievement in support of governance (Usage 4). Most importantly, in *Trow*'s view, are the internal usages of accountability. While financial and legal audits are necessary, of course, external academic accountability (i.e. Usage 4) is assessed by *Trow* to have a limited impact:

"[...] external academic accountability in the United States, mainly in the form of accreditation, has been irrelevant in the improvement of higher education; in some cases it has acted more to shield institutions from effective monitoring of their own educational performance than to provide it; in still other cases it distinctly hampers the effort of institutions to improve themselves. It encourages institutions to report strength rather than weaknesses, their successes rather than their failures — and even to conceal their weaknesses and failures from view".

Trow amplifies here a view of *Herbert R. Kells* regarding evaluation measures (Kells, 1995), and he states:

"If internal reviews and assessments are to be more valid and fruitful than those done by outside accreditors, it is necessary that the institution subject itself and its units to serious and recurrent internal review, with real teeth and real consequences. The loss of institutional autonomy is both cause and consequence of the abdication of responsibility by colleges and universities for managing their own affairs".

Accountability measures or accreditation can be seen as special or related cases of performance funding. Institutions — or institutional programs — need accreditation for funding purposes and to attract students. Performance evaluations for funding purposes or for accreditation cause very similar responses — or escape patterns — on the part of academics and academic administrators. *Martin Trow* specifically criticizes funding modes by the Higher Education Funding Councils (see Appendix D.1), the practice of funding departments instead of researchers or research groups, and the negative impact such funding modes have on the cohesiveness and collegiality within a department:

"The UK is the only country [...] that assesses whole departments for funding purposes. Research is done by individuals and research teams (increasingly interdisciplinary), not departments. Britain's funding arrangements [...] confuse an administrative unit with a research unit, and introduces new pathologies into the life of departments — for example by discouraging interdisciplinary research".

And at another place in the paper, *Trow* states:

"[...] we know how cleverly academic departments manage their reports to the [Higher Education Funding Council]: the care with which they sort out the sheep from the goats on their staff (with what effect on the morale of the goats?); the intense interest that has arisen around gaining certified publication before closing date [...]; the recruitment of stars trailing clouds of publications and glory in their train. And on the teaching side, the anxious rehearsals for a forthcoming site visit, whole days given to walking through the visit, with every moment and conversation choreographed and planned for the fullest effect [...]".

External evaluations in the name of accountability and as bases for accreditations and performance funding measures are judged to be flawed for a range of reasons: incentives point in wrong directions, systems adapt to circumvent or even to undermine external performance measures[32], and these in turn cannot serve as substitutes for a healthy competition among higher education institutions or systems.

Competition. The observation that there is lacking competition in higher education has some merit. If one looks at the supply side of higher education, there is clearly less diversity within European higher education than within the US, as scholars such as *Clark* and *Trow* have professed (see p. 80). To be sure, there are stratified higher education systems, e.g. binary systems in Germany, in The Netherlands, or in Switzerland, or trinary systems in France, and this stratification may be mistaken as constituting diversity.

Two or three strata, to be sure, cannot constitute diversity. Compounding that, within a particular stratum, institutions often lack profile: they tend toward uniformity and common standards rather than toward diversity. Uniformity and common standards are defended on the grounds of quality assurance, but diversity does not mean institutions of diverging quality standards. Diversity means institutions of differing missions and disciplinary foci which address various student populations. It is an illusion to believe that institutional quality can be maintained — let alone raised — simply through the association with a particular stratum of the higher education system. Not even accrediting boards can accomplish this. Institutional quality is dependent on the will to raise quality, and this willpower has to be found in the institutions themselves.

From a supply point of view, institutional competitiveness is dependent on institutional diversity. If institutions are diverse, if institutional profiles are distinct, institutions meet one major requirement which facilitates competition. The other major requirement refers to what US Supreme Court Justice *Felix Frankfurter* called the fourth essential academic freedom, namely to have institutional control over admissions (Herbst et al., 2002, p. 97). We should note that admission standards and active admission practices serve as reasonable proxies for the 'price-tag' of educational ser-

---

[32] It can be observed that institutions or institutional systems adapt to performance standards. In a sense, this is what performance funding is about. But their adaption frequently perverts the original aims. For instance, once resources distributed to Australian institutions were tied to publication counts in the mid 1990s, publication rates soared, particularly marginal, low impact publications (and average impact decreased). See (Butler, 2003).

vice. While many European universities do not exercise this freedom, and while active admission management under the name of *numerus clausus* is frequently frowned upon, a range of schools in Europe do engage in this practice quite naturally: art institutes, design or architecture schools, music conservatories, but also many other educational institutions in the non-university sector — in the fields of social work or health sciences, for instance, where students are frequently recruited from diverse backgrounds[33].

If institutions are diverse, with different entry requirements and different 'price-tags', demand could form in relation to what the higher education market offers, and supply and demand could be brought to match. It is evident that within the European systems these opportunities to reform higher education have hardly been pursued in comparison with other public management reforms — and in particular performance funding. While there is an ongoing discussion relating to voucher systems (Frey, 1997) and the marketization of schools (Woodfield & Gunby, 2003; Fiske & Ladd, 2000), in particular regarding primary and secondary schools, there is no corresponding comprehensive debate regarding alternative funding modes in the field of higher education and regarding equity issues.

Equity. An inordinate interest in a solution which calls for higher tuition and fees has come to the fore in Europe, but the efficacy of this solution within a European context is not deeply researched and the social side effects of such measures have barely been addressed. The proponents of higher tuition and fees are likely overestimating the impact of this measure, while the financial effects of active admission management remain largely unexplored. In higher education, a range of equity issues have arisen:

- equity with regard to students' access, and

- with regard to research funding, to the funding of disciplines, or to the funding of institutions.

At the university level, active admission management is generally not practiced in continental Europe, and it is purported to stand in the way of eq-

---

[33]The demand for an active admission management at the university level has been voiced, of course: "Die Universität sollte sich ihre Studierenden wie die Fachhochschulen selbst auswählen können [...]" ("The university and non-university type higher education institutions ought to be in a position to actively recruit their students [...]"; my translation). See (Rusterholz & Liechti, 1998, p. 43).

uity[34]. Because of this seeming consensus among the various political factions, raising tuition and fees has become an issue in today's debates. If open access is to be retained, the pressure to raise tuition and fees will remain strong; and conversely, it is unlikely that a resistance against raising tuition and fees can be maintained without addressing the question of active admission management.

The second major group of issues pertains to research funding. Equity in this context would mean that research proposals of equal merit have equal chances to be funded. While such aims are clearly difficult to implement, it appears that research foundations are doing a much better job of pursuing the goal of equitable research funding than research funding councils do. Research foundations fund research of — possibly interdisciplinary or even inter-institutional — teams[35], and research funding councils fund institutions or academic departments. To be clear, research foundations and research funding councils have slightly different aims in mind: while the former have a focus on funding individual research projects, with some overhead possibly covered, the latter have a focus on funding research infrastructures as well as on non-focused, basic research. The funding approach of research foundations, as science history has shown, supports changing locational foci of research, whereas research funding councils exhibit a tendency in support of the status quo.

Lastly, with regard to funding, equity concerns are brought forward as an argument in favor of formula-based funding modes. As mentioned, formula-based and performance funding are frequently found to be twin solutions of a same approach, with formula-based funding applied to (undergraduate) education and performance funding reserved to pursue particular aims or to fund research. Because formula-based and performance funding are so intertwined and difficult to separate in this particular context, they often promote a similar doctrine. Equity needs to be addressed, of course, in various contexts, and in the particular context of the base funding of higher education institutions. However, formula-based funding modes by themselves cannot serve as the operationalization of notions of equity.

---

[34]The *Grandes Écoles* in France form an exception, and elite universities in the UK practice admission management. Exceptions pertain also to certain fields of study, such as medicine, veterinary medicine, or dentistry.

[35]There is the open issue as to whether to fund on the basis of research reputation or on the basis of research prospects. A conservative funding strategy will base its decisions more on the research reputation of the principal investigators, whereas more risky funding strategies will focus on the proposal itself. A strategic research investment portfolio should follow a balanced approach.

Chapter 5

Alternative Governance and Management Modes

The principal opportunities for increasing productivity lie in changing those who manage production, not those who produce.

Michael C. Geoghegan and Russell L. Ackoff (Geoghegan & Ackoff, 1989)

PERFORMANCE funding — and in large measure also formula-based funding —, is not so much a measure to distribute funds equitably, but rather an instrument used to steer and manage higher education systems or institutions[1]. With such an aim, performance funding — or performance budgeting — is offering itself as a substitute for, or a new form of, governance and management. A substitute replaces the original approach, and a new form modifies older ways. But which original approach, and which older ways? Higher education has not known a singular governance and management approach, but a plurality. Some of these governance and management approaches are in need of reform because higher education systems or institutions steered by such approaches do not perform well or appear endangered in the future. Other approaches, however, seem reasonably adequate if one takes the performance of the corresponding institutions or institutional systems as a guideline.

---

[1] Here, I deviate from *Burke*'s distinction between 'performance funding' and 'performance budgeting' and use the two terms interchangeably. See Chapter 4, p. 70. I also take the liberty here to subsume formula-based funding in the general discussion under the concept of performance funding.

The question is not so much whether performance funding or performance-based budgeting should be used as a substitute for (or a new form of) existing concepts of governance or management. The question is rather how to select the necessary elements from a broad spectrum of governance and management approaches which could work as an ensemble in a given setting and which foster creative adaptation and change (Clark, 1998, 2004b). Performance funding came into being as a remedy for governance and management approaches which were judged to be deficient in attempts to properly steer and manage higher education systems. We can presume that there was generally more consensus on the symptoms of the problem (the perceived deficiencies within higher education or the forecasted shortcomings), than on the associated diagnoses and treatment plans. But there was also a consensus that some actions had to be taken, and because performance funding was promoted by a vocal group of advocates, performance funding measures were eventually considered or chosen.

Outside the US, performance funding appears to have gained some credence as a general solution without looking, in greater depth, at alternatives. Some of these alternatives look sensible and feasible, but they fail to generate a greater resonance. Solution approaches designed to foster a healthy competition among institutions receive scant attention, irrespective of the fact that all work reasonably well in the US. Instead, measures are contemplated or introduced, performance-funding systems for instance, to artificially create competition and a quasi-market of higher education. One possible explanation for this phenomenon is the perceived link which binds higher education cultures to specific sub-sets of solutions. In other words, solutions are sought conditional on given higher education cultures, however defined, and not solutions which affect the 'core' of the cultures themselves. From a systems analysis point of view, this is a crucial limitation. We know that solutions look different depending on the boundaries of the systems under investigation, and we have to select both boundaries and solutions with care.

I suspect that the relative scantness with which certain themes or issues are being discussed in a range of European nations is due to a general reservation to address the core values of the respective higher education cultures (Woolf, 2003). In Germany, for instance, a range of themes appear outside the focus of current debates, such as the existing chair system, the open admission policy, and the diversity of higher education institutions, particularly universities. There are good reasons to suspect that the current chair system stands in the way of a proper departmental orientation and a true collegiate culture; the open admission policy stands in the way of institutional admission management and budgetary controls; holding onto nationwide concepts of attributed — instead of tested — quality stands in the way of diversity and performance, both in teaching and research; and all these factors together endanger the prosperity — if not the survival — of established and well respected higher education systems[2]. If these issues are not addressed or properly discussed, the space for feasible solutions is artificially curtailed and the chosen solutions are very likely suboptimal.

In Chapter 2, I have sketched the basic reasons for the present challenges of many modern higher education systems: the increasing student populations (Section 2.1), and the difficulties of most societies in funding ever-expanding higher eduction systems. In Section 2.2, I addressed the funding crises and why I think that one of the widely mentioned means to combat such crisis, raising levels of tuition and fees, should not be counted as belonging to the set of effective — and equitable — solutions, at least not as long as other viable options remain unexplored. In Section 2.3, I discounted hopes, particularly as far as they relate to research universities, that technological development — and a possible shift from a labor intensive form of instruction to a more capital intensive mode of education — will bring about a change in this pattern. And in Section 2.4, I sketched the specter of an ever-growing loss of quality if we continue to be ineffective in combating the funding crisis which has engulfed many higher education systems.

The current chapter will not attempt to be prescriptive regarding specific solutions or solution packages. However, I would like now to point out issues which, from my point of view, require attention and should form the focus of more intensive discussions. Governance and management cultures in higher education are rich, diversified, and well documented, leaving ample space for comparative analyses and for the exchange of concepts across national boundaries. It is mandatory that we constantly observe and study these cultures, in order to learn, and through our learning, to improve higher education systems or institutions for which we express concern, of which we are part, or to which we provide guidance.

---

[2]The issue of diversity has recently come to the foreground with the call for so-called 'elite' institutions (see the Foreword, p. xiv). History has shown that excellent research universities cannot just be founded, they must develop (Kerr, 2001a, 2001b; Keller & Keller, 2001). And successful development depends on proper structures and policy frameworks.

5.1   Resource Flows into Higher Education

In order to explore the spectrum of possible solutions, and in order to pinpoint themes or issues which deserve deeper discussions and public debate, I shall address governance and management issues from a funding perspective. In doing so, one has to distinguish levels of funding. The first level concerns funds which flow into higher education systems, and I shall focus on the general case, with several public sources of funding streams, some of which are domestic and some of which are international[3]. Subsequently I shall cover the second level: it concerns the distribution and allocations of funds within institutions (Section 5.2). I shall confine myself here, as I said before, to problems affecting public higher education, not because I am an opponent of private institutions[4], but because this is the focus of the entire volume, and because I take the position that private institutions are complementary to — and no substitute for — public higher education.

Funding Regimes. If we look at public funding streams flowing into institutional systems or institutions, we first ought to distinguish between two major — and overlapping — cultures of how to organize research: research concentrated within universities, and research concentrated in dedicated research institutes[5]. In the present context, I shall focus on research concentrated within universities because a more encompassing view would

---

[3]In federal systems, such as those of Germany, Switzerland, or the US, funds originate at the state and the federal levels: *Länder* and *Bund* in Germany, *Kantone* and *Bund* in Switzerland, and States and Federal Government in the US, while in more centralized systems, such as those of the UK or the Netherlands, there is one primary domestic source. In the European context, a range of programs — regarding research, technology transfer, and mobility, et cetera — have to be taken into consideration in addition to domestic sources.

[4]In the European discussion regarding private institutions, the distinction between nonprofit and for-profit institutions is frequently lacking, perhaps because authors are unaware of such a distinction. One should note that the private US research universities, which are frequently referred to as examples to emulate, are all non-profit institutions. The distinction between public and private US research universities is far smaller, and the difference between public US and public European universities far greater, than many European observers believe. It is true that in the US, private universities such as Harvard, MIT, Stanford or the California Institute of Technology form an elite. But it is equally true that the large US state universities provide educational and research opportunities which allow them to compete rather effectively with Ivy League institutions, and which puts them far above most continental European institutions. See also footnote 6 on page 47.

[5]Such as those of the Centre National de la Recherche Scientifique (CNRS) in France; the Consiglio Nationale della Ricerca (CNR) in Italy; the Concejo Superior de Investigaciones Cientificas (CSIC) in Spain; or those of the the the Max-Planck-Gesellschaft (MPG) in Germany.

easily break the framework of topics dealt with here.

Public funding of higher education institutions destined to support teaching and research follow various schemes. We notice that some of these schemes are designed to cover base funding of teaching and research activities, while others cover teaching activities only:

- The first scheme is common in countries like Germany, Switzerland or the UK, where the institutional base funding covers not only teaching activities, but perhaps half of the research activities of research universities as well[6], including research infrastructure.

- The second scheme is common in the US where base funding is almost exclusively used to fund teaching activities, while research activities will have to be funded on the base of external grants or contracts by science foundations or industry, respectively, and where institutions 'tax' the research income of their principal investigators to cover costs of infrastructure[7].

The first scheme is said to be more gentle for new faculty members, in giving them generally more time to integrate themselves into the competitive "publish or perish" world of research production, and it is also said to favor longer-term, riskier research projects, particularly in the basic sciences. But the first scheme also poses the problem of a resource allocation rationale, which is addressed, for instance, by performance funding. The second scheme may be harsher on junior faculty members initially, and it demands attuned science foundations, but peer reviews of research proposals generally guarantee not only funds allocations based on merit but also the reasonable absence of discriminatory factors. This gives younger, not yet established researchers or faculty members, better chances to progress in the hierarchies of the academic world.

Aldo Geuna and *Ben R. Martin* have published a valuable overview on funding systems, with information on institutional systems in Western and Eastern European countries, as well as on those located within the Asia-Pacific region (Geuna & Martin, 2003). They focus on the dichotomy of performance funding versus indicator-based funding and explore the continuum between the two extremes. Not explored are funding systems, such

---

[6]The remainder of the research activities is covered by third party funds, distributed by national or international science councils or by industry.

[7]The 'taxing' of research grants by the institution of the principal investigator to cover infrastructure and general overhead is specifically prohibited by the Swiss National Science Foundation (SNF), for instance.

Table 5.1: CLASSIFICATION SCHEME OF UNIVERSITY SYSTEMS (Research Universities), by Regimes of Base Funding, based on (Geuna & Martin, 2003).

	FUNDING SCHEME	
BASE FUNDING	indicator-based and negotiated arrangement	indicator-based and performance-based
for teaching & research	REGIME 1: Universities of Finland, Germany, The Netherlands, Norway, Sweden or Switzerland	REGIME 2: Universities of Australia, Hong-Kong, and the UK
for teaching only	REGIME 3: most US research universities	REGIME 4: few US research universities (e.g. University of South Carolina), affecting a minor portion of the budget

as those of the US or Switzerland, where the allocation of base funds is basically subject to negotiations within the relevant decision-making bodies. If we classify the various national schemes according to whether or not performance funding is being applied, and if we combine the findings of *Geuna-Martin* with our own, we can distinguish four primary regimes of resource allocation (see Table 5.1)[8].

Regime 1 has been the primary mode of resource allocation in Europe in the past, until the 1980s at least, when the UK higher education system switched to Regime 2. Within Germany, we can perceive a current to make this switch in the immediate future (Leszczensky, Michael, 2003b, 2003a), and in Switzerland there are strong tendencies visible to move in this direction as well. In the US, in contrast to Europe, Regime 3 has been the basic

---

[8]*Geuna* and *Martin* list the advantages and drawbacks of performance-based funding modes (Geuna & Martin, 2003, 297–298). They feel that performance-funding may have merit during the early years of implementation, but after some years, "everyone will need to run faster just to stand still". From this point on, the costs associated with the system will exceed the benefits. They advocate a hybrid system, "based partly on performance (incentive-creating) and partly on educational size (cost-minimizing)" which they see implemented in The Netherlands, Finland or Denmark.

mode, because US colleges or research universities had — and retained —
a strong teaching focus, and the growing research orientation of universities was supported by separate research funding organizations, such as
the National Institutes of Health (NIH), which started to appear around
the end of the 19th century[9]. The natural separation of funding streams
for teaching and research was emphasized after World War II (Bush, 1945)
and after the passage of the National Science Foundation Act in 1950[10].
Only recently have there been signs of jumping onto the bandwagon of
performance funding and switching to a Regime 4 (see Appendix D.2), but
because US basic funding schemes are so different from those found in Europe, the effects of performance funding seem only marginal.

While the current focus of debate within continental Europe concerns
the shift from Regime 1 to Regime 2 funding, the possible alternative —
namely the shift from Regime 1 to Regime 3 funding — remains relatively
unexplored. A shift from Regime 1 to Regime 3 might be associated with
disadvantages I have referred to on the previous pages (publish-or-perish
pressures, shorter horizons for research planning, etc.), at least from the
vantage point of some observers of higher education, but it would also
bring major advantages:

- the vast majority of research funds would be distributed on merit,
  on the basis of peer review and a qualitatively-oriented competitive
  system;

- researchers and research groups would be funded for research, as it
  should be (Trow, 1996), not departments or universities;

- the 'natural' competitive environment for researchers and research
  groups would be broadened and strengthened, young investigators
  could move more independently to further their academic careers,
  and a wider spectrum of faculty members could be supported;

---

[9]Some Latin countries' schemes, as indicated above, might be seen to fall into the same
category as those of the US, but since we are dealing here with research universities, this is
not the case. It is true that most research in France, for instance, is concentrated in dedicated
research institutes (of the CNRS) and, hence, universities can be seen to be financed mainly
for teaching. However, in contrast to US research universities, French universities are not
(in general) research oriented; and the research funding of national research institutes (such
as those of the CNRS) is not competitive or merit based. A more encompassing investigation would have to assess the relative return on investment in research universities versus
dedicated research institutes. Unconfirmed theses appear to indicate that investments into
research universities are likely to be associated with higher returns (see also Sections 2.4
and 6.2).

[10]see: www.nsf.gov/od/lpa/nsf50/history.htm.

- as a consequence, the competition among institutions would be more directly dealt with by the researchers themselves; and

- new institutions, departments or institutes could emerge more spontaneously, in accordance with the prowess of their faculty and students; established institutions or groups could not easily lean back and would have to compete; and a natural diversity of institutions would emerge (Clark, 1997; Trow, 1997).

The shift from Regime 1 to Regime 3 funding should not be seen as a rejection of the Humboldtian idea of the unity of education and research. Quite the contrary: it should be seen as a form to strengthen this bond[11].

Funding and Institutional Morphology. However, funding regimes are not the only criterion by which to distinguish between higher education cultures. Neither are they the sole factor that affects the performance of higher education systems. As I have indicated elsewhere, organizational structures (Ben-David, 1991) — or morphologies, as *Pierre Bourdieu* (Bourdieu, 1988 (1984)) calls them — play a role[12]. The point now is that funding regimes on the one hand and organizational structures or morphologies on the other are only loosely tied. Funding regimes are not dependent on particular morphologies, and vice versa, and we cannot bring about the latter by choosing the former. A shift from Regime 1 to Regime 3 funding, for instance, will generally not affect structural or morphological indicators, such as student-faculty or staff-faculty ratios, unless the funding principles of the corresponding science councils specifically aim for this and prove effective:

- In order to promote young faculty members — and women —, the Swiss National Science Foundation (SNF) sponsors faculty positions for a specific period, covering the salary of an assistant professor as well as supplemental resources in support of research assistantships and infra-structural facilities. These programs do affect the gender distribution among the faculty to some extent, and they have a minor effect on improving the career paths for younger scholars[13]; but they

---

[11]*Gerhard Casper*, the former President of Stanford University, and a native German, referred to the better implementation of the Humboldtian system as the primary reason for the prominence of the US higher system.

[12]See also Section 2.4, and in particular the paragraph on "Achievement in Tertiary Education", pages 33–36.

[13]Career paths of young scholars can only be improved if the university budget covers significantly more permanent faculty appointments.

will unlikely affect the morphology of institutions in a sustainable way.

- In order to make improvements sustainable, it might be better to make a constant stream of research funds available, with the specific intention to sponsor a broader spectrum of principal investigators. Furthermore, if institutions were allowed to tax research grants to cover costs of infrastructure, institutions would have a clear incentive to employ as many fine faculty members as possible, in order to increase their research base and to broaden their research portfolio[14].

Hence, while the choices of funding regimes and the selection of measures to affect the morphology of institutions constitute separate courses of actions, and while the choice of one course does not imply or predispose the choice of the other, it is conceivable that a European Regime 3 funding which is specifically geared toward smaller research teams and better student-faculty ratios will prove more productive than a Regime 2 funding approach.

If Regime 3 funding were to find greater resonance in Europe, not only the funding policies of research foundations would have to be reviewed but also the institutional base funding itself[15]. Base funding would have a focus on the teaching-learning nexus, and in this context two options present themselves:

- the provision of funds in accordance with the size and educational orientation of the student body; the option is formula-based, in that funds are allocated as a function of some input or output measures, i.e.:

---

[14]There is the counter-argument which states that it is practically impossible in Europe to find well-qualified faculty members who would be willing to work with a small staff of a few doctoral students and post-doctoral fellows. I doubt this. For one, most faculty members in fields such as mathematics, theoretical physics, humanities and social sciences already work in small teams. Second, faculty candidates who look for larger teams — and the working conditions of institutes of the Max-Planck-Gesellschaft — may not be the most productive (provided the productivity measurement is not biased toward principle investigators). If talent is fostered early, and if the tenure track system is used to select highly qualified senior faculty, a new higher education culture could evolve in Europe in which smaller, more effective teams become the norm, even in fields (of engineering and natural sciences) which are characterized today by rather large groupings of subordinates.

[15]The Swiss National Science Foundation (SNF) has decided to overhaul its basic structures and has launched a project "SNF 2008" to pursue this aim. The project is directed by *Hans Peter Hertig*. See: www.snf.ch/de/com/prr/prr_cur_mai17.asp.

  – the number of students enrolled or credit-units subscribed to (input measures) or

  – the number of graduates (output measure);

- the supply of resources necessary to run an educational facility of a given size.

While orthodox proponents of performance-funding would opt for the second version of the first option, neither of these versions are really designed to foster performance and both are easy victims of manipulations[16].

The second option would entail a contractual arrangement between funding body and institutional system or institution. This contract would assure a steady flow of resources[17] in return for the assurance that within well-defined annual fluctuations, a specific number of students[18] are being enrolled. The option is dependent on the institutions' or institutional systems' sovereignty to select its own students and to practice an active admission management. Institutional systems or institutions need not grow if demand for study places exceeds the available slots, provided students can enroll somewhere within the relevant higher education system.

Coordination and Planning. Thus far, I have not covered an issue which received — and still receives — great attention and which forms a central part of most discussions on governance: the issue of coordination (Ursprung, 1997; Kleiber, 1999; Sporn & Aeberli, 2004). Coordination is said to be necessary because of a perceived market failure: higher education institutions or systems are said to adapt sub-optimally to changes within the sciences or in response to a changing environment, and coordination is seen as a means to strengthen higher education systems. For example, certain sciences or sub-disciplines are being offered at various institutions without reaching the required critical mass for effective teaching and research. In this situation, coordination would help to avoid unnecessary duplications and concentrate forces on a subset of programs in order to strengthen these, and close the remaining ones. Or, programs are being offered at various institutions which have an aura of being 'outdated' and whose resources may better be invested in newer fields. Here, enlightened coordination would limit the succession of old, 'outdated' programs in order to redirect resources to newer fields. Alternatively, coordination may also mean to pool resources of institutions in order to offer joint programs.

---

[16]See footnote 15 on page 53, for instance.

[17]An annual lump sum, guaranteed over a given planning horizon.

[18]Defined in terms of full-time equivalents.

In the case of binary or trinary systems, coordination or cooperation between educational levels would become necessary. In a more comprehensive sense, coordination or cooperation would have to be based on longer range planning activities and associated longer range plans. These plans would regulate the interplay between the two or three levels of higher education, and between peer institutions, but they may even include the entire spectrum of education (see Appendix D.3). Coordination and cooperation should complement each other, and cooperation should play a dominant role. Successful cooperation among institutions and higher education systems is based foremost on an open information policy which goes beyond mere accountability measures. By disseminating information in an open and clear fashion, institutions do not simply meet accountability requirements. They also gain profile: it becomes clearer how institutions understand themselves, how they comprehend and translate their mission or purpose, and what they do and do not do. In addition, it becomes clearer who their potential collaborators and partners are. This clarification of institutional profiles frequently levels the path for mutually satisfying cooperative institutional arrangements.

If coordination is seen as a way to manage change, the question regarding who is to coordinate stands in the foreground. Normally, governing bodies are assigned the task to coordinate, and if appropriate governing bodies do not yet exist, they are thought about or created. Indeed, coordination may be seen as a prime reason to create governing bodies in charge of a system of institutions. To coordinate via coordinating or governing bodies is to coordinate 'top down'. But there are other ways to coordinate, in bilateral or multilateral — i.e. cooperative — ways, whereby institutions find each other on an equal basis to accomplish common tasks, for instance to design and to launch a joint degree program or to found and finance a common research center. If institutions find each other to pursue a common task or a common mission, they act on the basis of their own initiative — and not on the basis of directives which they may resent. Hence, 'top down' coordination may not be as effective as its proponents may think, and coordination may not be the best reason to form governing bodies.

5.2   Resource Flows within Systems or Institutions

Funds flowing into institutional systems or institutions for the purposes of an annual base funding will have to be distributed down the line. This internal allocation of funds is not a trivial matter and it shapes, to a great extent, the character and performance of an institution.

Funding and the Chair System. If we look at the European university of the past, funded according to Regime 1, this internal fund allocation problem does not appear to take on a prominent role. A university had a number of fields it would cover, and for each field there was a chair to be funded. If the person holding this chair retired, a new promising chair holder was sought who could continue and develop the course of research and bring it to new heights. In this way, lines of successions could be drawn, from one chair to the next, not unlike those of royalty. Gradually, as science expanded, new fields would be incorporated into the university and new chairs created and funded, but after such occasional creations the system could evolve as it had before. In such a context, intra-institutional resource allocation was a simple matter and was handled in good part not by the institution itself but by the corresponding governmental funding agency[19].

While the existing universities of the Humboldtian tradition may have softened their stand on the chair system and on the succession of chairs, the historical picture just sketched is not one of the past. Many features of a system that *Joseph Ben-David* decried as "woefully out-of-date" (Ben-David, 1991) are still in place and they threaten the vitality — if not the survival — of the university as we know it. Internal resource allocation mechanisms have proved to play a central role in the management of institutions, and allocation systems which tend to emulate past structures are not suited to provide universities with the means necessary to adapt successfully in a highly dynamic and complex world. Elsewhere, I have formulated the hypothesis that existing European higher education structures, i.e. their morphologies, are suboptimal[20]. Not addressed properly is the question of how to move or change systems, and how to lift those from a locked self-replicating, suboptimal mode, to a mode which allows for pro-active adaptation and enlightened change.

In the context of the US higher education system, *William F. Massy* is perhaps the most knowledgeable and creative thinker on intra-institutional resource allocation (Massy, 1996, 2003). I have referred to his contributions in Chapter 4, and in particular in the paragraph on "intra-institutional allo-

---

[19]Budgeting, or better quasi-budgeting, took place through the control and planning of faculty positions, i.e. chairs. With such a system the institution could easily replicate its structure (or morphology), but it could not easily change it. It was also difficult — but not altogether impossible — to change disciplinary foci (ETHZ, 1991).

[20]See e.g. Section 2.4, and in particular the paragraph on "achievement in tertiary education", page 33. There is some evidence to give the hypothesis credit, but it is clear that more evidence will have to be accumulated to assess this phenomenon.

cation of resources" (see page 85). *Massy* and his collaborator *Robert Zemsky* refer to two "cost diseases" of universities which have general validity. The first, the "administrative lattice", refers to a natural tendency toward ever-better work quality and professional improvement. The second disease, termed the "academic ratchet", is of particular significance in a Humboldtian higher education environment. As I explained previously, the "academic ratchet" refers to a process of increasing funding expectations on the part of principal investigators and senior faculty, and the disease appears particularly virulent or powerful in a system characterized by a strongly-regulated supply of members of the professoriate. In such systems, the chairs become 'fat' and 'fatter' over time, gradually absorbing resources which could have been funneled to other fields, to new research groups, to riskier endeavors[21].

A strongly-regulated supply of members of the professoriate seems appropriate if

- quality concern demands a strict limitation on the population of faculty;

- student-faculty ratios do not affect teaching quality and learning effectiveness;

- research output is unaffected by staff-faculty ratios, i.e. by the size of the research group which works under the supervision of a faculty member.

But evidence mounts that all three of the above statements are false. First, Europe could produce more able faculty members than are currently employed. Indeed, there is evidence that many of the brilliant young scholars have left — and leave — Europe for good, not only for a period of scholastic growth. Moreover, many a talent leaves the field of higher education altogether because of a lack of career opportunities. Furthermore, had Europe more effective higher education systems, talent could be recruited earlier and developed better, increasing the supply of appropriate candidates for

---

[21]To give an example, between 1979 and 2003, ETH Zürich experienced growth in various sectors: number of students (75.9%), number of staff (51.9%), and number of professors (36.4%); see www.ethz.ch/about/bginfos/annualreports. In other words, over this period, staff and faculty grew by a smaller percentage than student numbers, and student-faculty, student-staff and staff-faculty ratios increased. The lower growth rate of staff and faculty in comparison to students may be interpreted, falsely from my point of view, as an increase in productivity. The same interpretation can be given to the lower growth rate of staff in comparison to faculty. In contrast, I call this the 'adipose process' of faculty teams.

faculty positions[22]. Second, there is ample evidence that student-faculty ratios do affect teaching quality and learning effectiveness. With more faculty, more modern teaching-learning modes can be pursued, broader and new curricula offered, and faculty-student interactions improved. Third, there is evidence that current European chairs are not 'lean' enough, to borrow a term that is so frequently employed in the context of public administration[23]. Large chairs effectively remove the chair-holder from research, or significantly reduce his or her involvement in that activity because other activities loom in the foreground: supervision, coordination, grantsmanship, committee work, work on editorial boards of journals, or because of peer review assessments, et cetera. As *Terrence R. Russell* observes (Herbst et al., 2002, p. 123):

> "[...] the costs of maintaining the large group constantly ratchets upward, and demands on the principal investigator's time and energy grow also, unless the principal investigator is able to pass the burden on to someone else (the growth of the 'administrative lattice')".

There is also the danger of perceiving and presenting the research of subordinates as one's own research.

In other words, the highly regulated access to faculty positions and the corresponding creeping adipose processes which steer an "academic ratchet" may affect teaching, learning and research performance within higher education systems negatively.

Institutions versus Faculty. If a certain consensus is reached regarding this matter, we are still confronted with the problem on how to change the situation as assessed. Here, one ought to distinguish between two positions:

- the position of the institution; and

- the position of the individual faculty member.

If we expect an increase in research productivity (on a per head or FTE-employee basis) if more (qualified) faculty were employed and research teams (i.e. staff-faculty ratios) were smaller, institutions should pursue the

---

[22]On the surface, the highly selective system to recruit faculty guarantees quality. But this is unlikely the case. We have no foolproof systems to detect quality, and the current chair setup and faculty recruitment systems may not only guarantee quality of faculty but may also be responsible for reducing the pool of qualified applicants.

[23]This statement, perhaps, ought to be limited to the fields of natural sciences and engineering. But there are also examples in the social sciences where the research groups under the supervision of a professor are too large.

goal to restructure their morphological setup. Frequently, faculty will fight this measure, because the documented 'productivity' of principal investigators will decrease as a consequence of such measures, but average and total productivity should increase: principal investigators profit today a great deal from their large research groupings. If institutions want to restructure their morphological setup, a new understanding must govern the role of the faculty. Not only publications should count as contributions of faculty members, but the entire spectrum of services: research, teaching, textbook development, student advising, work in committees, et cetera[24]. Also, not only the productivity of principal investigators should count, but the productivity of the entire institution.

The recognition of the positional differences of institution and faculty member is necessary for a strategy on how to reconcile these differences. It is natural for a faculty member to profit as much as possible from the staff, from the doctoral and post-doctoral students under supervision, and from the prestige which is associated with a faculty position. It might even be natural, to some extent, that faculty members opt or fight for a large staff. A large staff empowers them to do more than they could do with a smaller grouping. But large groupings might not be the most effective or productive setup if viewed from the institution's standpoint, and it should also be clear that the institution must have a different standpoint. The leadership of an institution is focused on maximizing the objective function of the entire institution and not of individual faculty members, unless the latter would imply the former. Anecdotal evidence suggests that rectors and presidents of institutions try to further their institutions by providing ample resources to a select group of high-profile faculty. But there is also evidence, referred to previously (see Section 2.4), to suggest that this strategy is not successful if followed exclusively.

5.3 Funding Systems and Change

In his comments on earlier observations regarding the sub-optimality of European, Humboldtian-oriented higher education systems of today, *Terrence R. Russell* asks (Herbst et al., 2002, p. 124):

> "Given the assumed advantages of the small-group model [i.e. the small research group], why does the large-group model persist? [...] Hierarchical pure research institutions maintain themselves through internal disciplinary

---

[24]This is something which has to be defined in a 'faculty book', or in a umbrella contract between institution and faculty regulating appointments.

boundaries, and a complex and stable set of internal arrangements and rewards that makes life within them predictable. So long as outside funds are
politically mandated to be distributed on a disciplinary basis, there is no particular impetus for change [...]".

In other words, if European, Humboldtian higher education systems are indeed suboptimal in their setup, as I believe they are, they appear to be
locked in this suboptimal mode. All the arrangements designed to nourish
and foster the system — the general funding arrangements, the way chairs
are formed, faculty appointed, research grants awarded and research funds
distributed — eventually have the effect of replicating the suboptimal system's structure, to reproduce a morphology which has evolved over time.
The simple infusion of additional funds into higher education, necessary
as it is, will not change this affair significantly. Additional funds unac-
companied by morphological changes will likely increase total output of a
higher education system, but they will not raise productivity and they will
not reduce or bridge the productivity gap which is separating the US from
continental Europe.

During the past two or three decades, we have witnessed a new movement to reform European higher education, a movement which was in-
spired by New Public Management or associated endeavors and which
leads to ideas of performance-based budgeting or funding. This reform
movement had performance as its particular focus, and it purported to
provide means and measures to increase performance. Unfortunately, the
proponents of the movement failed to study the link tying performance to
a range of performance enhancing measures systematically. Indeed, this is
difficult and would entail a great and extended research effort. The proponents' analyses, as I have tried to show in the two previous chapters,
appear unconvincing to many respected exponents of the social sciences,
and the proponents' normative notions and recommendations leave grave
doubts concerning the effectiveness of the proposed measures. Specifically,
the reformers have not addressed morphological aspects as they relate to
performance and, consequently, their reforms do not touch — or change —
the morphology of the university.

In order to raise the effectiveness of institutions or institutional systems, in order to advance universities (Frost, Chopp, & Pozorski, 2004),
one has to do a range of things. Among those, one has to pay attention
to structure, to morphology, in order to allow other aspects to develop as
well. Particular cultures can only develop if conditions are conducive for
this development, and if we have particular higher education cultures to
foster in mind, we ought to make sure that the required preconditions are

met[25]. There is ample evidence that European higher education systems demand a change which allows these systems to prosper, but there is also evidence that the major reform movements within Europe might not bring what they profess. Other paths will have to be pursued, paths perhaps which stress less the uniqueness of national higher education systems and more the commonality of higher education.

The task to point to common aspects of future higher education systems is not a simple one and will require elaboration and debate. I shall mention, from my point of view, three aspects to focus on:

- diversity of higher education systems and transnational orientations;

- disciplinary orientations, inter-disciplinary foci, and the relationship and interplay between institutional base funding (by governmental agencies or funding councils) and research funding (by science foundations);

- leadership and institutional policies in support of more suitable morphologies in the case of research universities (i.e. improved student-faculty and staff-faculty ratios).

Diversity, Equality and Stratification. Diversity within higher education systems is an old requirement, and it has gained renewed momentum with the advent of mass higher education. As more students enroll in higher education, higher proportions of the relevant age cohort attend institutions of tertiary education. As a widely diversified student body is involved —

---

[25]A recent article points to an inherent problem of modern Humboldtian institutions (Schwendener, 2004). The problem arises when institutions try to minimize permanent staff positions (other than faculty) without increasing faculty positions. The policy to minimize permanent staff positions has many advantages (too numerous to point out here), but it also has the major disadvantage that institutions lose valuable — or even critical — know-how when time-contracts expire (quite apart from the disadvantages which accrue to the leaving staff members). *Richard Ernst*, the Swiss Nobelist, is quoted as saying: "[...] we follow a kind of hybrid system that is situated somewhere between the German institutional system [with few professors] and the US American system with a high number of professors heading small teams but without workers on permanent contracts [...] We try to combine the advantages of both systems but tend to ignore the fundamental incompatibility of the two systems. We think we have vanquished the German system but we are still a long way from the American one". To be consistent, the article quotes *Ernst* to say, "the permanent, independent layer of scientific staff positions would have to be abolished and the number of professors tripled [...] Naturally, funding would not be tripled and that would mean, on average, professors would have less funding at their disposal [...] The problem of the scientific staff employment can only be solved if we decide on either the old German approach or the American one with many more professors. There is no middle way".

apart from the traditional adult students, and in particular also women, in pursuance of degree courses which were interrupted or to engage in further or continuing education —, institutions or institutional systems have to respond to this diversity and will have to diversify themselves (Trow, 1979, 1997). This diversity can take two forms: (i) within the institutions themselves, in that programs are started which cater more to non-traditional students or to newer academic professions; and (ii) between institutions, in that institutions gain a specific profile which they may have lost since mass higher education.

Diversity within institutions can more easily be pursued by larger universities. Indeed, the large and prestigious US state universities are models of internal diversity. They sustain a broader spectrum of educational programs, from arts and sciences or engineering to nursing, education, music, public health and social work. With this orientation, they are in a position to cater to a local population and to local needs, but they can also position themselves on the national agenda or assume an international or transnational role[26]. The institutions are large enough to pursue both orientations, without having to fear a loss of quality. Indeed, by incorporating a broader spectrum of disciplinary fields, they can exercise greater control on the quality of emerging or newly implanted academic fields. This dual role holds great promise for regional economic development. Alternatively, smaller institutions located in the same region may be in a position to bundle their separate profiles, with possibly similar effects, provided proper bilateral or multilateral cooperative agreements are adhered to or implemented[27].

In the US context, diversification of institutions is a direct consequence of a relatively free higher education environment. Diversity evolved over time, and today a rich ecology of higher education institutions exists. In the more regulated European environment, and in a culture where a certain equality of higher education institution is valued and promoted, institutional diversity is not a primary aim to pursue. Many aspects of the European, Humboldtian higher education system directly depend on a notion of institutional equality[28], and some ideas contained in the Bologna decla-

---

[26]The recent report by Avenir Suisse concerning Swiss universities proposed a segregation of institutions by their geographic reach (Sporn & Aeberli, 2004).

[27]Not all cooperative arrangements need a formal agreement. A tacit agreement may suffice. Tacit agreements are normally based on a fairly open information policy guiding players or actors involved.

[28]For instance, the practice of the *Habilitation*, the right to teach. This right is bestowed by a given institution, not necessarily by that which appoints the new faculty member.

ration are strongly based on notions of equality. Diversity and equality are not that easy to reconcile, and many of the implicit issues will come to the foreground during the further implementation of the Bologna process[29].

As institutions diversify, they also stratify themselves. Some institutions have an international reputation, they are in a position to attract a larger share of international students, and they can recruit their faculty and staff worldwide. This in turn enhances their productivity and their stature. Diversified and stratified higher education systems can act like a percolator to extract and to accumulate talent[30]. The recent call for elite institutions in Italy and Germany, or for a hierarchically structured higher education system, recognizes the fact that continental European institutions have lost ground; and it also recognizes the fact that elite institutions cannot be that easily furthered in a culture of institutional equality or uniformity. What has yet to be recognized and discussed in Europe is the role of diversity. Elite institutions have generally not been built on the sheer desire to form such institutions: they were no top-down inventions[31]. The research universities within the top stratum of institutions generally evolved: they have a longer history, and they developed their current position persistently, over an extended period of time, by developing their own specific profile (Bergier & Tobler, 1980; Keller & Keller, 2001; McCaughey, 2003).

Disciplinary Orientation and Inter-Disciplinary Foci. Research universities have a disciplinary base. Disciplines are cultivated within departments, and these in turn are grouped into faculties or schools. As time passes, as the sciences mature and as the disciplinary spectrum remains relatively stable, scientific endeavors will likely be focused toward sub-disciplinary aspects and inordinate specialization may result. This process may eventually be reinforced by a practice to fund teaching and research jointly (Regimes 1 and 2).

---

[29]The Bologna process specifically promotes study abroad or exchange student programs through a newly formed European Credit Transfer System (ECTS), presumably relying on a general open admission policy (and equal higher education standards) and without addressing the issue of institutional admission management.

[30]As one looks at the biographies of famous US scientists or scholars, one frequently notices their humble beginnings. They may have started out at a non-elite college or state university, and gradually moved up the ladder of institutions.

[31]History knows of attempts to form elite institutions from scratch, so to speak. The State University of New York at Stony Brook, for instance, was to be the UC Berkeley of the East, mandated by the State Board of Regents in 1960 to become a university that would "stand with the finest in the country". And the Canadian University of Waterloo, established in 1959, achieved early on a very fine reputation. In England, the newly formed University of Warwick plays a formidable role.

In the past, or up to World War II, the disciplinary orientation of universities did not stand in the way of interdisciplinary work. Indeed, if one looks at the work of the extended Vienna Circle, for instance, or at the cooperation of *John von Neuman* and *Oskar Morgenstern*, we can see that interdisciplinary work took place almost in a natural way. Similarly, transdisciplinary work is not a new phenomenon. The social sciences, to give just one example, oriented themselves early on the natural sciences. Additionally, economics focused on physics to derive new impulses, and to develop new methodologies as well as new tools of analysis[32]. However, in recent decades, as the science enterprise has grown, and as gratifications regarding professional advancement, et cetera, became more disciplinary centered, the proclivity toward interdisciplinary work suffered. It is well-known that science progresses often at the fringes of established fields, at the intersection of two or more disciplines, and the inordinate focus on sub-disciplinary matters may draw resources and manpower away from more adventurous or more promising lines of research (van Vught, 2004, pp. 99–101).

Modern research universities cannot easily count any longer on a natural tendency to engage in interdisciplinary work. This change is particularly pronounced in Europe where disciplinary boundaries are more entrenched[33]. The entrenchment of these boundaries is due, in great part, to the regime of funding: large portions of funds for teaching and research flow into departments organized along disciplinary lines[34]. Research institutes are organizational units which are normally part of — and not separate from — the respective department. As a consequence, cross-disciplinary work frequently takes place only if funds specifically directed for these purposes are allocated by research foundations.

In contrast, the US research university allocates — or derives — its

---

[32]The newer tendency within economics is to focus on psychology and biology and derive impulses or modeling approaches from these sciences. Trans-disciplinary approaches are easier to initiate and to implement if aspects of a 'foreign' science are imported to enrich a given discipline. That is, the initiative for trans-disciplinary work ought to be associated with the importing discipline. The opposite approach, the export of concepts, from a given discipline onto a 'foreign' science, is normally resented by the discipline at the receiving end. Successful trans-disciplinary approaches are frequently based on interdisciplinary collaborations.

[33]The tendency is also visible elsewhere and affects career paths and tenure of young scholars. Faculty members up for promotion may feel pressured to research discipline-specific problems and to publish in their own discipline, rather than to pursue interdisciplinary work.

[34]In the form of Regime 1 or Regime 2 funding.

funds in a different matter. Departments and corresponding faculty receive a base funding for teaching which is organized along disciplinary lines[35]. Each department, or each discipline, may offer a range of degree programs in this context[36]. In addition, research funds flow to principal investigators, as independent agents so to speak, who have more options to organize themselves and to collaborate in an interdisciplinary way with peers from neighboring disciplines. In this way, the academic departments and the research institutes form a true matrix organization. The academic departments responsible for degree programs receive a base funding, and the research institutes, through their principal investigators, procure funds from research foundations or industry. Interdisciplinary research centers, in collaboration with departments, may even offer specialized courses or entire post-graduate programs.

It appears clear that funding modes affect not only the dynamics of change, they also affect tendencies to engage in interdisciplinary work. Because interdisciplinary work is growing in importance, and because the promising foci of research are changing faster than the disciplinary boundaries, organizational structures and corresponding funding modes which allow for easy adaptation and change lead the way.

Leadership, Productivity, and Morphological Change. I have mentioned above that we have to distinguish between two positions when we address the issue of productivity: the position of the institution, and the position of the individual faculty member. In economics, we may rephrase this to call the first the position of the common good, and the second, the position of the individual. In certain economic situations, the two positions are not in conflict with each other, namely then when the pursuance of the individual position will implicitly further the common good. But this is not always the case, as the theory of games shows. If the two positions differ, one has to find regulatory measures to keep the individual in line and keep him from defecting (Barash, 2004).

Our societies are full of regulations which keep individuals — or individual economic agents — in line, and this for good reasons. In the cases where the pursuance of an individual agenda is detrimental to the common good, regulations are crafted and enforced to protect the society. In the field of higher education, we have indications that systems with amply

---

[35] As a rule in the form of Regime 3 funding.

[36] Internal funds allocation, and the inter-departmental flow of services and funds, is not a trivial matter and may depend on rather elaborate accounting schemes. See in this respect (Whalen, 1991) or (Massy, 1996).

staffed faculty chairs are in conflict with institutional — or national — productivity, and that if the latter is of importance, the former will have to be changed and regulated to work differently. In other words, the institutional morphology requires change[37]:

- in the natural sciences or in engineering, i.e. in the fields that are normally 'well-stocked' so to speak, an internal reshuffling or reallocation of resources could take place, and where well-funded separate research institutions exist next to less well funded universities, as in France or in Germany, a merging of universities and research institutes could be considered (Butler, 2004);

- in the social sciences or the humanities, where resources are often scarce, additional resources are likely to be required, but admission and program management might help to limit the funds needed.

Similar to the case of cooperation, a change in institutional morphology need not be based on formal regulations. Indeed, a tacit agreement, a new practice, suffices to change the system.

Institutions may be skeptical regarding a new practice, even if their leadership sees the advantages of a morphological setup which is based on smaller research groups in the sciences and in engineering, correspondingly more faculty, and flatter hierarchies. They fear that their institution would suffer and lose out competitively if they fail to offer large startup grants and ample staff positions to future faculty members of their choice. Faculty are known to play a game whereby they try to negotiate better salaries or research conditions with a range of institutions simultaneously, in order to put pressure on their own institution, or in order to move eventually to an institution which offers them a better contract.

There is nothing wrong with this game. It is generally in the interest of an institution to attract some high-profile faculty. Wrong, however, is the institutions' apparent inability to extract themselves from the pressures implicit in the faculty game. Research universities are not at the mercy of faculty and prospective faculty, at least not in the longer run. If leading scholars are in short supply, the research universities themselves are in a position to see to it that a new — and possibly enlarged and better educated — generation of scholars emerges. This new and enlarged generation can only find employment at the leading European research universities if a reshuffling of resources is pursued, i.e. if the higher education system

---

[37]See also footnote 25 on page 111.

reduces or limits the resources with which to aliment an average faculty position.

Once governing agencies and institutional leadership agree on change to restructure higher education institutions, ways have to be found to accomplish this task. As I have indicated, two broad courses of actions should be considered:

- a gradual change of a Regime 1 (or Regime 2) to a Regime 3 type funding, extending over one or two decades, whereby funding streams are partially redirected in favor of research funding agencies (see Table 5.1 on p. 100);

- Regime 3 funding, as far as it pertains to institutional funding (and not to research funding of principal investigators), is generally directed toward departments — and not to individual faculty members —, and a corresponding focus on junior faculty, tenure track positions is pursued.

The detailed exposition of this or other options is a different matter. It entails further research and debate. But options to the current higher education situation in Europe do exist, and they need not rely on performance-based budgeting or funding.

Chapter 6

Inertia and Challenges

> *[T]he future of universities rests in their self-reliance.*
> *[...] universities will largely get what they deserve. The*
> *lucky ones will have built the institutional habits of change.*

Burton R. Clark (Clark, 2004a)

IT HAS BECOME COMMON to view higher education as a system characterized by a high degree of inertia[1]. *Burton Clark* states that, "[w]ith many reasons to stay in the traditional box, with steady-state inertia wedding institutions to the *status quo*, a large number of globally dispersed universities, perhaps the majority, will not venture very far down the road of self-induced major change" (Clark, 2004a). This perception, unfortunately, is not unfounded, and it may serve as the major cause for the widespread call for performance-based budgeting and funding measures.

Inertia in university systems is basically tied to three factors: the lack of a competitive environment within which higher education systems operate — or at least the unwillingness to recognize or perceive a competitive environment; the reluctance to really pursue quality and to adopt instead a satisficing point of view (Simon, 1957); and finally inappropriate management and governance structures. The lack of a competitive environment is particularly evident in Europe. Institutions see no real need to change or adapt, especially if they are guided by a short-range planning horizon and lack future scenarios. Almost no market forces compel institutions to alter or modify their course. Their experience has been that their common

---

[1]See the footnote 24 on p. 60.

reactive adaption strategies work reasonably well and that there is no obligation for fundamental pro-active ventures. If the outside — or market — forces are too weak to influence the course of institutions, an inner vision, an institutional quality focus could provide the fuel for a pro-active future orientation, but it is apparently easier to embrace a common satisficing strategy. All these points are compounded by often ill-fitting governance and weak management structures.

If institutions see no need to change, why should they? Whose business is it anyhow to tell institutions what they should do or not do? The answers to these questions are not simple. In the past, most European institutions were tightly controlled, even run to some extent, by government agencies. In contrast, the modern tendencies point to a clear separation of tasks: if we assume ideally designed higher education systems, the public, i.e. the government, would be responsible for the setup of a framework within which higher education institutions, public or private, could operate at their own volition. If the public is not satisfied with the operation or performance of institutions, the government has as its sole option to change the legal and financial framework; it cannot run any longer — or should not coerce — the institutions directly. But a basic requirement for this separation of tasks to work is an open and broad discussion regarding all matters which touch the mission and operation of higher education; the discussion in turn requires public access to data which describe or characterize higher education systems; and access to data presupposes the availability and maintenance of corresponding data banks. Furthermore, a public debate on higher education requires professionals who are in a position to study higher education systems in a comparative context (Herbst, 1997): e.g., students of higher education systems, educators, higher education administrators, economists, policy scientists.

Any discussion on the mission and performance of higher education systems ought to recognize the values of the various actors or stakeholders representing higher education. Institutions do not intrinsically pursue a particular set of commonly shared values. Instead, the various actors pursue separate goals, depending on their own roles and self-interests. The values and aims of the faculty are not the same as those of students and aspiring scholars; rectors and presidents have aims separate from those of the faculty; and the government's goals may not necessarily match those of the other actors. "Universities will discharge their delegated responsibilities", writes *William F. Massy*, "when and only when their value functions truly reflect the public good" (Massy, 2004). This is perhaps more easily said than operationalized. But if one accepts *Massy*'s dictum, all in charge of and interested in higher education will have to ponder the form of such 'value functions' and the content of the 'public good' in question. This I shall try to do in the remainder of this last chapter by addressing — on the fly, so to speak, with a best-practice orientation and in an illustrative way — various issues which loom in the forefront of today's higher education debate.

6.1 Formulaic Steering

The gist of this volume centers on performance funding measures. Performance funding has a dual purpose: to fund tertiary education systems or institutions and, through funding, to direct them. Performance funding gained proponents because of an apparent rift in the perception of how to govern and manage higher education. Particularly those outside the institutions themselves — government officials, politicians, and occasionally members of buffer organizations or interface agencies — subscribed to increasingly different views than those held by institutional representatives and faculty. A gulf opened up between the two viewpoints, threatening the social contracts that bound together higher education institutions and their respective societies.

Massy (Massy, 2004), following *Stephen A. Hoenack* (Hoenack, 1983), distinguishes three forms of principal-agent relations: regulatory, formulaic, and persuasive[2]. The first of these principal-agent relations has also been referred to as the 'state control model', while the other two were subsumed under the 'state supervising model' (van Vught, 1989). Regulatory forms of governance and management were very common in Europe (and other countries outside the US) until recently, but they are gradually being phased out and replaced by other forms of control. The general consensus is that tight regulatory controls are not suitable to guide higher education any longer, but there are obvious differences in the way national systems chart their paths toward alternative guidance mechanism (Chevailier, 2004; Teixeira, Rosa, & Amaral, 2004). As an alternative to regulatory controls, formulaic principal-agent relations were proposed and are being used, i.e., measures which I address and critically review in this volume under the heading of performance-based budgeting or funding. As a second alterna-

---

[2]I refer here strictly to the terminology of *Massy*. Particularly the term 'formulaic' is critical in this context. *Massy* does not refer here to intra-institutional, quantitative budgeting or resource allocation models (Massy, 1996; Whalen, 1991). But I assume that his stance on formulaic principle-agent relations has been shaped by his creative work on intra-institutional resource allocation.

tive we cite the persuasive form of principal-agent relation which is most commonly found in the US. It is generally viewed as a successful model, at least within the US context, but in recent years it has become subject to a critical assessment as well, aimed to modify the model rather than to replace it (Burke, Joseph C. and Associates, 2004; Massy, 2003).

The clash of views, the differing perception of higher education by government officials and politicians on the one hand and by institutional representatives and faculty on the other, may have a long history, but it is safe to assert that the conflicting views of the two parties gained profile with the spreading of mass higher education in the 1980s. In Europe, governments were seeking ways to gradually release institutions from the regulatory controls which characterized the governance of higher education systems up to that point in time (Höltta & Nuotio, 1995; Bauer, 1996). Retrenchment was the answer to ever growing budget figures spawned by mass higher education, and formulaic budget allocation mechanisms were, and are being, favored by government officials as a substitute for tight regulatory controls. Furthermore, formulaic approaches to budgeting are also being welcomed in an attempt to 'transfer' budgetary responsibilities and 'involve' agents in budgeting and resource allocation decisions: following the formulaic schemes, the universities themselves are seen in control of their resource allotments.

Persuasive principal-agent relations, with few exceptions, were rare in Europe, but they are still the norm in the US. While one can observe a move from regulatory controls to formulaic approaches in Europe or Australia, similar, but weaker, tendencies can be observed in the US where persuasive forms of principle-agent relations are being replaced by formulaic approaches[3]. Some of these tendencies in US higher education can be tied to government reform measures (Klitgaard & Light, 2005), which I cover in Chapters 3 and 4, and some can be tied to insights which were gained by (former) university administrators (Whalen, 1991; Massy, 1996, 2003; Burke, Joseph C. and Associates, 2004). Particularly *Massy* extended his insightful normative notions regarding the intra-institutional accounting of

---

[3]The reader should recognize that the tripartite characterization of principle-agent relations employed here is rather ill-defined and dependent on a subjective judgment. When I claim that US universities are dominantly governed by a 'persuasive' mode, I do not imply that States do not exercise regulatory controls. Of course they do. What I am saying is that regulatory controls of US State governments, by and large, far less affect the management and budgetary autonomy of universities under their supervision than corresponding government-university relations in Europe. A consequence of this comparative abstinence of US government intrusion in the internal affairs of institutions, perhaps, is a rather dense set of rules which regulate the internal affairs of a university (March, Schulz, & Zhou, 2000).

resource flows and and their eventual allocation to the case of government-university relations. Referring to his tripartite segmentation of principle-agent relations, he states:

> "The first two [principle-agent relations] — regulation and strictly formulaic funding — are problematic in higher education. That leaves the third approach, persuasion. But persuasion cannot work without something on the line. If one likens persuasion to 'jawboning', to use a term familiar in the US, the jawbone must have teeth.
>
> I believe 'performance-based steering' is the answer. The idea is very simple: allocate a small amount of funding based on the subjective evaluation of key elements of performance — and make the evaluations public. Experience shows that a few percentage points of annual appropriation can refocus universities in important public goals, without undermining their responsiveness to the markets [...] Constructive dialog on [...] issues would help align the university's objectives with the public good, and the ensuring financial allocations and attendant publicity would underscore the seriousness of the exercise" (Massy, 2004, p. 31).

In other words, *Massy* is a proponent of a middle ground. He does not want his "approach [to be] confused with the many formulaic approaches that have been proposed or implemented in higher education" (p. 32). He rightly wants to fight inertia and academic complacence, intra-institutional "cost diseases" — the 'administrative lattice' and the 'academic ratchet' — which I covered at various places within this volume, and he is cognizant of the fact that the notion of the university as a public good requires interpretation[4] by the various stakeholders of higher education. He favors a system which, in *Burke*'s assessment, has a limited impact (see 'The US Experience' in Section 4.2), but he sees potential in this 'limited impact' because "Performance-based steering leverages small increments of funding to nudge universities in the right [sic] direction without disempowering them" (p. 32). Clearly, we lack empirical evidence to assess *Massy*'s notion, but my feeling is that proper negotiations and eventual contracting between steering agencies on the one hand and institutional systems or institutions on the other, i.e. the undiluted persuasive option of *Massy*'s principle-agent relations, is more honest and much more effective (in a comprehensive way).

---

[4]One could also say: operationalization, particularly if one wants to quantify certain aspects.

6.2   Distribution and Concentration of Resources

Performance-funding measures are tools introduced to correct a perceived market failure. They do not address directly the aims of higher education, the mission of institutions, the approaches to teaching, learning, research or services. They are an indirect attempt to bring higher education closer to the market — by introducing a quasi-market. And yet, while higher education operates outside the open market (see Chapter 1), there are many aspects of higher education which share, or potentially share, the characteristics of a market. Before quasi-markets are introduced, it might be more fruitful to develop those aspects of higher education which are naturally closer to a market orientation and to focus, head-on and directly, on improving the performance of higher education.

Diversified Higher Education. Both *Clark* and *Trow* are eloquent proponents of a diversified higher education system (Clark, 1997; Trow, 1993; Levine, 1993). "By diversity of higher education", writes *Trow*, "I mean the existence of distinct forms of post-secondary education, of institutions and groups of institutions within a state or a nation that have different and distinctive missions, educate and train for different lives and careers, have different styles of instruction, are organized and funded differently and operate under different laws and relationships to government" (Trow, 1997, p. 15). In the face of mass higher education, a broader spectrum of institutions and teaching-learning approaches is called for in order to match the broader client structure of today's and tomorrow's tertiary institutions: an enlarged percentage of age cohorts of students has to be addressed, a broader spectrum of talents and interests, domestic and international students, traditional first cycle students as well as older undergraduates and post-graduate students, and so forth. But in contrast to the US, European diversification, like higher education in general, has traditionally been highly regulated: the proliferation of a broad spectrum of higher education institutions in response to mass higher education has been curtailed and restricted.

There are strong cultural aversions against tendencies to diversify European higher education, aversions which may differ in degree from country to country. Many of these are rooted in noble sentiments regarding the role and function of education. Particularly equal opportunity or egalitarian principles, but also a concern for quality and quality assurance, can be seen to block diversification in Europe. From the viewpoints of proponents of diversity, these aversions appear misguided because the noble political stances regarding educational opportunities and quality are shared. Only through diversification can institutions address the needs of such a diversified student population (Ratcliff, 1996). Only through diversification, they claim, are societies in a position to address the financial impasse in which higher education systems find themselves. "No country can support a system of mass higher education at the cost levels of the elite universities", writes *Trow*, "and this has been a problem for many European countries and a constraint on the expansion of their system" (p. 22). "[...] governments should demand greater diversification and hierarchy of their system of universities", write *Luc E. Weber* and *James J. Duderstadt*: "Clearly all universities should not aspire to become world-class universities" (Weber & Duderstadt, 2004a, p. 244). The lack of structure, ill-directed ambitions, and inappropriate ideals produce a landscape of undistinguished institutions unprepared to elevate their mission of teaching and research. Universities find themselves "overloaded and underfunded", wrote *Jürgen Mittelstraß* over a decade ago with reference to Germany, and this situation has not changed since (Mittelstraß, 1994, p. 13). The very idea of the university, the Humboldtian ideal itself, seems to stand in the way of reforms which would institute diversification.

Segmentation of Higher Education. The European answer to diversification appears to be segmentation. With the broader definition of the tertiary sector of education, with the redefinition of former secondary schools as higher education institutions in the last decades of the past century, and with the formation of two or three tier systems in various European countries, a segmentation of higher education institutions took place. Each tier was to address a specific segment of the student population. In the UK, polytechnic schools were integrated into the higher education sector before being transformed into universities. In France, universities and university institutes of technology (IUT's) joined the *grandes écoles* to form the higher education sector. In Germany and Switzerland, *Fachhochschulen* were formed to provide a "separate but equal" path to higher education, while in The Netherlands the *Hogeschool* took on the same role as the *Fachhochschulen* in the pursuance of professional, as opposed to academic, education.

A similar segmentation can be observed in the US, although not in such strict terms. There are community colleges for vocational training and lower division academic transfer programs, colleges of various standards providing a liberal education or graduate education, comprehensive universities offering academic or professional foci, and research intensive universities (Zemsky, 2004). Segmented systems pose the problem of permeability; students of promise who start out at a lower tier ought to have the opportunity to continue their studies at higher-tier institutions. Talent or drive may not be apparent initially and may only surface during the course of studies or later on in life. On the other hand, academic orientation or research may not be on everybody's mind and a more practical, vocational pursuit may provide greater satisfaction and better income prospects. US higher education systems solve the permeability problem in that they are reasonably liberal regarding the acceptance (and the credit transfer) of students. This is a direct consequence of their market orientation[5]. In Europe, students are frequently locked within a tier of institutions, although the recent Bologna reforms try to address this situation.

Permeability is one problem of segmented higher education systems; mission, or academic, drift is another. Mission drift may be caused by different forces. Universities may find their research orientation, and their teaching and learning modes, challenged by enrollment growth they cannot control because of their open admission policy. In fact, open admission policies and enrollment growth downgrades their mission: they lack the resources for proper teaching and the support of active learning, and they lack the resources for their research orientation. The faculty resents and tries to fight mission drift by various measures, many of which are detrimental to education. Students are viewed as a burden, large lecture courses abound, seminars are overcrowded, knowledge transfer stands in the foreground. We frequently observe in Europe that research output, research quality, and educational progress is inversely related to the number of students enrolled: the respective indicators are high in fields which attract relatively few students and low in 'popular' disciplines. Of course, this phenomenon cannot be attributed to enrollment figures alone. Fields with comparatively fewer students, and in particular the natural sciences, receive more resources, not only because they require more resources on a per-head basis but also because the fields are particularly valued, and hence better funded, by society. I presume that many of the reported performance deficits in Europe in the humanities and the social sciences are the result of "overload and underfunding" (to use the wording of *Mittelstraß*).

---

[5]The market orientation of US institutions is not necessarily tied to high tuition and fees, as one would suspect. The Yale School of Music, for instance, plans to "permanently stop charging tuition to its students". A gift is used to cover the tuition foregone. Its Active Dean observes that "Yale is expensive and there are talented students all across the country who would never think of applying here because of the expense, so now we've removed a barrier [. . .]" (di Mento, 2005).

Mission drift is attributed to universities which place undue weight on their research and negate their teaching focus. This, as I have just indicated, is the result of the growth in student population and the corresponding squeeze of the resource base. It is also the result of a performance funding philosophy which idolizes output indicators. However, mission drift is normally attributed to former polytechnic institutes, *Fachhochschulen* or *Hogeschoolen* which aspire to be (research) universities. Here, the issue is complicated by official policies regarding what constitutes a proper mission. In an attempt to blur the boundaries of a segmented system, the "separate but equal" paths to higher education receive misleading signs and corresponding questionable missions. In the UK, the blurring of boundaries is perhaps most advanced in that the former polytechnics were formally integrated into a unitary university system. In the case of the binary systems of Germany and Switzerland, an undue separation of tasks results from one class of institutions focusing on professional education and the applied sciences, the other on academic education and the pure sciences[6], negating the fact that universities prospered in Europe (and elsewhere) exactly because they harbored the professions[7]. Somehow to counteract this ill-formulated separation of missions, the Swiss law amplifies the informal blurring of boundaries between the two tiers of higher education in that it requires *Fachhochschulen* to engage in applied research and development[8]. Research and development are generally tied to doctoral and post-doctoral students, for good reasons, and it is clearly disjointed to require institutions to engage in research and development without giving them the right to offer doctoral programs[9]. The blurring of boundaries is also questionable

---

[6]It is interesting to note that, in English translation, the institutions of both classes tend to use the term 'university' to refer to their own institution. Hence, *Fachhochschulen* or *Hogeschoolen* are likely called 'Universities of Applied Sciences' instead of 'Colleges of Applied Sciences'.

[7]Physiology, medicine and law early on, but also education, certain applied sections of the social sciences, engineering and architecture (in newly founded polytechnic institutes or, later on, technical universities). The Netherlands do not make this inappropriate semantic distinction when referring to their higher education institutions. Regarding the relation between professions and higher education institutions, see also (Abbott, 1988, Chapter 7).

[8]"Bundesgestz über die Fachhochschulen vom 6. Oktober 1995 (Version of October 4, 2005)", in particular Article 9; see: www.admin.ch/ch/d/sr/4/414.71.de.pdf. The German laws are here more ambivalent in that they 'allow' research to take place.

[9]This is no argument for *Fachhochschulen* to grant doctoral degrees (which they are not normally allowed to). If a research orientation is part of the institutional mission, doctoral programs are a must; conversely, if doctoral programs are not part of an institution or a higher education tier (again for good reasons), one should not call for a research focus or a research mission.

from an economic point of view: it makes sense to distinguish between (lower-priced) teaching institutions and (more costly) research-oriented institutions. The reality, however, is often such that university education has become less costly (per student enrolled) than at some of the more vocational institutions under the same jurisdiction, a possible indication that the corresponding universities enroll too many students to ensure a quality education.

Agglomeration Economies. If outputs were proportionally related to local resource inputs, one would not have to be concerned about the distribution of inputs. Research results and educational outcomes could be harvested wherever resources were allocated. One would not have to think about the concentration or distribution of resources or about economies of scale. Institutional missions would not stand so much in the foreground because the requirements could be met at the micro-level, practically at each location. In such a world, there is no need for segmentation or diversification.

And yet, we know not only that profiles of higher education institutions differ, we know also, or presume, that they are unevenly productive. We lack a clear conception of a production function of universities, but we can assume that agglomeration (or urbanization) economies play a role in making them productive (Fujita et al., 2001; Fujita & Thisse, 2002). Cities exist because of agglomeration economies. In cities we observe that antiquarian shops or stores selling secondhand books tend to cluster; the same is true for fashion stores selling brand names. Larger cities tend to have an over-proportional concentration of cultural facilities. Certain regions specialize in research or development: the Silicon Valley (in California) or areas around Route 128 (in Massachusetts) (Lampe, 1988; Saxenian, 1994), the Research Triangle (in North Carolina) or the science park of Sophia Antipolis (in France). The clustering of entities such as antiquarian shops, cultural facilities or computer companies cannot be explained simply by economies of scales. There are added elements playing a role which one tries to capture by concepts such as agglomeration economies: clustering has economic advantages.

Similar phenomena can be observed in the university environment. Although allegiance to institutions seems to wane and a disciplinary sense of belonging appears to gain ground (Elton, 1996), it is clear that certain institutions play a prominent role in attracting faculty or students. Prospective faculty members do not only chose a particular department to work in; they also choose a university or a general intellectual environment defined by the standing of colleagues in associated departments or by the quality of students in general. Students associate with students they want to study with and they choose faculty who can best further their understanding or their career. Prospective doctoral students try to enroll in doctoral programs which fit their talent and aspirations, and strong doctoral students tend to choose strong mentors (Zuckerman, 1996 (1977)). Universities that view their students not only as clients but also as factors of production are keen to attract a student body of promise. Larger universities may be in a position to draw a diversified population of students and scholars because there is ample space for academic subcultures or clusters. Smaller universities or institutions may provide only one dominant cluster.

A focus on agglomeration economies appears essential to further the attractiveness and productivity of institutions. Limited funds have a more pronounced impact when concentrated. 'Bloated' universities, i.e., universities with too many students in relation to their mission, cannot be as effective and as productive as properly sized institutions with the same budget. Bloated universities are deficient regarding their teaching-learning nexus (and hence the quality of graduates), they are less effective in bringing their students to graduation (higher drop-out rates and longer study durations), and they are less productive in their research. In the case of cities, we have no criteria for defining optimal sizes, and the same is true for universities. Some of the cities are thriving and some are not, some of the cities are urbane and some are not, almost irrespective of their size, and corresponding observations can be made about universities[10]. Bloated universities operate way below their productivity frontier. They either need more resources to match their "load" (in the diction of *Mittelstraß*), or reduce their load — or change their mission — to match their resources. I presume that many of the European higher education institutions, perhaps even most, fall into this category of 'bloated' universities.

Because of historical reasons, and because resources are constrained, some European countries concentrate research in dedicated research institutes or research societies (Hammerstein, 1999; Andrey Allakhverdov and Vladimir Pokrovsky, 2004). In Germany, basic research is concentrated to some extent in institutes of the Max-Planck-Society and applied research

---

[10]The size of first rate universities varies considerably. The California Institute of Technology, for instance, has a bit more than 2,000 students (to use the number of students as a size-measure), the Swiss Federal Institute of Technology (Lausanne) has more than 6,000 students, the Massachusetts Institute of Technology roughly 10,000 students, Oxford University has a student population of over 18,000, the University of California (Berkeley) has close to 33,000 students and the University of Michigan (Ann Arbor) close to 40,000 students.

in institutes of the Fraunhofer-Gesellschaft. In France there is a concentration of research activities in units of the *Centre national de la recherche scientifique* (CNRS). Because these institutes do not engage in teaching (other than graduate or doctoral education) and because they are normally adequately funded, the problem of "overloaded and underfunded" — i.e. bloated — universities is circumvented, at least in these institutions. However, the concentration of funds in dedicated research institutes bleeds universities of required resources. And it is even questionable whether dedicated research institutes are as effective as are well funded and well organized research universities[11]. Tendencies to change this division of labor and to move universities and non-university research institutes closer together are met with stiff resistance (Balter, 1999; Casassus, 2005) because it is feared that in the case of a more unified system, non-university research institutes would lose whatever strength they now have without any gain in compensation[12].

Structure and Morphology. Even if institutions are not "overloaded and underfunded", they may not operate at their productivity frontier. This is, of course, a major potential concern of overseeing bodies and politicians. In fact, the proper funding of institutions may lull institutions and cause inertia[13]. Proper funding is a relative matter in any case: what is proper for a complacent institution is insufficient for an entrepreneurial, ambitious university trying to broaden its funding base (Clark, 1998, 2004b).

   Inter-institutional (and international) analyses reveal that there exist very large differences in the research output and research productivity of universities (Da Pozzo, Maye, Roulin Perriard, & von Ins, 2003; Herbst, 2004b)[14], and we can presume that similar pronounced differences exist re-

---

[11]See in this respect Section 2.4, pp. 30.

[12]Two quotes may amplify this sentiment: "The last place to put research in France is in the universities [...] The French university system is straight out of Kafka" (Harry Bernas); "[t]o do university research the way it is done in the United States is illusory. French universities don't have real autonomy and the teaching load is too heavy" (Claude Cohen-Tannoudji, see: (Balter, 1998)).

[13]When I once asked *Herb Kells* how one could move institutions to adopt change, he advised to reduce their budget by 20%. The advice, of course, was kind of 'tongue-in-cheek'. By reducing the budget, institutions would have to reduce slack, reorder their priorities and focus on things which really matter. This would constitute rational adaptation. Afterwards, the retained resources could be reinvested along the lines of newly defined priorities. My experience, however, is that such reactions by institutions are unlikely and would require excellent leadership (and active admission management). Under normal conditions, nothing of the sort would happen, just a reduction in quality and a 'bloating' of the institution.

[14]Differences in research productivity of individual scientists have long been observed.

garding the teaching-learning nexus. Many of these differences are tied to funding and the associated 'bloating' phenomenon. But some differences result from the way universities internally organize themselves, i.e. to their 'morphology' (Bourdieu, 1988 (1984); Wüthrich, 2003; Carayol & Matt, 2004a). I have referred to this phenomenon elsewhere in some detail (Herbst et al., 2002). The phenomenon occurs at reasonably well funded European institutions which are characterized by inordinate academic hierarchies[15]. These hierarchies are mainly a byproduct of a particular interpretation of the Humboldtian culture, and they are dysfunctional (Ben-David, 1991, pp. 127–139) and characterized by large student-faculty ratios and large staff-faculty ratios[16].

Hierarchic setups are dysfunctional because they place students too far away from faculty so that personal guidance and mentoring of students becomes infeasible; academic fields or subfields are frequently represented by just one faculty member which severely restricts the choice of students and the potential for research and excellence; hierarchical in-group work takes precedence over horizontal multi-group work; risks inherent in appointments and research activities cannot be distributed over a spectrum of faculty; inter-disciplinary or trans-disciplinary research is constrained; doctoral and post-doctoral students lack intimate working relations with faculty members and the principal investigators of research projects; faculty members are overloaded with administrative chores, with grantsmanship, or with service in committees; career options of the new generations of scholars are significantly, and artificially, reduced; and talent leaves academia.

6.3 Governance and Collegiate Culture

With such a broad agenda of issues confronting higher education systems, and with the frequently stiff resistance — on the part of faculty and students — against change, performance funding (and steering) is welcomed by many as a relatively neutral measure to move tertiary education. In the previous chapters, I have argued that performance funding is inherently deficient and the strange equivalent of a Stachanovian system within a So-

---

See in this respect (Lotka, 1926).

[15]Affected are primarily the natural sciences, medical sciences and engineering, but also some social sciences.

[16]Institutions which are not that well funded and which practice open admission are often simply characterized by large student-faculty ratios: they lack the funds to support large staff-faculty ratios (i.e. they are 'bloated').

viet economy. Too great are the dangers that performance funding will not help to move but will lock institutions in their mode of affairs; that measures and goals get undermined, circumvented or perverted (for good or bad reasons); that bureaucracy will increase; that institutions will be guided by opportunistic instead of entrepreneurial principles; and that institutional systems under such regimes will lose out against cultures which steer their institutions in a more enlightened way. "The increasing intrusion of state and federal government in the affairs of the university, in the name of performance and public accountability", writes *James J. Duderstadt*, "can trample on academic values and micromanage many institutions into mediocrity" (Duderstadt, 2000, p. 239). *Frank A. Schmidtlein* anticipates that "[t]he questionable assumptions underlying performance-based budgeting [...] seem to thwart this 'reform'. Like other fads that have afflicted higher education it seems likely to end up in the 'trash heap' of history" (Schmidtlein, 1999). With performance funding implemented on a broader scale, Europe would not likely regain its lost ground against the US, not to speak of the role it might play vis-à-vis the newly emerging science nations in the Far-East (The National Summit on Competitiveness, 2005).

Other avenues will have to be pursued. Ways will have to be found to support a healthy competition among institutions and institutional systems to fight complacency, undue satisficing behavior, and to foster enlightened governance and management. In the remainder of this chapter I shall refer to a number of issues which, from my point of view, require closer scrutiny.

Long-Term Perspective. Universities have been described as some of our oldest institutions. They not only cherish traditions, they are also champions of survival. Apparently, universities can adapt and change traditions sufficiently to shoulder new burdens or to take on new challenges. Universities can change, but they change slowly. Furthermore, effects or implications of their activities may only be discernible years after. Discoveries may turn into product development and come to fruition two, three, or four decades after they have taken place, and the quality of graduates of higher education institutions may pay off only gradually from a societal point of view. A long-term perspective, and a concerted and unremitting effort, is required if one wants to significantly improve the quality and standing of higher education institutions or institutional systems.

The desire to change things in European higher education is fueled by a notion of inadequacy (van Vught, 2004). The recent broad call for so-called 'elite' universities in Germany, Italy or Russia may constitute a testimonial.

Proper elite universities were not decreed or founded to take on this role[17], they slowly evolved. The declaration of goals alone does not change much. Spurred by the prospect of the new millennium, perhaps, European heads of state and governments met in Lisbon in the year 2000 to launch a series of reforms and to make the European Union "the most dynamic and competitive knowledge-base economy in the world" by the year 2010[18]. Now, more than half-way through this process, "[...] the results are [seen as] not very satisfactory. The implementation of reforms in the Member States", says the European Commission, "has been quite scarce [sic]". One cannot achieve goals which are outside one's reach, and it is illusionary and counter-productive to set such goals. Europe cannot quickly create new elite institutions (Clery, 2006)[19] but, if some institutions or institutional systems and their governing agencies have the vision and stamina to pursue a true quality agenda over a prolonged period of time, the future European higher education landscape may show more promise.

Quality Focus and Benchmarking. Any change, any development toward a goal, predisposes a reasonably correct assessment regarding one's own position. This is not only true for navigational exercises in the air or on the ground, it is also true for science policy or higher education systems (Herbst, 1999). The position one wants to change needs to be assessed or described, preferably in the same terms as one would like to portray the desired state, the goal. In the fields of science policy or higher education, such portrayal is not a trivial task, and a broad variety of descriptive (and analytic) approaches have been established for such purposes.

In order to assess the standing of US research in a comparative context, a joint US committee of the National Academy of Sciences, the National Academy of Engineering and the Institute of Medicine (COSEPUP) concluded that "the most effective means of evaluating federal research is expert review" (Committee on Science, Engineering, and Public Policy, 2000). This expert judgment is to be supported by, but not based on, quantitative appraisals of citations, publications, or prizes received. "[...] quantitative indicators commonly used to assess research programs — for example, dollars spent, papers cited, and numbers of scientists supported — are useful information but [...] by themselves they are inadequate indicators of leadership", the committee noted. The committee also focused on aspects which are frequently ignored from being assessed: "[...] if all the interest-

---

[17]See Section 5.3, and in particular footnote 31 on p. 113.

[18]See: http://europa.eu.int/growthandjobs/intro_en.htm.

[19]see: http://europa.eu.int/comm/education/policies/edu/eit/index_en.html.

ing research in a country is being done by senior researchers, that country might lack sufficient young researchers to develop accomplishments in the future". Furthermore, COSEPUP set reasonable standards for leadership and for second-best, satisficing or fast-follower behavior. It is impossible, even for a strong science nation such as the US, to lead in every field, and a fast-follower position may suffice. Such a position allows domestic institutes to absorb quickly new developments which take place elsewhere and to replicate results, perhaps in a matter of weeks[20].

Proper and realistic assessments of relative positions in the landscape of science, conducted by international panels, are mandatory for universities and nations. They are based on quantitative analyses of science indicators and they form the starting point for diagnostic activities which try to trace cause-and-effect patterns. These in turn, then, form the azimuth by which to reach solutions and to find courses of actions designed to strengthen science. The same holds true for higher education.

Internationalization. Science is international. Knowledge spreads fast, and publication cultures are designed to review scientific work and to disseminate pertinent information. Particularly the natural sciences and engineering have spearheaded the way toward internationalization, and the social sciences and humanities have followed suit. Information, scientific results or ideas are not only exchanged. People move or are driven away from their origins or are attracted by destinations. Some countries have benefited a great deal from the influx of foreign academics and students, particularly the US (Levin & Stephan, 1999; Djerassi, 2004). But these countries may have benefited for good reasons; they welcomed foreign students and scholars and furnished the opportunities and attractive working environments (Medawar & Pike, 2000).

And yet, while the internationalization of science appears as an ideal, the reality may look different. International student exchange, a prime target of the Bologna process, is low. In France, for instance, only roughly 1% of students study abroad (Balter, 2001). In other populous European countries, the picture is not significantly different. While many universities have adopted a policy of not selecting their faculty from their own ranks in order to fight 'inbreeding', career paths at the same university are not uncommon: doctoral studies often take place at the same institutions

---

[20]COSEPUP refers to the breakthrough at the IBM Research Laboratory in Rüschlikon (Switzerland) concerning superconductivity which was quickly replicated (Nowotny & Felt, 2002). In the year 1987, J. Georg Bednorz and K. Alexander Müller received the Nobel Prize in Physics for their work on superconductivity at the IBM Research Laboratory.

where undergraduate studies have taken place, as well as post-doctoral work at the same institution where the doctorate was pursued, frequently even under the same supervising faculty member. Students tend to choose institutions in the vicinity of their place of residence, and faculty are recruited primarily from the pool of domestic applicants. No wonder that parochialism abounds in many higher education institutions, even in those which aspire to be research universities[21].

The impact on science can be devastating. Not only productivity as such is likely to be affected, the very fabric of science is threatened. History has given us examples of 'national' sciences which have flourished during Nazi or Soviet times, to the detriment of science (and to the detriment of humanity)[22]. Some disciplines, such as law or accounting, may have a strong national or local affinity, but this affinity relates more to the practice of the discipline and less to its scientific part. Localized cultures of science are dangerous because they undermine an international flow of ideas and concepts across boundaries. In a sense, localized cultures of science are self-sufficient, and they stand in the way of intellectual development[23].

Learning and Innovation. Learning is multifaceted. Learners are guided in their pursuit by teachers and mentors, but eventually, and most importantly, learners will have to learn how to learn. To bring learners to this stage is perhaps the most challenging aspect of higher education. It is also one of the most important. In autobiographies of scholars we are told that perhaps the deepest learning takes place while teaching or preparing a course, while researching a subject. We cannot teach others unless we ourselves have surveyed or mastered the subject.

Before one reaches this stage of a self-led learning, guidance is necessary. "[...] education is not to be viewed as something like filling a vessel with water but, rather, assisting a flower to grow in its own way",

---

[21]It is clear that language barriers form a problem. Still, some (continental) European universities have managed to attract international faculty. I should stress here that the tendency toward parochialism was less prevalent in the 19th century when the leading universities of those days were much more international (Helfenstein, 2001).

[22]A range of studies exist which trace Nazi or Soviet versions of localized sciences, some of which still affect academic life now.

[23]A recently published (2004) anthology on Austrian university reform may provide an example of such a localized culture. The volume of circa 450 pages contains more than 20 papers by different authors, mostly academics (law or social science professors). It contains 633 footnotes or references; of these, only 11 refer to sources written in a language other than German. A book which has to deal with 'best practice' or with management questions in relation to higher education ought to cover experiences in other settings. It is the celebration of ignorance here which is indicative of the localized culture.

writes *Noam Chomsky* in reference to *Dewey* and *Russell* (Macedo, 2000, p. 38). Knowledge transfer, still so dominant in many curricula, should not be overemphasized. We need some lexicographic knowledge, but not too much. One cannot hope to capture exponentially growing theories and facts with the limited capacity of a human brain, and one should not attempt it. Modern curricula should not force students to cram facts and figures, but many still do. One needs instrumental knowledge, knowledge about how to go about learning and how to do things, because one needs tools in order to be in a position to study phenomena or to create concepts or machines. Students will also have to acquire skills necessary in the pursuit of scholarship, and the development of skills needs practice.

Scholarship and personal growth takes place in an environment conducive to the development of knowledge acquisition or creation. Universities may lose the most talented students if they neglect their specific needs, and the more normal students can easily be misled. Teaching ought to be a priority of all institutions, research oriented or not, but teaching should not be confused with eloquent lectures in front of large audiences. *William B. Wood* and *James M. Gentile* (Wood & Gentile, 2003) state that "[...] traditional lecture, laboratory and recitation courses [...] are relatively ineffective at helping students master and retain the important concepts of their disciplines over the long term. Moreover, these practices do not adequately develop creative thinking, investigative and collaborative problem-solving skills that employers often seek". Students require an easy access to faculty; active, inquiry-based learning ought to be a priority; collaborative learning has proved to be more effective than individualized learning; and information technology should be used now to assist the learning process.

A necessary, but not sufficient, condition for this to take place is that of sensible student-faculty ratios. Student-faculty ratios have long been seen as indicative of teaching quality (Astin, 1993). The leading US research universities have retained their student-faculty ratios over a period of 150 years or longer without major changes. On average, roughly 10 to 20 students could be counted per faculty position, irrespective of the period and irrespective of the financial position the universities found themselves in. This is in stark contrast to the European situation where student-faculty ratios generally deteriorated over time. As I have said elsewhere (Herbst et al., 2002, Chapter 8), it is ironical that this teaching focus would eventually prove central regarding the pursuit of research (Herbst, 2004b).

In properly funded research universities, sensible student-faculty ratios imply sensible staff-faculty ratios. Sensible staff-faculty ratios mean relatively small research groups composed of doctoral and post-doctoral students assisted, perhaps, by some non-academic staff[24] and headed by an academically autonomous faculty member. The function which traces productivity of research teams in terms of group size is roughly bell-shaped: output per researcher increases first, reaches then a maximum (at a team size of roughly 5–9 people), and tends to decline with increasing group size and associated costs of coordination, communication and administration (Pelz & Andrews, 1976; Hurley, 1997; Carayol & Matt, 2004a). The composition of the research group plays an important role, of course: experienced principal investigators working with younger, perhaps foreign, people for a restricted period are likely to be more productive than groups whose composition remains stable over a prolonged period (Carayol & Matt, 2004b).

But the major advantage of systems based on small research groups versus systems which rely on large research groups appears to be related to their adaptive power. Systems with a culture of small research groups are potentially much more dynamic and adaptive than corresponding systems characterized by larger research groups: they provide a more attractive career pipeline and testing ground for young scholars who gain academic autonomy earlier, institutes can much more easily be formed or closed, patronage can better be fought or meritocracy pursued (Bonaccorsi, 2005), knowledge more easily propagated, or know-how bequeathed to new generations of scholars (Abbott, 2001). Research groups ought to be large enough in order to profit from the necessary division of labor (and interdisciplinary work), but not much larger[25]. The "Matthew Effect" (Merton, 1973, Chapter 20) might provide principle investigators with an outstanding research record better chances to exploit the grantsmanship game and to recruit talented staff, but in the longer run, prudence is likely to be a good safeguard of quality. Finally, a policy to support smaller sized research teams enhances the diversity of ideas and, presumably, serendipity (Merton & Barber, 2004).

6.4 Prospects

A range of issues will have to be addressed in oder to revitalize European higher education. Foremost on the agenda are ideas and measures de-

---

[24]Non-academic staff (technical staff functions, secretarial work, et cetera) can normally be shared by more than one group.

[25]Many large research groups are not large because their task requires the particular size; prestige, income or social standing may demand a large number of subordinates. In the case of the development part of R&D, a strategy to work with larger — or sets of — teams might prove fruitful, however.

signed to empower institutions to transform themselves. The university cannot remain a "republic of kingdoms" (Gugerli, Kupper, & Speich, 2005) if it wants to prosper in the 21st century, and its feudal vestiges still prominent in European university cultures — its obsession with rank, titles, and insignia — will have to vanish and be replaced by an unpretentious meritocracy. *Frank H.T. Rhodes* observes that "[...] major change [...] seems inevitable. Universities tend to share a model of internal governance that is medieval and ecclesiastical in its origin, nomenclature, and offices [...] and cumbersome and conservative in its operation" (Rhodes, 2001, p. 233), but he sees the successful university as "[d]entralized, feistily independent, uncoordinated, pluralistic, [...] adaptive, creative, and responsive to new opportunities" (p. 13). A similar anarchic energy is required if European universities are to continue their mission as centers of intellect.

Change and transformation presupposes, as I have said above, a "realistic assessment of relative positions in the landscape of science" and proper normative notions of higher education institutions. The broad class of institutions which are called universities needs to be subdivided or classified further, in order to identify mission orientation, desirable aspects to emulate or undesirable features to avoid. One basic requirement for healthy universities, however, is the autonomy of institutions. No reform plan will get very far without a thorough discussion, and revision, of the prevailing concept of autonomy. Most European higher education institutions are far from being autonomous, and particularly research universities suffer from this situation.

Institutions to Focus on. A simple attempt to classify institutions in accordance with the criteria discussed above is given by the 2×2 Table 6.1, defining four (ideal-type) institutional classes. Classes 1 and 2 refer to properly funded institutions. Class 1 encompasses teaching institutions characterized by low student-faculty ratios (say, 20 students per faculty), but also by low staff-faculty ratios (say, not more than 1–2 teaching assistants or administrative staff per faculty). Class 2 covers research universities (I) which have proved to be effective; these are characterized by a student-faculty ratio in the range of 10:1 to 25:1, and by a (academic) staff-faculty ratio in the range of 5:1 to 10:1[26]. Class 3 covers what I have termed 'bloated' — i.e. "overloaded and underfunded" — institutions, that is institutions characterized by high student-faculty ratios (such as 60:1 or 80:1) and by relatively low (academic) staff-faculty ratios (lower than in Class 2). And

---

[26]These are averages characteristic of the natural sciences and engineering; in the humanities and the social sciences, the figures are likely to be somewhat lower.

Table 6.1: Classification Scheme of Higher Education Institutions, by Resources Demand Indicator (Student-Faculty Ratio) and Resources Supply Indicator (Staff-Faculty Ratio)

	STAFF-FACULTY RATIO	
STUDENT-FACULTY RATIO	low	high
low	1: teaching institutions	2: research universities I
high	3: 'bloated' universities	4: research universities II

finally, there is Class 4 of institutions (research universities II) characterized by moderately high student-faculty ratios (say, 40:1) but also relatively high staff-faculty ratios (perhaps twice the rate of Class 2)[27].

In a dynamic context, Classes 1 and 2 are relatively stable, unless funds are withdrawn. Class 1 ought to be cherished as a class of good teaching institutions. Research can take place in moderate amounts if only faculty members (and perhaps non-doctoral students) are involved (and no staff) and to the extent is does not conflict with the teaching mission of the institution. If academic drift affects a Class 1 institution, it is likely to move into the (undesirable) direction of a Class 3 institution. Class 2 is an ideal-type of the research university. Class 3 encompasses the many "overloaded and underfunded" universities which have generally evolved, over time, from Class 2 institutions in that growth in enrollment outpaced funding. Class 3 institutions operate sub-optimally regarding teaching and research, and they should be transformed into teaching institutions (Class 1) or proper research universities (Class 2) by reducing enrollment[28], by a change of funding regimes (see Chapter 5), by increased funding, or through the merging with dedicated, non-university based, research institutes (see Section 6.2). Finally, a few universities belong to Class 4. They are relatively well funded in relation to their enrollment, but they operate sub-optimally in teaching

---

[27]For a discussion on student-faculty and staff-faculty ratios, see (Herbst et al., 2002, Chapter 4).

[28]Through active admission management.

as well as in research. Because the institutions of Class 4 are relatively well funded, they should be in a position to transform themselves, without outside help, into Class 2 institutions.

Reform plans, hence, will have to focus on institutions belonging primarily to Classes 3 and 4. Class 3 institutions, i.e. perhaps the great majority of European universities, have the most arduous task confronting them: they have to match their resources with their mission. This may entail choosing a mission to match their available resources or, conversely, greatly enlarging their funding base in support of their current mission. The "[...] process of redesigning the university will be the reclamation of its central mission", says *Donald Kennedy*; "[p]lacing students first is a simple design principle, but it has great power" (Kennedy, 1997, p. 287). If the mission is to be adapted to the resources available, a transformation of Class 3 into Class 1 institutions may have to be envisaged, or the split of a large institution into two units: a teaching unit, and a proper research university. Because institutions within the same region are potentially affected by these reform processes, a multi-institutional perspective, involving universities, teaching institutions, and non-university research institutes, is probably beneficial. A continuation of the present ambivalent posture is likely to undermine the future of European higher education.

Class 4 institutions appear to occupy an envious position within the current landscape of higher education institutions, but their days are numbered: within a decade or two, they may find themselves as Class 3 institutions. Class 4 institutions have the clear option to transform themselves and to re-frame their position outside the national context as European, or worldwide, players in education and research. This window of opportunity is open now, perhaps for a decade or two as I said, but it will close if no concerted reform plans are instituted and if the will is not harnessed to change matters and to look forward.

Academic Autonomy. Any reform of higher education will have to rely on academic and institutional autonomy which is still lacking in a range of higher university systems (Mora, 2001). While some academic rights are commonly upheld, at least to some degree, under the umbrella of the "freedom to teach and to research", one academic right is not that common: the institutional right to determine "who may be admitted to study"[29]. In fact, this "fourth academic freedom", as *Felix Frankfurter* called it, has a negative connotation as *numerus clausus*, invoking perhaps admission quotas as they

---

[29]US Supreme Court Justice *Felix Frankfurter* in the Sweezy vs. New Hampshire case, US 234 (1957).

were applied in the 19th and the first part of the 20th century to limit the enrollment of certain ethnic groups (e.g. Jews, Blacks) or women (Karabel, 2005).

Admission management or *numerus clausus*, as some people choose to call it in Europe, stands in contrast to open admission. Open admission policies allow students with (certain) high school certificates to enroll in universities of their choice, at least within their own country[30]. Open admission policies made sense, and were even mandatory or necessary, when relatively few students attended universities, perhaps 5–6% of the corresponding age cohorts, and when student populations were rather stable[31]. With the advent of mass higher education, and the swelling of student populations with corresponding measures of retrenchment, open admission policies were directly instrumental in the creation of "overloaded and underfunded" research universities. The spectrum of students to be admitted, covering perhaps 30–60% of the corresonding age cohorts (depending on the country), was too broad for single institutions and their specific educational missions, and institutional adjustments had to be dysfunctional if one views the broader mission of higher education.

While some stakeholders clearly see the negative side of open admission policies, open admission is seen as a guarantor for non-discriminatory admission practices. This is questionable, and one would have to compare discriminatory effects of open admission against corresponding effects of admission management to assess the issue. Open admission to tertiary education institutions is discriminatory to the degree that high school education is discriminatory. High school education in Europe is frequently discriminatory in that it attracts, for a range of reasons, an over-proportional representation of students from higher-income families, and an under-proportional representation of low-income and immigrants' families, a distribution which cannot be fully explained by differences in talent or achievement. Admission management by institutions or institutional systems can

---

[30]It is an open issue to what extent the Bologna process will in fact institute an open admission policy on a European scale. Admission management is being practiced in certain fields within universities (such as Medicine) or professional schools (e.g. Music, Art, Design, etc.). *Luc E. Weber* and *Pavel Zgaga* say in this respect: "Obviously, an institution with high academic requirements will not accept students who have accumulated any number of credits if they have been acquired at an institution that they [i.e. the institution students apply to attend] do not consider of a relatively equivalent level" (Weber & Zgaga, 2004, p. 33).

[31]This was the case in the first part of the 20th century or, in Europe, prior to 1965.

counteract these tendencies to include a well balanced student population which fits the mission of the institution[32].

Admission management also serves to fit the available budget and, without admission management, no European research university of standing is likely to survive. Admission management is frequently tied, by proponents or adversaries alike, to tuition and fees designed to cover a substantial portion of the costs of education. This is a false conception. Admission management is not dependent on tuition and fees and can be practiced irrespective of how tuition and fees are handled. Conversely, tuition and fees require admission management to combat discrimination. Elevated levels of tuition and fees are basically advocated for two reasons: to raise the income of institutions and to induce students to take their studies seriously. I have already covered the issue (in Chapters 2 and 5, and in Appendix D), and my position is that higher levels of tuition and fees are normally not required or are even outright detrimental to the quality of institutions, and that admission management, coupled with proper course management systems, have the effect of raising students' motivation and their educational success[33].

While the control over admissions is perhaps an obvious requirement for research universities to balance income and expenditures, opponents of admission management might argue that the public ought to cover the costs associated with an open admission policy or that tuition and fees be raised. Post World-War-II history has shown, and *Martin Trow* has stated above, that the public is not in a position to finance tertiary education at the cost levels required to sustain true research universities[34], and that societies will have to concentrate the available resources. Furthermore, raising tuition and fees will not substantially alter this picture[35]. However, admis-

---

[32] A good example of a well balanced student population is provided by the Berkeley campus of the University of California. See in this respect (Herbst et al., 2002), in particular the discussion on pp. 99–101 and pp. 174–175 (Appendix A.4), covering both the questions of balance and imbalance (in Swiss high school population). Of course, the underlying problem of unequal (non-meritocratic) chances of educational progress will have to be addressed by enlightened forms of primary and secondary education.

[33] 'Chosen' students have a different sense of allegiance as compared to students freely admitted. Furthermore, properly implemented course-credit systems can easily assure study progress, or else the student is ex-matriculated. The term *numerus clausus*, because of its wrong connotation, should not be used to designate admission management.

[34] Not addressed here is the question which portion of students ought to enroll in research universities.

[35] I deviate here partially from prominent scholars of higher education. For instance, *Luc E. Weber* and *James J. Duderstadt* note that "[...] the payment of fees by students actually yield a better allocation of resources (on both the supply and demand sides of higher education). [Furthermore], free access to higher education produces a regressive impact on the

sion management is but one measure to take control of the budget. In order to maintain academic autonomy, institutions and institutional systems will have to broaden their notion of academic autonomy to include the supporting foundation, the resources of the university. Institutions must be prepared to extend their funding base, to act in an entrepreneurial way (Clark, 1998, 2004b), and to professionalize their internal management and budgeting systems (Whalen, 1991; Massy, 1996, 2003).

Governance and Leadership. Institutions or university systems prosper during phases of well-supported growth. The German university of the 19th century prospered because it was in a position to expand, and the expansion was properly funded (Ben-David, 1991, Chapter 6). The US universities prospered for the same reasons after World War II (Freeland, 1992). Growth, if only qualitative in nature, is much more difficult to sustain during periods of limited resource availability, or even retrenchment, and enlightened and competent governance and management is required to guide institutions.

A basic requirement for adaptation and institutional change is an adequate distribution of power and the setting of proper priorities. Presidential systems of universities, guided and fostered by trustees, have proved to be better suited to combat the storms in the sea of higher education than systems with rectors at the helm elected by a faculty senate. However, trustees, regents and boards of governors have to have a proper concept of their function, presidents need associates with whom to fight the storms, and all together have to have appropriate tasks to perform in concert.

Because the experience with higher education autonomy is rather new in Europe, and because trustees, governing boards, and institutional executives cannot easily refer to well-established traditions or practices, a period of experimentation is likely to characterize the coming years of European higher education. My limited perspective suggests that some mistakes which have surfaced in the past result from this lack of experience and they are likely to occur in the future. In particular, there is a tendency to mistake management for governance. Governance is not management, and the two activities should be kept separate. Governing boards do not fulfill the function of fall-back management executives, and they should not

---

income distribution of a country. These are two strong arguments in favour of raising student fees, provided that sufficient need-based financial aid is provided to prevent fees from becoming a barrier to low-income students, and provided as well that governments do not simply offset the additional income from raising student fees by reducing public funding in higher education" (Weber & Duderstadt, 2004a, p. 249).

engage in micro-management. "Governing boards should focus on policy development rather than management issues. Their role is to provide the strategic, supportive, and critical stewardship for their institution" (Duderstadt, 2000, p. 257). Governing boards and trustees define, as governmental representatives in Europe, basic institutional missions, they appoint chief executives (or terminate their tenure), and they oversee the operation of the institution. But most importantly, governing boards and trustees have a fiduciary role to play, as guardians or protector[36], and as advocates of the institution under their supervision in the society at large (Rhodes, 2004).

Chief executives are likely to suffer from the same ailment as governing boards: they attempt to manage themselves what should be delegated:

> "Leadership is dispersed throughout academic institutions, through department chairs and program directors, deans and executive officers, and influential leaders of the faculty and student body" (Duderstadt, 2000, p. 249).

Chief executives lack the time to engage in detailed management. They should be concerned with major issues, with the broad lines of development of an institution, with 'cultural' aspects, or with fund-raising. While cultures may change "from below", cultural change may be mandated or should be signaled "from above". If women are heavily under-represented in our institutions, it may require a presidential stance to clearly state that such a culture is undesirable and that long range and effective measures are needed to change this situation. If diversity is a culture to be defended or sought, presidential leadership is a must (Kennedy, 1997, pp. 280–281). If the quality of faculty appointments is to be assured or raised, time is wasted for presidents if they focus too much on the appointment process itself. It is wrong to think that they can ensure quality by trying to 'own' the appointment process. They need to support or enlarge the framework which guide appointments, they ought to foster quality assurance measures or career paths patterns of young scholars[37]. In general,

> "[a] president is expected to develop, articulate, and implement visions of the university that sustain and enhance the quality of the institution. This

---

[36]In particular: of a proper legal framework, and of a sufficient funding base.

[37]This may imply a change in how faculty positions are funded (or resources secured) or faculty roles are to be perceived. If faculty positions (and associated resources) are essentially handed over, from an emeritus to the new incumbent, not much change is possible and a true quality perspective is severely restricted (even if the new faculty member is very well qualified). Such lines of succession are very common in European universities, and they practically lock institutions into their class (as described in Table 6.1 above).

includes bold and creative long-range thinking about a broad array of intellectual, social, financial, human, and physical resources, and political issues
that envelope the university" (Duderstadt, 2000, p. 252).

A sense of service needs to be revived. In the world of politics, history has shown instances of statesmen securing their position by skillfully
and opportunistically adapting to what they read as the public mood and
the signs of time. These politicians artfully ride and dance on the crests
of the waves of political turmoil like surfers on Malibu Beach. Chief executives of higher education institutions should not be recruited from this
class of surfers. To stay in office is not the major aim. Presidents and rectors
ought to be visionaries, realistic and thoughtful visionaries. They should
surround themselves with like-minded, able and professional people, with
independent and creative thinkers, not with mandarins. Leaders are leaders to the extent they are able to see and foster the quality and creativity
in others, and to the extent that they have courage enough to pursue the
paths of their conviction.

Managing Change. Tertiary or higher education, in one sense, institution-
alizes change in a *laissez-faire* mode. There are research universities and
non-university research institutes charged with staying at the frontier of
scientific development, and science and scientific fields change while pursuing this goal. Research universities as well as comprehensive universities
and teaching institutions constantly acculturate and incorporate scientific
paradigms and novel professional practices and hand them over to ever
new generations of students. Faculty are basically in charge of this process,
in that they shape the research agenda, design curricula and courses, and
supervise students and their learning processes.

When higher education is accused of inertia, the claim is not that science does not move or that research does not progress. Rather, it is claimed
that tertiary education organizations do not adapt properly in a dynamic
world: their organizational setup and their hierarchies are seen lacking,
the allocation of resources appear misguided, promotion and reward structures seem outdated or dysfunctional and the guidance and management
of the institutions not up to its tasks. If one conceives of two areas within
higher education,

- the academy in the narrower sense (e.g. faculty and students, curricula and courses, knowledge and research agendas), and

- the necessary support structures (institutes, departments or schools;

funding systems; appointment and admission procedures; executive boards and supervision, etc.),

it is primarily the second area which is being questioned and invited to change.

Higher education institutions cannot be run 'top down' in a command-and-control mode, because the know-how is concentrated in the middle-ranks, i.e. the faculty (Etzioni, 1975). The faculty, individually or collectively, makes most decisions regarding teaching and research and, implicitly, also regarding organizational goals. However, the faculty, as such, are not professionals regarding organizations or tertiary education institutions[38]. They have to professionalize themselves gradually if they take on duties of department chairs or deans, of provosts or rectors, and become institutional executives. Most university executives are recruited from the ranks of the faculty, for good reasons, and they are assisted by a host of administrators of various ranks.

Modern universities have become complex organizations. A range of service offices have to be staffed which may not have existed a few decades ago, dealing with technology transfer, patents and licensing, the organization of symposia and conferences, external communications and public relations, fund-raising, budgeting and planning, institutional research, student admissions, computer-aided instruction, and so forth. The functioning and productivity of institutions depends on the functioning of these service units, and it depends on a proper organizational setup of such units. How does one form, or close down, departments? Should institutions be subdivided into schools and these in turn into departments, or is it preferable to leave out the level of schools in the hierarchy of the university? What should be regulated by statute, what by rules or regulations? Who is to invoke change?

Experience has shown that universities are fertile grounds for 'bottom-up' induced change. A legal and financial framework is required to support this, and institutional executives are responsible for creating a supportive cultural climate within their institutions to encourage new ideas and entrepreneurial stances among faculty, staff and students. Statutes, rules and regulations should be framed so as not to constrain viable change. If institutes are legally constrained to be subunits of departments, to give an example, inter-disciplinary, and trans-disciplinary, work is severely restricted and the dynamics and progress of research artificially curtailed. If

---

[38]The exception, of course, are faculty in fields which cover the operation of organizations, such as management, higher education, law, etc.

no provisions are implemented to account for the inter-departmental flow of resources, inter-disciplinary and inter-departmental course programs are difficult to implement. If faculty members are allowed to make decisions which affect the institutional budget after their retirement, institutions will lose necessary options to allocate their resources in an appropriate and effective way. If the legal framework of an institution is too tight, or if 'bottom-up' initiatives are too frequently deterred, sensible change may be suppressed.

Universities may have standing, or *ad-hoc*, committees to advise the board of executives on matters of development or change. Committees require a mandate, a charge, and they need to be able to accept the aims of this mandate to do their work effectively. Standing committees demand some authority, and they gain it over the long run through transparent and thoughtful work in the service of the academic community. Executive boards have the duty to evaluate the recommendations of committees, but they should not often have to negate their advice since this will undermine the committees' authority and self-respect. A standing committee whose recommendations are notoriously being negated is a sign of misfit; it will eventually lead to the dissolution or demission of the committee, or to a closer check of the executive board through the board of trustees.

To manage change, a proper conception of the problem situation is required (Herbst, 1970, 1999). Failure to assess a problem situation properly results in a mis-allocation of managerial resources and the call for or implementation of inappropriate solutions. The perception of problems is a managerial art and a complex business. If problem situations are inappropriately assessed, if problems are not 'seen' or even negated over prolonged periods, no viable solution strategies can be pursued. A proper notion of the *status quo* is a basic requirement of any managed change. This is not only a matter of 'facts & figures'; it is also a matter of judgment and experience. In the field of medical practice, a proper diagnosis is a prerequisite for a treatment plan; the same applies to higher education. Higher education officials have to assess and benchmark the institutions under their jurisdiction, in a hopefully unbiased and comprehensive way[39]. National benchmarks will not suffice any longer, because education and research is destined to become a global enterprise. Poor performance indicators should be reflected, not negated. Good performance indicators should not affect the vigilance with which one observes and monitors the scene; complacency is the wrong position to take.

---

[39]Institutional rankings or league tables, so popular now in magazines, may not help them to pursue this aim (Herbst, November 2, 2005).

The *status quo* may affect the way we see the future, particularly if we basically cherish the *status quo* and fear the unknown. Proper diagnoses of the higher education systems at hand will clarify strengths and weaknesses, and will embolden us to think about opportunities and threats[40]: it will help to sketch a desired future. The desired future, a joint product of many actors and not under the exclusive control of higher education officials, should be feasible and attainable. It is not effective, and perhaps even misleading, to picture a vision without thinking about the path one will have to pursue in order to transform a given state of a system into a desired state. A vision of higher education's future without corresponding studies of the political, economic or pedagogic ramifications is likely to produce a poor vision. Likewise, it appears shortsighted to think about transformations, or 'treatment' plans[41], without a clearer conception of what the transformation is to accomplish and how progress is to be measured.

Advice and Counseling. In higher education and in many other fields, there cannot be treatment plans or prescriptions without corresponding visions of desired states and proper diagnoses of the givens, of the *status quo*. In European higher education, the situation is complicated by the fact that there exist at least three major cultures (British, French and German) which have shaped tertiary education, not only in their own direct spheres of influence and not only in Europe alone. The general comments on higher education contained herein are not intended to imply a solution; for that, they are much too general. Nonetheless, comments on alternative governance and management modes (Chapter 5), on the distribution and concentration of resources, on governance and collegiate culture or on prospects of higher education (this Chapter), may have significance in a wider context.

General comments refer to classes of problems, to shared problems, which span, perhaps, major cultures of higher education. A range of scholars have had the courage to address not only specifics, like student retention, curriculum development or faculty time allocation, but more encompassing, 'cultural' aspects of higher education, and the implication is that descriptive insights may have normative significance. *Chris Duke* focused on "institutional learning" as a new paradigm (Duke, 1992). *Henry Etzkowitz* and *Loet Leydesdorff* addressed the broader context of "university – industry – government relations" (Etzkowitz & Leydesdorff, 2001

---

[40]The approach is commonly called SWOT-Analysis (strength, weaknesses, opportunities, threats).

[41]Like the Bologna process, for instance.

(1997)). *Burton Clark* has tried to synthesize vital elements which make diverse institutions "entrepreneurial" (Clark, 1998, 2004b). *Barbara Sporn* has searched for features which allow institutions to be "adaptive" (Sporn, 1999). *Lisa Lattuca* investigated ingredients of "interdisciplinarity" (Lattuca, 2001). *Derek Bok* explored the "commercialization of higher education" (Bok, 2003). And *Michael Shattock* has focused on "managing successful universities" (Shattock, 2003).

My own research has a propensity to be comparative and to focus on structural, or morphological, aspects of higher education institutions or systems. Because of my professional background, I also dwell on how to fashion change or on how to move within a changing environment. Since higher education or higher education institutions are so tradition bound, no future orientation is really effective without a thorough understanding of past developments. In this respect, I am greatly indebted to *Joseph Ben-David* whose writings tower over much of what is being published in the field (Ben-David, 1972, 1991). Regarding the sociology of science, *Robert K. Merton* has left a vacancy which has yet to be filled (Merton, 1973, 1996). I have also benefited from the work of historians who focused on higher education (Ringer, 1990 (1969); Weisz, 1983; Hammerstein, 2000; Schwinges, 2001; Schalenberg, 2002), or from biographies, personal recollections or statements, or institutional monographs (Arrow, Cottle, Eaves, & Olkin, 1996; Kennedy, 1997; Duderstadt, 2000; Bonner, 2002; Kerr, 2001a, 2001b).

In order to advance higher education and higher education institutions, we need a deep understanding of the underlying forces which shape higher education and its environment. Shortsighted and ill-informed reforms may not point in the right direction and may cause irreparable damage. Any engagement for higher education will also require a devotion for the subject matter which should not be construed to stand in the way of 'objective' inquiry. Good teaching predisposes a penchant for the course content being taught and an affection for the student. Good architecture requires insight and taste. Science demands inquisitiveness and determination. Like teaching, architecture or science, higher education is a noble enterprise, and one should aspire to let it develop and mature, for the benefit of new generations and the society at large.

Appendix A

Background Information

> *The view that universities are businesses needs to be challenged [...] While its educational services yield private returns to individual students, the greater part of its activities yield social benefits and cannot easily be captured by market arrangements.*

Peter Karmel (Karmel, 2003)

THIS APPENDIX assembles information to illustrate some aspects of the context of higher education, specifically regarding tuition & fees, research rankings of institutions, and departmental foci. The following five tables are included:

- Tuition & fees at selected US state universities; tuition & fees at selected US private universities (Table A.1); research rankings of selected US state universities; research rankings of selected US private universities (Table A.2). Note that tuition & fees and research rankings do not correlate.

- Faculty of Departments (Schools) at the University of North Carolina at Chapel Hill (see Table A.3). I provide here a historical example, some 20 years old, of a fine but by no means elite university: the graduate school of the University of North Carolina at Chapel Hill (of the year 1979-80) listed 66 departments and courses of studies, among them inter-departmental curricula.

These inter-departmental curricula were offered in the following fields: in Biomedical Engineering and Mathematics, Comparative Literature, Ecol-

Table A.1: TUITION AND FEES (IN $ PER ACADEMIC YEAR) AT SELECTED US UNIVERSITIES (2003–04), based on: chronicle.com/stats/tuition/.

PUBLIC INSTITUTION:	in-state	out-of-state
Georgia Institute of Technology	4,076	16,002
Indiana University (Bloomington)	6,517	17,552
Michigan State University	6,769	16,729
North Carolina State University	3,889	15,737
Pennsylvania State University (University Park)	9,706	19,328
Purdue University	5,560	17,640
Rutgers University	7,927	14,441
U of California (Los Angeles)	5,298	19,508
U of California (Berkeley)	5,250	19,460
U of California (San Diego)	5,508	19,718
U of Colorado (Boulder)	4,020	20,336
U of Illinois (Chicago)	6,934	17,080
U of Illinois (Urbana)	7,010	18,046
U of Maryland (College Park)	6,759	17,433
U of Michigan (Ann Arbor)	7,895	24,695
U of North Carolina (Chapel Hill)	3,993	15,841
U of Oregon	4,959	16,698
U of Pittsburgh	9,274	18,586
U of South Carolina (Columbia)	5,778	15,116
U of Texas (Austin)	4,188	11,268
U of Virginia	5,964	21,934
U of Washington (Seattle)	4,968	16,121
U of Wisconsin (Madison)	5,136	19,136
Virginia Polytechnic Institute	5,095	14,979

ogy, Folklore, Genetics, Human Services Administration, Marine Sciences, Neurobiology, Occupational Therapy, Operations Research and Systems Analysis, Physical Therapy, Recreation Administration, and Rehabilitation Counseling. At the time, the University had some 17,000 students.

Table A.1 (continued)

PRIVATE INSTITUTION:	in-state & out-of-state
California Institute of Technology	24,117
Carnegie Mellon University	29,410
Cornell University	28,754
Duke University	29,345
Harvard University	29,060
Johns Hopkins University	29,230
Massachusetts Institute of Technology	29,600
Northwestern University	28,524
Princeton University	28,540
Rensselaer Polytechnic Institute	28,496
Stanford University	28,923
University of Chicago	29,238
University of Pennsylvania	29,318
University of Southern California	28,692
Washington University	29,053
Yale University	28,400

Table A.2: RESEARCH RANKINGS OF SELECTED US UNIVERSITIES, by Percentage of Publications in Qualified Subfields (%) and by Number of Publications in Qualified Subfields (No.), based on CEST (www.cest.ch).

PUBLIC INSTITUTION:	Rank (%)	Rank (No.)
Georgia Institute of Technology	252	211
Indiana University (Bloomington)	159	61
Michigan State University	34	42
North Carolina State University	70	68
Pennsylvania State University (University Park)	75	36
Purdue University	45	48
Rutgers University	149	52
U of California (Los Angeles)	26	5
U of California (Berkeley)	8	8
U of California (San Diego)	9	10
U of Colorado (Boulder)	30	39
U of Illinois (Chicago)	319	168
U of Illinois (Urbana)	18	20
U of Maryland (College Park)	56	46
U of Michigan (Ann Arbor)	19	7
U of North Carolina (Chapel Hill)	31	24
U of Oregon	36	100
U of Pittsburgh	16	17
U of South Carolina (Columbia)	198	191
U of Texas (Austin)	33	38
U of Virginia	81	51
U of Washington (Seattle)	25	9
U of Wisconsin (Madison)	35	21
Virginia Polytechnic Institute	134	118

Table A.2 (continued)

PRIVATE INSTITUTION:	Rank (%)	Rank (No.)
California Institute of Technology	3	28
Carnegie Mellon University	17	70
Cornell University	23	15
Duke University	21	19
Harvard University	1	1
Johns Hopkins University	6	3
Massachusetts Institute of Technology	4	14
Northwestern University	51	33
Princeton University	10	32
Rensselaer Polytechnic Institute	85	181
Stanford University	5	6
University of Chicago	32	27
University of Pennsylvania	42	16
University of Southern California	20	26
Washington University	13	18
Yale University	12	13

Table A.3: FACULTY OF DEPARTMENTS (SCHOOLS) AT THE UNIVERSITY OF NORTH CAROLINA AT CHAPEL HILL (1979–80): by Professors [P], Associate Professors [AP] and Assistant Professors [aP], based on: (The Graduate School, 1979).

DEPARTMENTS (OR SCHOOLS):	P	AP	aP
Anatomy	11	7	9
Bacteriology & Immunology	14	11	11
Biochemistry & Nutrition	18	9	10
Botany	10	3	2
Chemistry	24	3	6
Dentistry (School)	36	22	20
Geology	11	–	6
Mathematics	15	12	4
Pathology	21	11	19
Pharmacology	14	13	4
Pharmacy (School)	11	8	8
Physics & Astronomy	22	5	2
Physiology	10	11	9
Statistics	7	3	1
Zoology	11	5	5
Biostatistics	10	14	7
Environmental Sciences & Engineering	18	6	4
Epidemiology	7	3	5
Health Administration	11	8	8
Health Education	3	2	3
Maternal & Child Health	7	1	1
Nutrition	2	2	1
Parasitology & Laboratory Practice	3	2	–
Public Health Nursing	1	5	2
Anthropology	7	1	5
Business Administration (School)	27	16	12
City & Regional Planning	10	3	2
Computer Science	3	4	2
Economics	13	13	5
Education (School)	22	25	13
Geography	4	4	2
Nursing (School)	5	17	17
Physical Education	4	4	5
Political Science	22	7	5
Psychology	28	17	13
Social Work (School)	4	8	6
Sociology	11	5	6
Speech Communication	2	3	4

Table A.3 (continued)

DEPARTMENTS (OR SCHOOLS):	P	AP	aP
Art	8	7	5
Classics	5	6	4
Comparative Literature	6	1	–
Dramatic Art	3	2	1
English	26	21	4
Germanic Languages	5	2	3
History	32	8	10
Journalism (School)	4	3	3
Library Science (School)	7	7	2
Linguistics	2	3	2
Music	9	7	7
Philosophy	6	5	4
Radio, TV & Motion Pictures	4	3	2
Religion	6	2	3
Romance Languages	13	9	6
Slavic Languages	3	1	2

Appendix B

Technical Notes

> *[. . .] efficiency is not a very helpful guide for teaching and research.*
>
> *Derek Bok (Bok, 2003)*

IN THE PRESENT report, a number of terms or concepts play a central role: efficiency and effectiveness; performance indicators; governance, management and accountability. Because all these terms are widely used, and because the usage in this report may differ from those the reader is accustomed to, I shall try to clarify meanings or ramifications of the terms in the present context. I do not want to enter into a deeper discussion here; a few remarks shall suffice.

B.1 Efficiency and Effectiveness

The term 'efficiency' is widely used in economics whereas the term 'effectiveness' is not (Pearce, 1989)[1]. 'Efficiency' is sometimes used in the context of a resource allocation discussion (Koopmans, 1957). Economists talk of efficient (and inefficient) patterns of output. In the context of linear programming (Dorfman, Samuelson, & Solow, 1958) and maximizing behavior, for instance, a set of choice variables is called inefficient if one or more of these can be increased without decreasing any of them. If a minimizing behavior

---

[1] To connote the term 'effectiveness', a range of definitions are employed, some of which are used synonymously with "goals' achievement": effectiveness is then the degree to which goals are attained. See in this context also the discussion surrounding the formula D.11 on page 199.

is modeled, the argument is reversed: we are looking for a set of feasible choice variables whose values cannot be further decreased without leaving the feasible region. It is this minimizing, cost reduction, model which appears to be in the foreground when popular reference is made to efficiency.

If we continue within the framework of linear programming, we might look at a primal problem in the form:

$$\text{minimize:} \quad C = \mathbf{cx} \tag{B.1}$$

subject to

$$\mathbf{Ax} \geq \mathbf{b},$$

where $\mathbf{c}$ is a $(1 \times n)$-vector of cost-coefficients, $\mathbf{x} \geq 0$ a $(n \times 1)$-vector of activity level variables, $\mathbf{b}$ a $(m \times 1)$-vector of targets to be met, and $\mathbf{A}$ a $(m \times n)$-matrix of coefficients. Specifically, we are looking for activity levels $\hat{\mathbf{x}}$ such that $\mathbf{A}\hat{\mathbf{x}} = \mathbf{b}$. This primal problem (B.1) can be interpreted as one designed to focus on efficiency: we minimize total costs C subject to the constraint that certain targets have to be met. I have called this problem situation the "outsider's" perspective on resource allocation, because it is mainly adopted by people outside the institutions under consideration — politicians, elected officials or legislators, namely "to provide a service — or a 'product' — as cheaply as possible" (Herbst et al., 2002, p. 26). If we look now at the corresponding dual problem,

$$\text{maximize:} \quad U = \mathbf{ub} \tag{B.2}$$

subject to

$$\mathbf{uA} \leq \mathbf{c}$$

where $\mathbf{u} \geq 0$ is a $(1 \times m)$-vector of (implicit) utility-coefficients, we can interpret the dual problem (B.2) as one designed to focus on effectiveness: we maximize the total utility U subject to the constraint that given unit costs are not violated. I have called this perspective the "insider's position, i.e. the position taken by responsible governing boards, presidents, provosts or rectors, deans and administrators of higher education institutions. [They] view the problem from the opposite direction: with given resources [or with given unit costs], they attempt to be as effective, as productive as possible".

At the optimum of problem B.2 we shall have $\hat{\mathbf{u}}\mathbf{A} = \mathbf{c}$. Duality theory tells us now that, at the optimum, the minimized value of C (of problem B.1) equals the maximized value of U (of problem B.2), i.e.

$$\hat{C} = \mathbf{c}\hat{\mathbf{x}} = \hat{\mathbf{u}}\mathbf{b} = \hat{U},$$

or, by substituting the values for **c** and **b**, we have $(\hat{\mathbf{u}}\mathbf{A})\hat{\mathbf{x}} = \hat{\mathbf{u}}(\mathbf{A}\hat{\mathbf{x}})$. In this sense — and in the context cited —, 'efficiency' and 'effectiveness' can be considered as dual concepts (Massy, 2004, p. 18).

Herbert A. Simon expressed his concern about the way the term 'efficiency' is used: "The term 'efficiency' has acquired during the past generation a number of unfortunate connotations which associate it with a mechanistic, profit-directed, stop-watch theory of administration. [...] Until practically the end of the nineteenth century, the terms 'efficiency' and 'effectiveness' were considered almost synonymous" (Simon, 1957). We could add to this that in the intervening decades the term 'efficiency' has lost much of its negative connotation that *Simon* sees — but it may also have lost its general meaning, at least outside the community of economists.

B.2 Performance-Based Resource Allocation

Performance Indicators. Performance indicators in higher education are generally tied to the framework of an input-output or a flow or process model (Astin, 1993). In analogy to an industrial plant, the higher education institution is seen as a processing unit by which 'raw materials' or 'semi-finished products' are transformed and value is added. The process model of higher education institutions distinguishes between input, process, output or outcome and the corresponding variables or indicators:

- *Input*: students (distinguished by various characteristics or 'qualities'), faculty and staff, infra-structural facilities, resources of various kinds (and origins), etc.;

- *Process*: unit-resources invested (e.g. faculty-student, staff-student or faculty-staff measures), throughput measures (time-to-degree ratio, drop-out rates), etc.;

- *Output*: degrees awarded (at various levels), publications of papers, journal articles or books, patents obtained, etc.;

- *Outcome*: career paths of alumni or outgoing staff and faculty, earning potential of graduates, citations generated by publications, scientific prizes procured, spin-off companies founded, etc.

Input variables (or indicators) might fall into two categories: (i) the primary 'raw material' or 'semi-finished' product to be transformed into the 'finished' product (e.g. the students if one focuses on educational processes or, if one focuses on the research process, the know-how present — however defined — in order to produce new scientific results) and (ii) co-requisites necessary (i.e. other resources, monetary or otherwise).

Process variables normally relate two input variables: the number of students taught per faculty member (student-faculty ratio, averages over a given domain), the number of doctoral students advised by and working under a faculty member, the number of staff members employed in the research groups of faculty members (staff-faculty ratio), the monetary inputs required to fund a student-year (measured in full-time equivalents) in a given disciplinary field, et cetera. They could also relate the effective time required to graduate with the norm-time required, or the number of students dropping out of programs with the numbers initially enrolled (drop-out rates). Process variables are frequently used as quality indicators of institutions. For example, student-faculty ratios are used in this way, or staff-faculty ratios. Institutions which pride themselves for having a teaching focus will draw attention to their low student-faculty ratios, and research-oriented institutions will invoke the notion of small research groups and intimate working relationships. Low time-to-degree ratios or low drop-out rates are also frequently seen as being indicative of quality education.

Performance indicators generally relate output to input — in the form of ratios or differences. If drop-out rates are low, we shall have corresponding high graduation rates (and vice versa). But they may also relate outcome to output, as when we compare citations generated by publications[2]. Performance indicators have to be intelligently assessed. If B and C are (real-valued) output and input measures, respectively, performance indicators are generally expressed in the form of $\frac{B}{C}$ or $B - C$ (if B and C have the same dimensionality). If, in the case of institutions i and j, we have

$$\frac{B_i}{C_i} - \frac{B_j}{C_j} > 0, \quad \text{or} \quad (B_i - C_i) - (B_j - C_j) > 0,$$

we might conclude that institution i performs better than institution j. But such conclusions are generally only reasonable when we have assurances that output and input measures were properly operationalized.

Take a performance measure "degrees awarded, by faculty member" (in a given time period, and a given departmental orientation), for instance. An institution with a higher ratio would seem to outperform an institution

---

[2]In this particular context, outcome and output can be redefined as the output and input, respectively, of a new process.

with a lower ratio, but only if degrees are really equivalent. Frequently, the institution with the lower ratio will produce qualitatively better degrees because of the more intimate faculty-student interaction. Output (or input) alone should also not be the criterium by which to judge. For instance, if one institution takes in students of lower academic standing than another, the output (or input) measure above will mask pertinent information. Suppose B_i and C_i denote (average) scores of an academic test administered at the time of graduation and enrollment, respectively (same scoring scale). If i is an institution with higher academic standing than institution j, we can expect $B_i > B_j$ (and $C_i > C_j$), and we might conclude that i performs better than j. If we measure the academic improvement of the students of institution i by $\Delta_i = B_i - C_i$, we could easily have $\Delta_j > \Delta_i$, that is, the institution with the lower academic standing — and generally lower test scores of its incoming or graduating students — might outperform the institution with the higher academic standing.

In this report, and in this technical note thus far, I have focused on performance indicators (or variables) in a strict sense (i.e. relating output to input). The term 'performance indicators' is also used (in the literature) in a loose sense, namely to refer to indicators used in the context of performance assessment. In reading or rereading through the literature, I came across terms such as "performance-based regulations" (Coglianese, Nash, & Olmstead, 2002). I should like to alert the reader to the circumstance that not all usages of the term 'performance-based' refer to the concepts addressed here. Performance-based regulations may refer to performance — or regulatory — standards, and these in turn may constitute a looser form of design standards, used in many fields, and enforced by corresponding regulating agencies[3]. Regulatory standards come into play when defining admissible levels of water or air quality, or of airline or power-plant safety, for instance, and they are under constant review. They specify an outcome, or a "performance level" in the diction of these regulations, and leave the choice of the specific measures required to the regulated agency; or they may even specify a code of practice. The setting of regulatory standards is very common — and very necessary in today's complex world, and it has an old history. But it would not be prudent to extend the meaning of such a concept to the cases and phenomena which form the focus of the present report.

---

[3]Regulating powers are frequently delegated to professional societies, particularly in the fields of engineering.

Performance-Based Resource Allocation. In the context of the present report, and in line with established notions (Burke, Joseph C. and Associates, 2002), performance-based resource allocation refers to allocation procedures which tie external or internal funding to performance indicators, via funding formulæ.

Analogous to the usage of 'performance indicators', I have noticed that the notion of performance-based resource allocation is also used in a less strict — and perhaps even misleading — sense. For instance, *Ingo Liefner* compares and analyzes six research universities, two Swiss, one Dutch, one from the UK, and two from the US (Liefner, 2003). Looking at the two Swiss universities, he concludes that the external and internal resource allocation is "not based" on performance. In the case of the two remaining European universities he states that the allocation of funds (externally as well as internally) are "partly" based on performance, and in the case of the two US universities he states that the external "allocation of public funds [is] based on performance" while in the case of the internal resource allocation "other competitive funding sources [dominate]" (Liefner, 2003, p. 476).

No doubt, all six universities are performance oriented and their funding agencies and management take performance into consideration. All six universities derive their external research support from similar sources, although to different degrees: the two US research universities derive practically all their research funding from external sources, whereas the European institutions are given resources (by their respective funding agencies) to fund research internally. But only one of the six, the University of Bristol, has been subjected to the performance-based resource allocation mechanisms that form the focus of this report (see Section D.1).

B.3   Information Systems

Accountability and accountability measures depend on properly designed and integrated information systems. Only a few years ago, different departments within the same organization or the same higher education institutions tended to have their own data system: student records, for example, would be kept separate from those of employees or faculty, and all three would be kept separate from accounting. In such non-integrated systems, it was impossible to answer such simple questions as how many people were associated with a university. Double counting was not easy to avoid because students were employed as assistants, or employees were enrolled as students, and the systems used did not permit proper identification of the intersections of the sets of students, employees and faculty.

Furthermore, the systems used could not easily track individuals holding different jobs at various departments, and they may have been unable to correctly calculate full-time-equivalent (FTE) employment figures.

However, properly designed information systems and proper management of records is not only necessary for accountability purposes, they are also mandatory for institutional management — or at least they should be. Until the recent development of the concept of the European Credit Transfer System (ECTS), a byproduct of the Bologna process initiated by the European Rectors' Conference (ERC), credit systems played no role in most European universities and their implementation is far from complete. As a consequence, FTE-student numbers could not be suitably defined, and many student-statistics reported inflated numbers (Pechar & Wrobleski, 2001), with implications also for accounting purposes and funding processes. At the same time, information was lacking to effectively manage courses or course systems which cross departmental boundaries, and the cost-effective matching of course programs and lecture halls or seminar rooms was practically impossible. The late introduction of credit systems in Europe is all the more perplexing when we realize that credit systems were introduced in the US (by the Carnegie Foundation) around 1905. Furthermore, the ECTS sets a focus on 'European credit transfer', as if credit transfer (from institution to institution) was the only a singular reason to introduce a credit system.

Credit systems are not the only tools in the teaching-learning field which have had difficulties establishing themselves in Europe. Course evaluations by students provide another example. Without credit systems, or without course evaluation systems, universities lack vital instruments to manage their own institution, and the general reluctance even to use the newly introduced ECTS for internal purposes signals a still prevalent hesitancy on the part of many European rectors or presidents to manage their institutions and make them transparent. That same hesitancy to manage appears to be tied to a reluctance to initiate pro-active, bottom-up change. The institutions' reluctance to change-management, in turn, provokes top-down initiatives on the part of supervising bodies or government agencies. Such actions are then often decried as micro-management, and are so resented by institutions or institutional systems[4].

---

[4]See the footnote 28 on p. 87.

Appendix C

The Atlantic Split

[O]nce employed in a specific environment, individual productivity soon conforms to the characteristics of that context [...] In almost all fields the most productive labs are the smallest, and the least productive labs may be small or large.

Nicolas Carayol and Mireille Matt (Carayol & Matt, 2003)

T HE THESIS OF THE ATLANTIC SPLIT regarding research productivity is not new; it has lingered on for some decades now. It states that US universities have a productivity edge. The thesis has to be reevaluated periodically because systems are in flux, and in recent years one can observe a tendency to challenge the thesis: non-US research institutions and universities have gained ground (Da Pozzo, Maye, Roulin Perriard, & von Ins, 2004; Da Pozzo et al., 2003, chapter 1), enough — some hope — to bridge or fill the cleft which separated in the past the US research enterprise from that of Europe or other regions.

However, reiterations of the thesis appeared (Da Pozzo, Maye, Roulin-Perriard, & von Ins, 2001; Herbst, 2004b). In what follows, I shall try to document the 'Atlantic Split' as it presented itself at the turn of the past century. The thesis is of relevance here because the productivity edge which separates US universities from those of the rest of the world was not brought about by performance funding measures (but by measures referred to in Chapters 5 and 6). Furthermore, there is no supportive evidence to assume that performance funding contributed to the closing of the productivity gap: other factors appear to stand in the foreground.

Table C.1: CEST-SAMPLE OF INSTITUTIONS (1998-2002).

Country	Institutions (numbers)
USA	217
Germany	59
Japan	56
UK	49
France	40
Italy	36
(others)	226
Total	683

The data to which I refer pertain to a data set compiled by CEST which is based on an original data set provided by Thomson Scientific, Inc., formerly Institute of Scientific Information (ISI). CEST extracted the most research productive universities (worldwide) and included thus 683 institutions in its own data set (roughly 2 percent of all institutions — universities, colleges and research institutes — documented by ISI). The country distribution of institutions included can be seen in Tables C.1, C.3 (alphabetical listing) and C.4 (listed by number of institutions included).

C.1 Indicators

The criteria (Criterion 1 and Criterion 2) by which this extraction occurred shall be explained below. CEST characterized the institutions by indicators, six of which are defined below (plus one definition of terms)[1]:

Number of 'Publications' Publications by institution. Publications cover journal articles (circa 71% of all publications), apart from other forms of written communications which are covered through ISI. Publications by institution is an output measure.

Fields or Subfields Current Contents of ISI distinguishes seven primary 'research areas' or 'fields': Engineering, Computing & Technology (ECT), Physical, Chemical and Earth Sciences (PCES), Agriculture, Biology & Environmental Sciences (ABES), Life Sciences (LS), Clinical Medicine (CM), Social & Behavioral Sciences (SBS), and Arts & Humanities (AH). Within these primary research areas ISI distinguishes

---

[1]Regarding the detailed definition of indicators and terms referred to below, see: http://adminsrv3.admin.ch/cest_ccs/introduction/method/method_2004.pdf.

'subfields': ECT (17), PCES (11), ABES (12), LS (18), CM (25), SBS (14), and AH (10); in total, hence, 107 subfields[2].

'P-Subfields' Number of Subfields with at least 50 Publications. Institutions may have one or more subfields where faculty, staff or students publish. If an institution has at least 50 publications in a subfield within the period (1998-2002) covered, the institution meets the first requirement for inclusion in the CEST-data-set (Criterion 1). P-Subfields is a kind of a performance measure.

'Relative Citation-Index' A citation-index is a quotient which links publications to the citations of these publications (citations per publication). The relative-citation-index standardizes these quotients for each field on a scale from 0 to 200 where the respective worldwide average (for each field) is defined to be 100. To qualify for CEST's own select set of institutions, CEST requires a relative citation-index of 120 (Criterion 2). The Relative Citation-Index is a performance measure.

'Number of Qualified Subfields' Qualified Subfields are subfields of institutions which meet the two criteria defined above (Criteria 1 and 2). Number of Qualified Subfields is a kind of a performance measure.

'QS-Publications' Number of Publications in Qualified Subfields, a kind of a performance measure.

'Publication Effectiveness' Publications in Qualified Subfields as a Percentage of Total Publications. The Publication Effectiveness is a performance measure.

C.2 Boxplots

Figures C.1 through C.12 below contain six pairs of figures (vertical boxplots) which visualize the distribution of subsets of the 683 institutions of the CEST-set along the axis of the respective indicators just described (see also Table C.2). These boxplots show the following:

- the axis of the values of indicator plotted (vertically);
- outliers below (if any);

---

[2]Each subfield is linked to an associated journal list which is used to 'define' the subfield.

Table C.2: SUMMARY STATISTICS OF THE INDICATORS REFERRING TO THE
CEST-DATA-SET OF INSTITUTIONS.

Indicator	Min	1. Quartile	Median	Average	3. Quartile	Max
Publications	57	1,678	3,556	6,108	8,073	76,140
P-Subfields	1.0	9.0	20.0	27.2	43.0	103.0
Rel Citation-Index	41.0	83.0	95.0	95.2	107.0	176.0
Qualified Subfields	1.0	1.0	4.0	8.5	10.0	79.0
QS-Publications	50	116	410	1,830	1,599	56,220
Publ Effectiveness	0.3	7.0	15.0	21.0	29.0	96.0

- smallest value (outliers excepted);

- first (or lower) quartile of values (beginning with the shaded area up
  to the median);

- median;

- third (or upper) quartile of values (up to the end of the shaded area);

- largest value (outliers excepted);

- outliers above (if any).

Each pair of figures contains a series of boxplots which are characteristic of
institutional distributions by country (organized alphabetically according
to country code — see Table C.3) to identify particular country boxplots;
and two vertical boxplots juxtaposing non-US and US institutions.

C.3 Findings

Number of 'Publications' If we look at the country distributions of institutional output (Figure C.1), we observe some institutions with many
publications (in particular, the University of London, actually a con-
glomerate of institutions, or institutions in the US or Japan). Institutions of a range of — mainly smaller — countries (e.g. those of Belgium, Canada, Switzerland, Germany, Israel, The Netherlands, Sweden or Singapore) show relatively high numbers of institutional publications. A juxtaposition of (466) non-US and (217) US institutions is
given by Figure C.2.

'P-Subfields' Again, institutions of a range of smaller countries (i.e. those of Belgium, Canada, Switzerland, Israel, The Netherlands, Sweden and Singapore) qualify for subfields with at least 50 publications in the period (1998–2002) considered (Figure C.3). Non-US and US institutions are compared in Figure C.4.

'Relative Citation-Index' Here, we look at the first true performance measure. Institutions of the following countries have a median greater than 100: Switzerland, Denmark, The Netherlands, Sweden, the UK, and the US (Figure C.5). Non-US and US institutions are juxtaposed in Figure C.6, and the median of the US institutions is above the value of the third quartile of non-US institutions.

'Number of Qualified Subfields' Institutions which qualify for the selection criterion of CEST (Criteria 1 and 2) assemble 'qualified' subfields most numerously in Canada, Switzerland, Denmark, Finland, Israel, The Netherlands, Sweden, the UK and the US (Figure C.7). Particularly Switzerland and The Netherlands score well. The US, and to some extent also the UK, have institutions in the top quartile which excel. Non-US and US institutions are placed side by side in Figure C.8; again, the median of the US institutions is above the value of the third quartile of non-US institutions. Furthermore, the forth quartile of US institutions is clearly much better placed than the corresponding non-US institutions.

'QS-Publications' If one looks at the number of publications in qualified subfields, the picture just sketched will show greater contrasts now: institutions of Switzerland and The Netherlands score well (if one looks at the respective population of institutions), and if one focuses on the top quartile of institutions, institutions of Canada, Japan, the US and the UK excel (Figure C.9). Placing non-US and US institutions side by side (Figure C.10)[3], the differences in the performance of the two populations of institutions become pronounced.

'Publication Effectiveness' This is the second proper performance measure. Institutions in Switzerland perform well on this measure (Figure C.11). Again, juxtaposing non-US and US institutions (Figure C.12), the differences in the performance of the two populations of institutions are pronounced.

---

[3]In Figure C.10, the 56,223 QS-Publications of Harvard University were excluded to show greater detail.

Table C.3: Number of Universities and Colleges Included in the CEST Data-Set of Institutions (1998–2002), by Code of Country (N = 683).

Country	Code	Institutions (number)
Austria	A	10
Argentina	AR	2
Australia	AU	17
Belgium	B	8
Brasilia	BR	3
Canada	CA	30
Switzerland	CH	9
Chile	CL	2
China	CN	11
Costa Rica	Costa	1
Czech Republic	CZ	4
Germany	DE	59
Denmark	DK	9
Spain	E	22
Estonia	EE	1
Greece	EL	3
France	F	40
Finland	FI	8
Hungary	HU	2
Italy	I	36
Israel	IL	5
India	IN	2
Iran	Iran	2
Ireland	IRL	3
Island	IS	1
Japan	JP	56
Kenya	Kenya	1
South-Korea	KR	6
Malaysia	MY	1
The Netherlands	NL	13
Norway	NO	5
New Zealand	NZ	7
Portugal	P	3
Poland	PL	3
Romania	RO	1
Sweden	S	12
Saudi-Arabia	SAr	1
Singapore	SG	2
Slovenia	SI	1
Turkey	TR	1
Taiwan	TW	9
United Kingdom	UK	49
United States	US	217
South-Africa	ZA	5

Table C.4: NUMBER OF UNIVERSITIES AND COLLEGES INCLUDED IN THE CEST DATA-SET OF INSTITUTIONS (1998–2002), by Numbers of Institutions in the Sample and by Country (N = 683).

Country	Code	Institutions (number)
United States	US	217
Germany	DE	59
Japan	JP	56
United Kingdom	UK	49
France	F	40
Italy	I	36
Canada	CA	30
Spain	E	22
Australia	AU	17
The Netherlands	NL	13
Sweden	S	12
China	CN	11
Austria	A	10
Denmark	DK	9
Switzerland	CH	9
Taiwan	TW	9
Belgium	B	8
Finland	FI	8
New Zealand	NZ	7
South-Korea	KR	6
Israel	IL	5
Norway	NO	5
South-Africa	ZA	5
Czech Republic	CZ	4
Brazil	BR	3
Greece	EL	3
Ireland	IRL	3
Portugal	P	3
Poland	PL	3
Argentina	AR	2
Chile	CL	2
India	IN	2
Iran	Iran	2
Singapore	SG	2
Hungary	HU	2
Costa Rica	Costa	1
Estonia	EE	1
Island	IS	1
Kenya	Kenya	1
Malaysia	MY	1
Romania	RO	1
Saudi-Arabia	SAr	1
Slovenia	SI	1
Turkey	TR	1

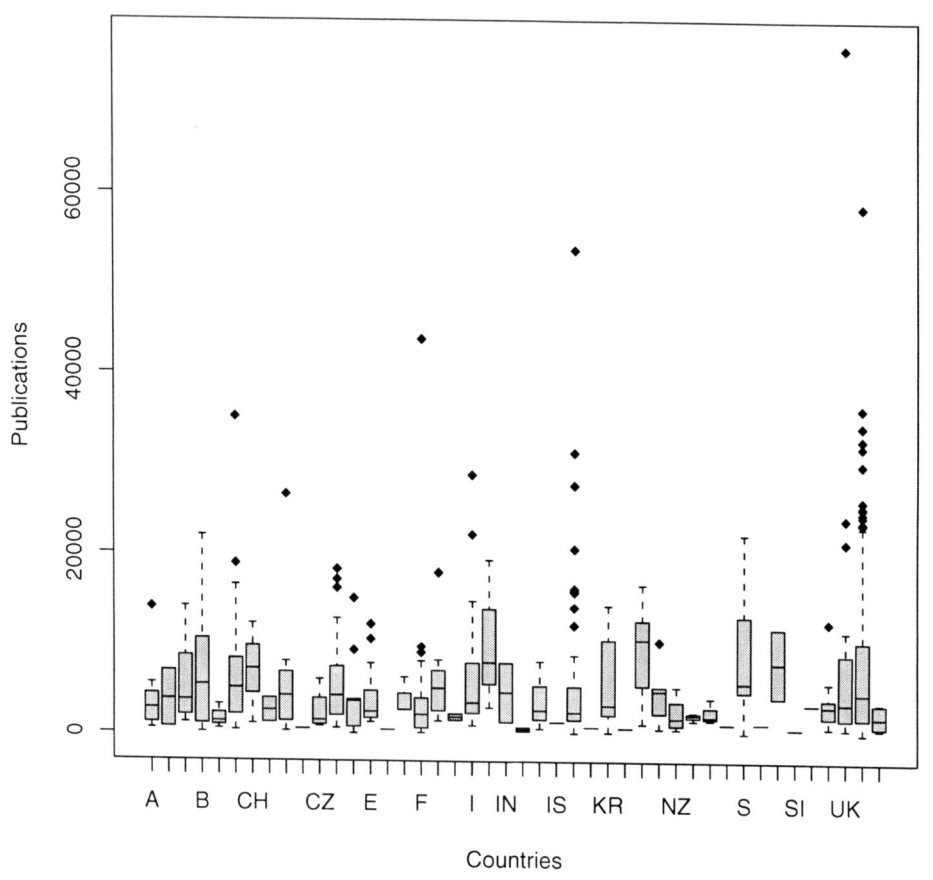

Figure C.1: BOXPLOTS OF THE NUMBER OF PUBLICATIONS OF UNIVERSI-TIES AND COLLEGES, by Country.

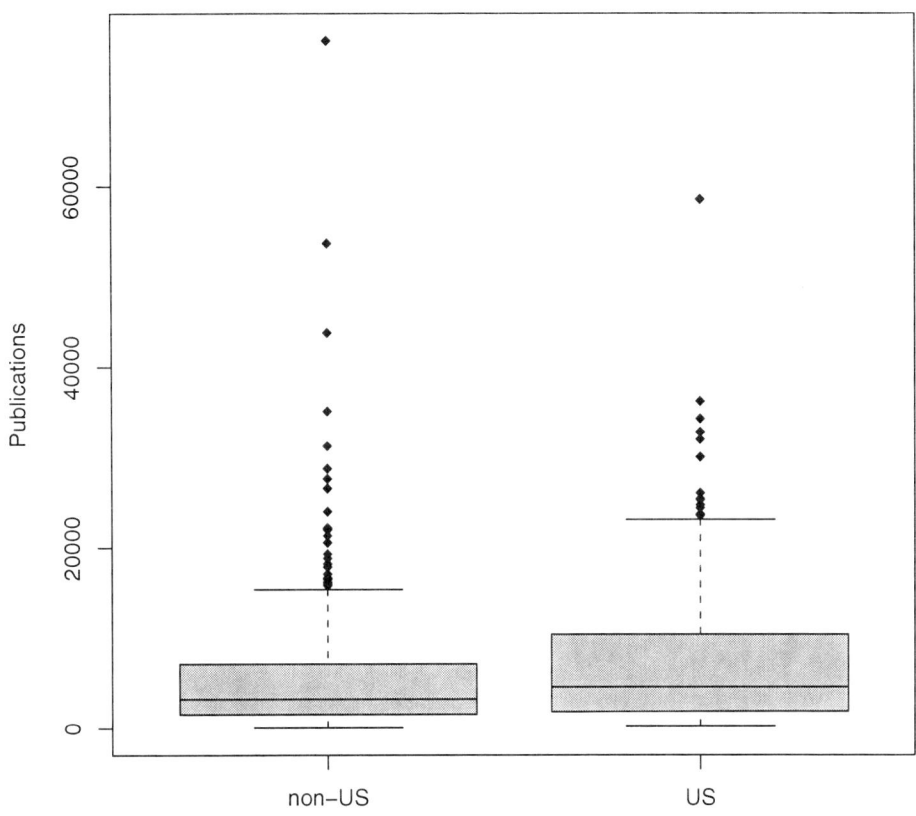

Figure C.2: BOXPLOTS OF THE NUMBER OF PUBLICATIONS OF UNIVERSITIES AND COLLEGES, by non-US versus US Institutions.

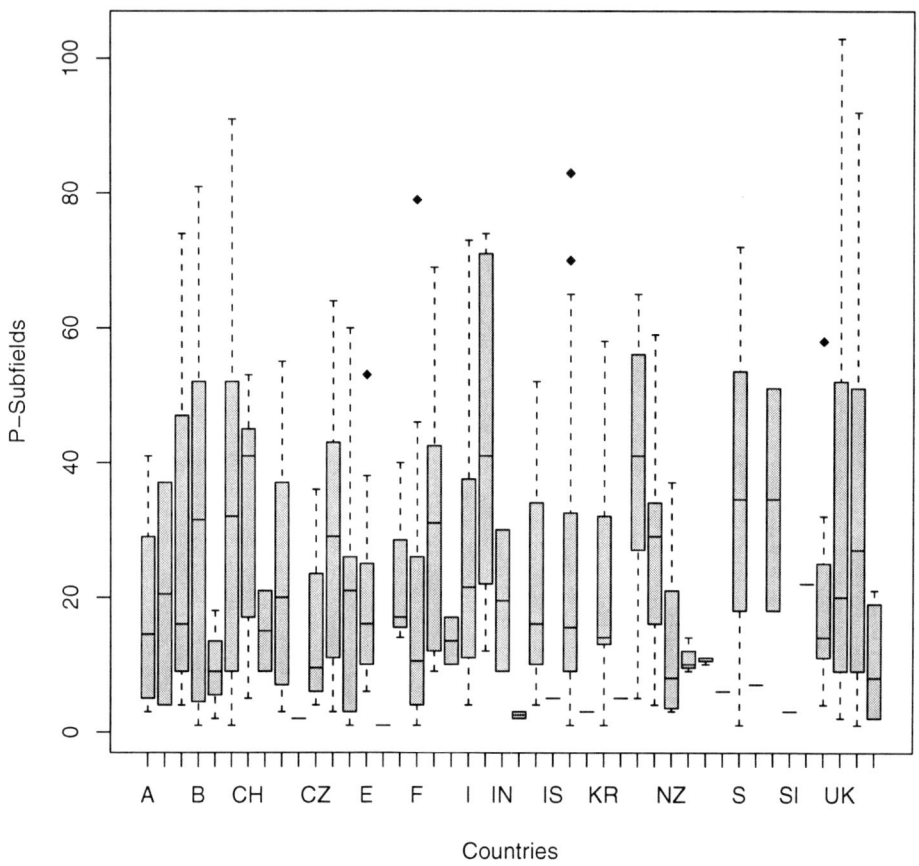

Figure C.3: Boxplots of the Number of Subfields with at least 50 Publications (P-Subfields) of Universities and Colleges, by Country.

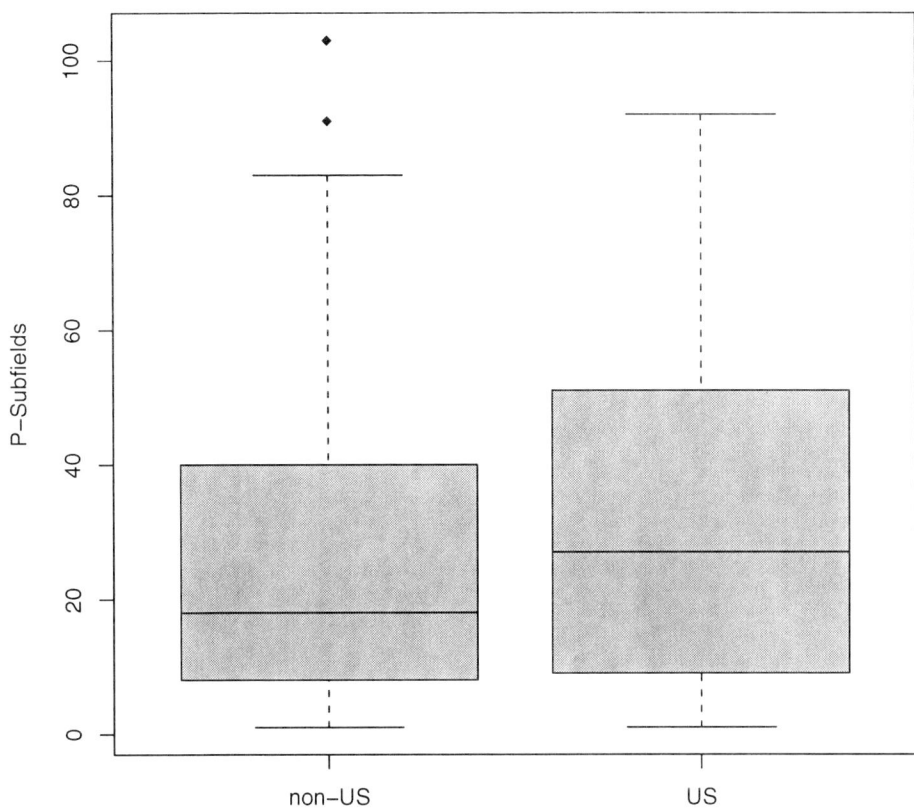

Figure C.4: BOXPLOTS OF THE NUMBER OF SUBFIELDS WITH AT LEAST 50 PUBLICATIONS (P-SUBFIELDS) OF UNIVERSITIES AND COLLEGES, by non-US versus US Institutions.

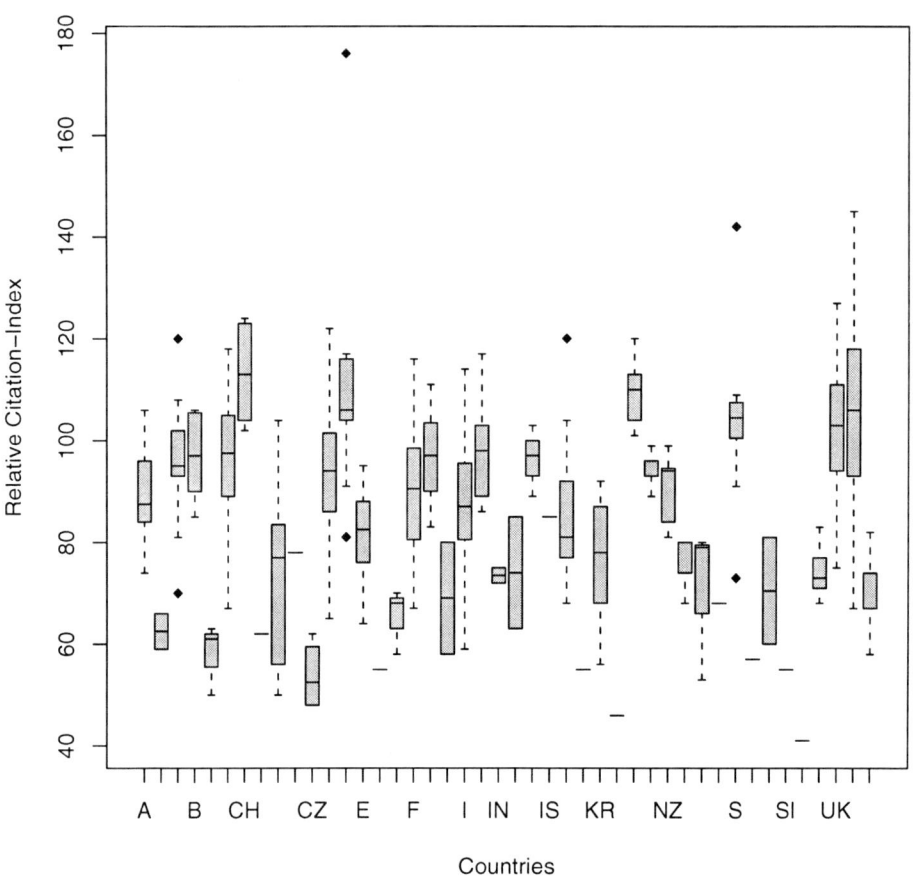

Figure C.5: BOXPLOTS OF THE RELATIVE CITATION-INDEX OF UNIVERSI-
TIES AND COLLEGES, by Country.

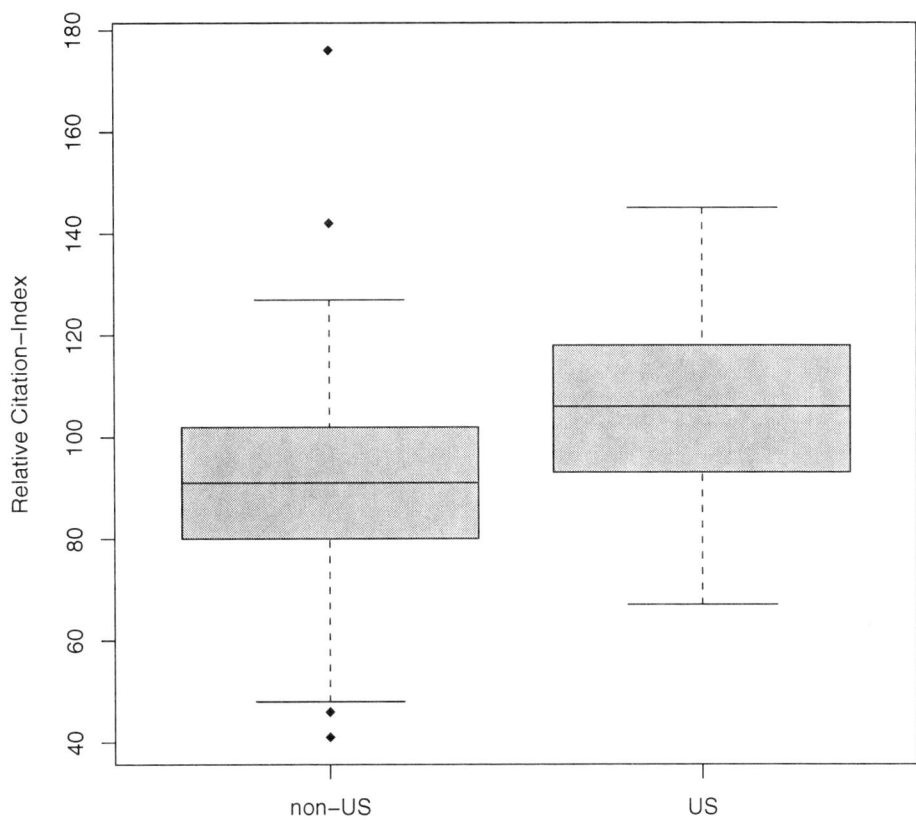

Figure C.6: BOXPLOTS OF THE RELATIVE CITATION-INDEX OF UNIVERSI-
TIES AND COLLEGES, by non-US versus US Institutions.

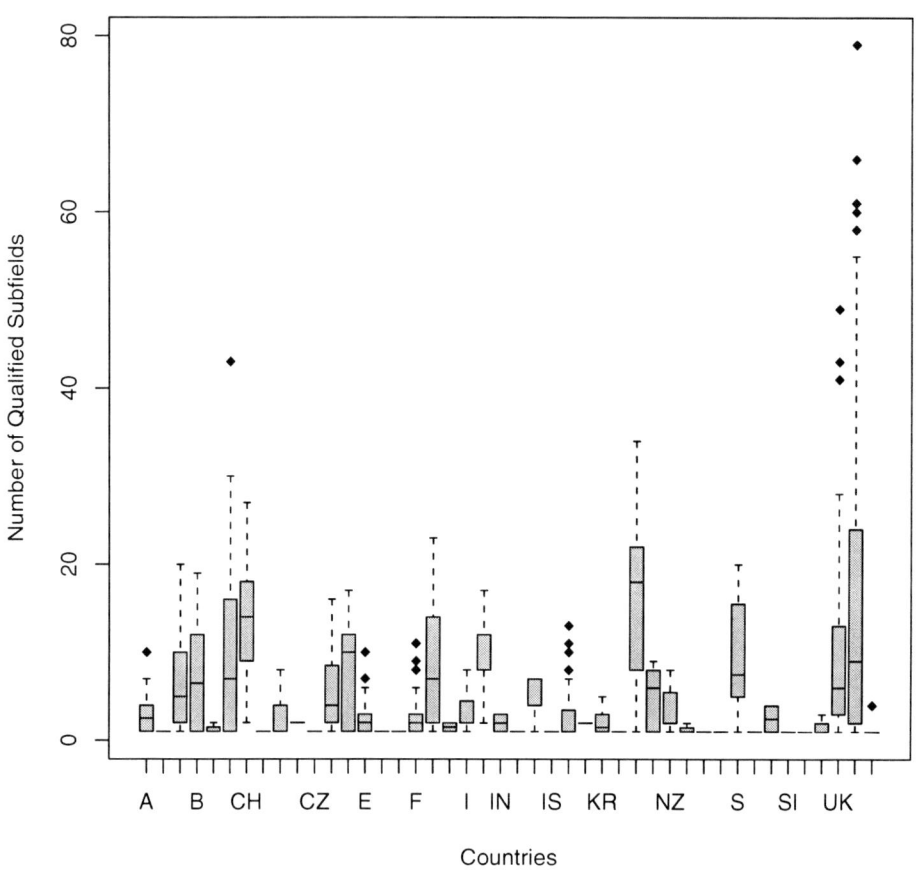

Figure C.7: BOXPLOTS OF THE NUMBER OF QUALIFIED SUBFIELDS OF UNI-
VERSITIES AND COLLEGES, by Country.

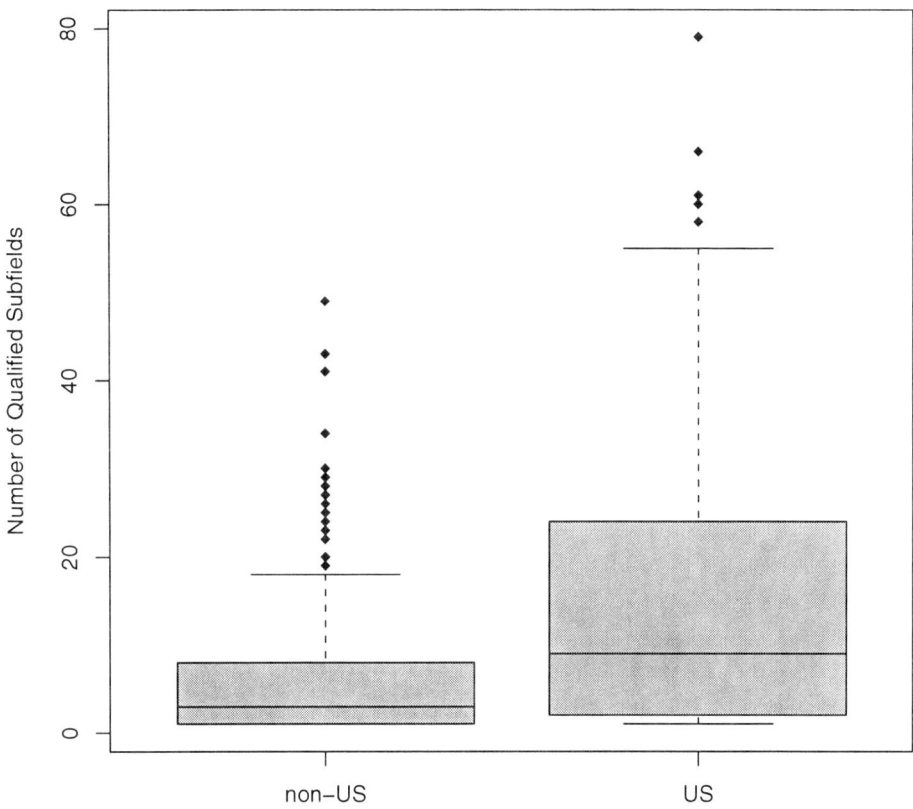

Figure C.8: BOXPLOTS OF THE NUMBER OF QUALIFIED SUBFIELDS OF UNIVERSITIES AND COLLEGES, by non-US versus US Institutions.

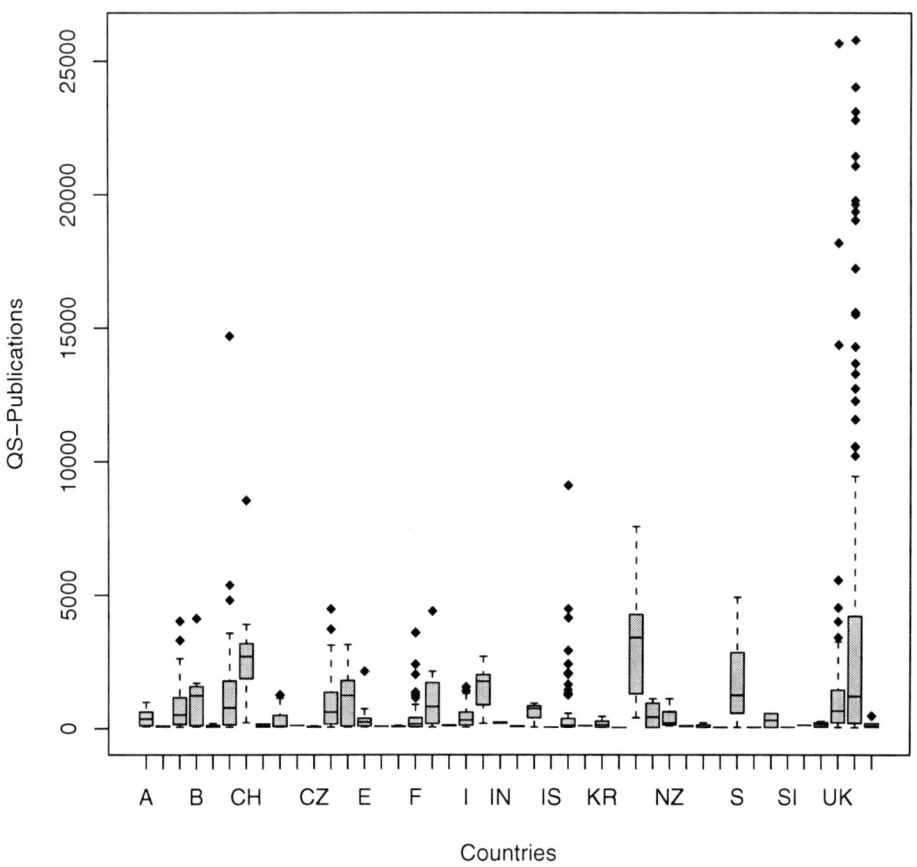

Figure C.9: BOXPLOTS OF THE NUMBER OF PUBLICATIONS OF UNIVER-
SITIES AND COLLEGES IN QUALIFIED SUBFIELDS (QS-PUBLICATIONS), by
Country (excluding the data of Harvard University).

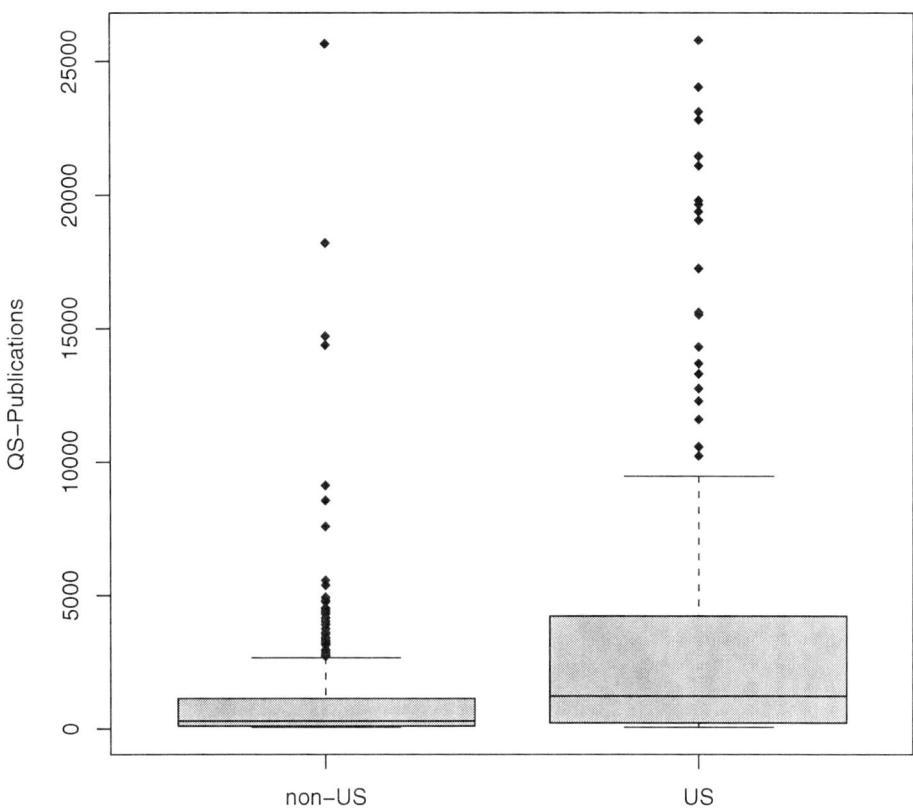

Figure C.10: BOXPLOTS OF THE NUMBER OF PUBLICATIONS OF UNIVER-
SITIES AND COLLEGES IN QUALIFIED SUBFIELDS (QS-PUBLICATIONS), by
non-US versus US Institutions (excluding the data of Harvard University).

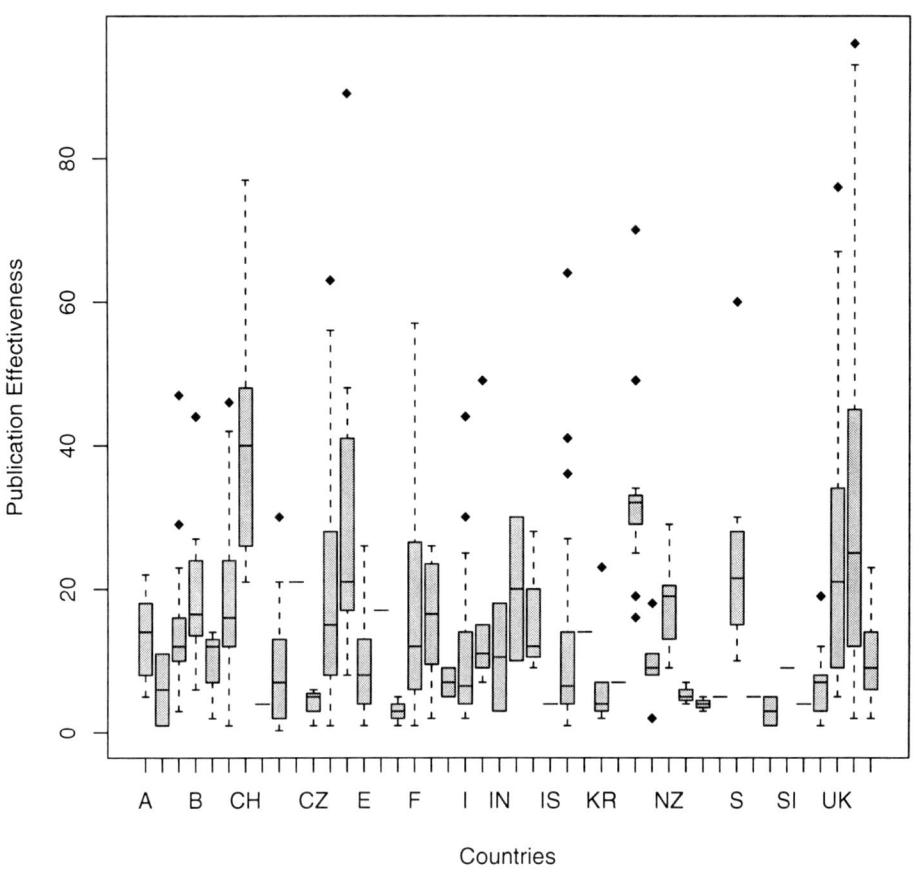

Figure C.11: Boxplots of the Number of Publications of Universities and Colleges in Qualified Subfields, as a Percentage of
Total Publications (Publication Effectiveness), by Country.

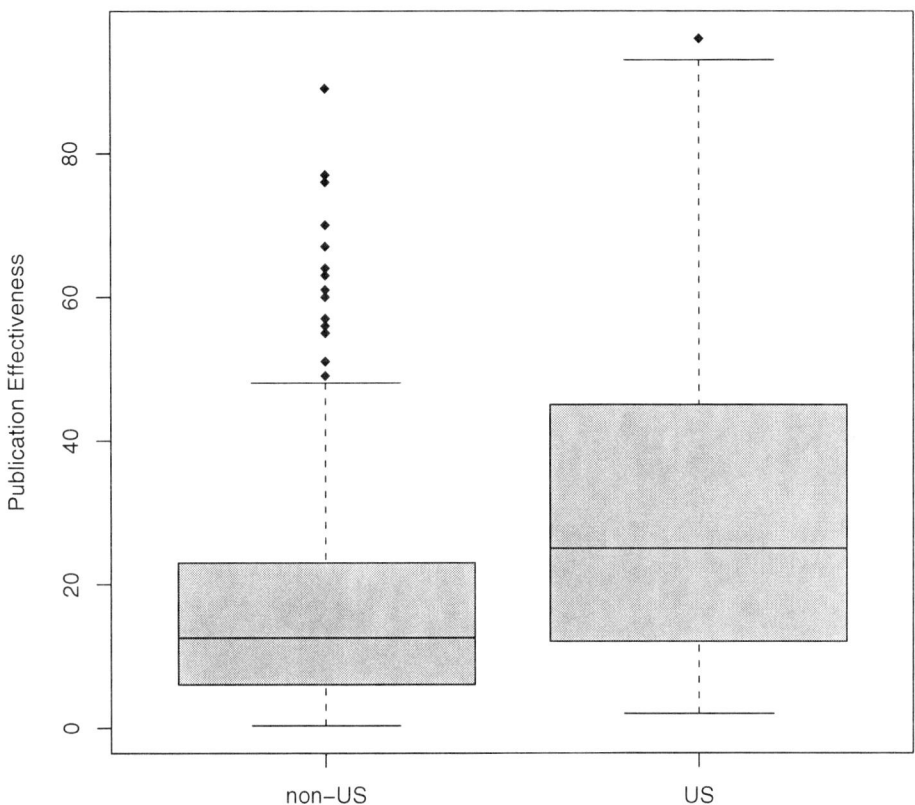

Figure C.12: BOXPLOTS OF THE NUMBER OF PUBLICATIONS OF UNIVER-
SITIES AND COLLEGES IN QUALIFIED SUBFIELDS, AS A PERCENTAGE OF
TOTAL PUBLICATIONS (PUBLICATION EFFECTIVENESS), by non-US versus
US Institutions.

Appendix D

Examples of Funding Systems

[...] reforms come and go like waves at the seashore, rarely leaving a lasting imprint [...]. The primary reasons these tides come and go is that there is little or no evidence on what works and why.

Paul C. Light (Light, 2002)

THE FOLLOWING sections contains technical descriptions of certain aspects of two funding systems: namely, aspects which pertain to the UK funding system, in particular, regarding the system used by the Higher Education Funding Council of England (HEFCE) (see Section D.1); and aspects which are related to the funding system employed by the US State of South Carolina (Section D.2). Lastly, an overview of the current master plan of the US State of California is given (Section D.3).

D.1 Funding in the United Kingdom

In the United Kingdom, as in other countries, higher education is funded through a range of sources, both public and private (see Table 4.3 on page 75). On the public side, the funding of higher education institutions is primarily channeled through three funding councils[1] and seven research councils[2] (HM Treasury, July 2002; HERO, December 2001): these funding

---

[1] Higher Education Funding Council for England (HEFCE), Higher Education Funding Council for Wales (HEFCW), and the Scottish Higher Education Funding Council (SHEFC).

[2] In 1992–93, UK Research Councils were established for the following fields: Biotechnology & Biological Sciences, Economic & Social Research, Medical Research, Natural En-

channels provide at most 90% of the public resources flowing into higher education and circa 50–60% of all resources (i.e. public and private; see Table 4.3).

Public resources are funnelled into higher education through four primary channels (Higher Education Funding Council for England, 2002a):

- Funding councils are responsible for distributing recurrent funds in support of teaching and learning activities at higher education institutions. In addition, they fund further education courses at other institutions. This allocation is formula-based.

- Secondly, funding councils are charged to fund research infrastructures and to provide a base funding of research, including the corresponding staff salaries. These appropriations are based on the Research Assessment Exercise.

- Thirdly, funding councils provide for special funding in support of particular development objectives and innovative projects. Special funding is provided over fixed project periods and is usually based on competitive bids from institutions.

- Lastly, research projects themselves are funded through the research councils.

This division of responsibilities between funding councils on the one hand and research councils on the other is known as the "dual-support system".

Mission and Role of Funding Councils. Funding councils are not only charged to act as the distributive arm of the government, i.e., to allocate recurrent funds for teaching and research or to fund special programs or projects. They also assume the roles of a 'buffer organization' mediating between government and higher education institutions. In this capacity, they are legally responsible for the quality of education, and they delegate this responsibility to the Quality Assurance Agency for Higher Education (QAA) which is in charge of the assessment of quality and standards of teaching within the UK. In addition, funding councils are directed to monitor — and to promote — the financial and managerial health of higher education institutions, to encourage good management practices, to ensure accountability, and to "develop detailed policies for higher education within

---

vironment Research, and Particle Physics & Astronomy Research, plus the Council for the Central Laboratory of Research Councils. In addition, there is an Arts & Humanities Research Board, established in 1998.

the broad guidelines set by the Secretary of State for Education and Skills" (Higher Education Funding Council for England, 2002a).

It would be of interest to take a look at one funding council's principles, the HEFCE for example (Higher Education Funding Council for England, 2002b, 2003). Grants for teaching and research are announced in March of a given year for the following academic year (which runs from August 1 to July 31); these are based on a three-year plan which is revised every other year. During the period of April to November, the HEFCE discusses trends and financial needs with the Department of Education and Skills, and in November the Secretary of State announces the funding volume available for the following year. During December, the enrollment figures of the current academic year are collated and processed to provide the necessary information to calculate the formula-based teaching grants for the following year. In January, the total volume of available funds is subdivided into the three main headings outlined above: teaching, research, and special funding. In February, decisions are taken, and in March they are communicated.

For the annual funding cycle of the 2002–03 academic year, a total of £5,076 million are earmarked to be distributed by the government[3], or an average of circa £5,360 per student (teaching, research, and special projects together)[4]. Close to two thirds of the available funding volume, i.e. 64.4%, flow into teaching; 18.5% are reserved to finance research; and 17.0% are earmarked to fund special projects (including 2.4% of the total reserved to reward and develop staff in higher education) (Higher Education Funding Council for England, 2002b, page 6).

Funds for Teaching and Learning: Funding Methods. While formula-based funding has been the practice for some time in the UK, current funding formulæ in England were introduced in 1998–99 for higher education institutions and in 1999–2000 for further education institutions (Higher Education Funding Council for England, 2002b, pages 3–15). Funds are basically allocated to institutions as a function of the number of students being taught. Students included in the calculation of teaching grants have their origin within the UK or a EU nation, they are academically qualified, and they do not receive funds from other public sources[5]. Student numbers are counted in terms of full-time equivalents (FTE) and weighed to account for factors affecting the funding formula:

---

[3]In addition to HEFCE grants, institutions receive tuition fees directly from students.

[4]Based on student numbers (FTE) for the academic year of 2001–02.

[5]Overseas students and those from outside the EU will have to pay higher fees to compensate for public funds foregone.

Table D.1: PRICE GROUPS FOR DIFFERENT SUBJECT CLASSES (TEACHING).

Subject Class	Description	Cost Weight
α_1	medicine, dentistry & veterinary sciences (clinical)	4.5
α_2	ditto (pre-clinical), science, engineering & technology (laboratory-based subjects)	2.0
α_3	subjects with a studio, laboratory or fieldwork element (such as geography, art & design)	1.5
α_4	all other subjects	1.0

- *subject-related premiums:* unit costs of teaching vary with the subject being taught: some subjects are more labor or more capital intensive than others (see Table D.1);

- *premiums pertaining to the duration or intensity of study:* enrollments in longer than norm courses have to be accounted for, administrative costs of part-time studies (per FTE) are higher, mature undergraduates[6] frequently need more support than their younger peers;

- *institutional premiums:* institutions within London are confronted with elevated operating costs, differences in pension schemes have to be accounted for, some specialist institutions[7] are confronted with higher than normal cost levels, small institutions[8] may experience raised costs of central administration, and institutions with old and historic buildings[9] are confronted with higher levels of maintenance, refurbishing and utilities.

In the following, the funding formula of the HEFCE used to allocate funds for teaching purposes shall be sketched. If X_{sj} denotes the number of students enrolled in a subject class $s \in S$ and institution $j \in J$ (measured in FTE), the number of students (in FTE) at a given institution is given by:

$$X_j = \sum_s X_{sj}, \quad \text{for all } j \in J. \tag{D.1}$$

---

[6]Mature students are defined as being 25 or older on entry.
[7]Defined as having at least 60% of their courses in one of two subjects only.
[8]Defined as having at most an enrollment of 1,000 FTE.
[9]Constructed before 1914.

Because unit costs of teaching, as indicated, are not uniform and vary by subject class, the HEFCE calculates subject-weighted enrollment figures

$$\hat{X}_j = \sum_s \alpha_s X_{sj}, \quad \text{for all } j \in J \tag{D.2}$$

where $\alpha_s \geq 1$ denotes the particular weight of subject class $s \in S$ (see Table D.1) applied to the corresponding enrollment in institution $j \in J$. In addition, the HEFCE calculates premiums as a function of characteristics pertaining to students and institutions. The student-related premium for an institution is defined as[10]

$$P_j = \sum_{dj} \beta_d b'_{dj} X_j + \sum_{dj} \beta_d b''_{dj} \hat{X}_j, \quad \text{for all } j \in J \tag{D.3}$$

where $d \in D$ denotes a premium class, $\beta_d \geq 0$ is the premium factor[11] and b'_{dj} and b''_{dj} are binary variables assuming the value of 1 if d is applicable to j, 0 else. And finally, there are — analogous to student premiums — institutional premiums to account for[12]:

$$I_j = \sum_{ij} \gamma_i c'_{ij} X_j + \sum_{ij} \gamma_i c''_{ij} \hat{X}_j, \quad \text{for all } j \in J \tag{D.4}$$

hence, $i \in I$ denotes a premium class, $\gamma_i \geq 0$ is the premium factor[13] and c'_{ij} and c''_{ij} are binary variables assuming the value of 1 if i is applicable to j, 0 else.

$\hat{X}_j$, P_j and I_j are defined in terms of full-time equivalents (FTE), the total weighted FTE for an institution is given by

$$T_j = \hat{X}_j + P_j + I_j \tag{D.5}$$

and that of all institutions by

$$T = \sum_j T_j. \tag{D.6}$$

The HEFCE now divides total available funds by T to calculate unit attributions (i.e., £ per weighted FTE) and the funding levels for each institution included in funding operations (issued annually as block grants).

---

[10]Certain student related premiums are defined in terms of number of students X_j, while others are defined in terms of weighted enrollment figures $\hat{X}_j$

[11]The range of values is currently set as follows: $0.25 \geq \beta_d \geq 0.05$.

[12]Again, some institutional premiums are defined by the HEFCE in terms of number of students, while others are defined in terms of weighted enrollment figures.

[13]The values normally fall into the following range: $0.1 \geq \gamma_i \geq 0.015$.

Quality-Related Research Funding.   Apart from funding teaching (and learning), i.e. apart from funding institutions in terms of student enrollment, resources are allocated in support of special projects or to enhance research. I shall focus here on the last aspect, termed "quality-related research funding", which in turn is based on the periodic Research Assessment Exercise (RAE).

Quality-related research funding, which covers roughly a fifth of all the funds allocated by the HEFCE, focuses on (i) funding research to reflect the quality and volume of research at institutions in different subjects (i.e., 88% of the total), (ii) funding the supervision of postgraduate research students (7%), (iii) providing a premium for institutions located in London (3%), and (iv) a supplement for departments which achieved the highest rating in the RAE of 1996 and 2001 (2%, pertains only to the year 2003–04) (Higher Education Funding Council for England, 2003, pp. 13–16).

I shall concentrate, for brevity, on the first of the four foci (and ignore the remaining three aspects). The distribution of these funds follows two stages:

- *Stage 1*: a funding volume is established which is to be associated with the different research fields or subject matters; and

- *Stage 2*: distributing these funds among the institutions in accord with the quality assessment of the RAE.

The RAE recognizes 68 different research fields (or subjects) to be assessed. In order to make the necessary calculations for Stage 1, the HEFCE takes into consideration only data of university departments (or assessment units) which meet minimum quality standards (i.e. departments that are being funded for research). Departments receive an overall rating on a scale spanning seven grades (see Table D.2)[14], from grade 1 to grade 5*. The lowest four grades (i.e. grades 1, 2, 3b and 3a) receive no research funding through the RAE channel and, hence, the data of university departments which receive any of these four grades are not taken into consideration when making the calculations for Stage 1.

For the subset of departments (or assessment units) of a given subject earmarked to receive funding, the "volume of research" is assessed. This 'volume' is operationalized in terms of research staff (in FTE) and subject

---

[14]The wording of the Description of Quality Standards in Table D.2 is quoted from (Higher Education Funding Council for England, 2001, p. 5). I failed to find any information on how funding weights (or funding multipliers) were set or derived.

Table D.2: RAE RATING SCHEME AND FUNDING WEIGHTS; see (Higher Education Funding Council for England, 2001, p. 5) and (Higher Education Funding Council for England, 2002b, p. 15).

Rating	Description of Quality Standard	Weight
5*	Quality that equates to attainable levels of international excellence in more than half of the research activity submitted and attainable levels of national excellence in the remainder.	3.357
5	Quality that equates to attainable levels of international excellence in up to half of the research activity submitted and to attainable levels of national excellence in virtually all of the remainder.	2.793
4	Quality that equates to attainable levels of national excellence in virtually all of the research activity submitted, showing some evidence of international excellence.	1.0
3a	Quality that equates to attainable levels of national excellence in over two-thirds of the research activity submitted, possibly showing evidence of international excellence.	0
3b	Quality that equates to attainable levels of national excellence in more than half of the research activity submitted.	0
2	Quality that equates to attainable levels of national excellence in up to half of the research activity submitted.	0
1	Quality that equates to attainable levels of national excellence in none, or virtually none, of the research activity submitted.	0

classes. Available research funds are then distributed over the set of recognized research fields (or subjects) in proportion to the "volume of research" in a given subject.

The formula which ties together research active staff for a given subject in assessment units earmarked for funding is as follows:

$$V_j = \sum_{i \in I}[1.0S_{ij} + 0.1A_{ij} + 0.15(1.75)P_{ij} + 0.191\frac{C_{ij}}{25000}] \quad j \in F \qquad (D.7)$$

where I denotes the set of institutions, F the set of research fields (or subject matters), V denotes the 'volume' of research, S the number of research active staff selected for assessment in the RAE (in FTE), A the number of research assistants or research fellows (in FTE), P the number of postgraduate research students (in FTE; the multiplier 1.75 is used as a factor to scale up funding to cover the average period of study of 3.5 years until graduation), and C stands for the amount of third-party funds (charities, in £) secured (and 25000 stands for the average salary [in £] necessary to cover a research position).

Next, research active staff V_j in a given research field has to be weighed by a cost factor to account for cost differences which separate subjects. The HEFCE recognizes three such classes of cost factors (see Table D.3). If the classes of cost factors are denoted by K, and the cost factors themselves by λ_s, the weighted research active staff $\hat{V}_j$ for a given research field is given by

$$\hat{V}_j = \sum_{s \in K} \lambda_s \beta_{js} V_j, \qquad j \in F \qquad (D.8)$$

where $\beta_{js} = 1$ if $j \in F_s \subset F, 0$ else. Available research funds, as I said, are then distributed over F in proportion to $\hat{V}_j$. This completes Stage 1.

Given the funds allotted to a given subject $j \in F$, funds will have to be distributed among the institutions which carry these research fields and which were rated to receive funding (Stage 2). In order to do this, the weighted 'volume' of research of a given assessment unit is once more weighed by a funding multiplier $\alpha_{ij} \geq 0$ which honors high ratings (see Table D.2). For any given institution $i \in I$ and any subject $j \in F$, this total weighted 'volume' of research $\bar{V}_{ij}$ is calculated analogous to equation D.7. To complete Stage 2, available funds for a given subject are then distributed among the institutions proportional to $\bar{V}_{ij}$.

Table D.3: PRICE GROUPS FOR DIFFERENT SUBJECT CLASSES (RESEARCH).

Subject Class	Description of Subjects	Cost Weight
A	high cost laboratory and clinical subjects	1.6
B	intermediate cost subjects	1.3
C	other subjects	1.0

D.2   South Carolina's Funding System

Beginning with the year of 1996, funding of the higher education systems within the US State of South Carolina changed with the passage of Act 359: it was mandated that a "performance system for determining institutional funding" (Commission on Higher Education, 2002a, p. I.3) be developed and used. South Carolina is a state of a bit more than 4 million inhabitants and a per capita income of 81% of the US average (year 2001) (Commission on Higher Education, 2002b). Its public higher education system encompasses three research universities[15], nine four-year colleges and teaching universities, five two-year regional campuses, and sixteen technical colleges. In the fall of 2001, total head-count enrollment in the public higher education system was close to 160,000, of which close to 60% — or ca. 92,000 — were enrolled in the twelve senior institutions (i.e. research universities and four-year colleges and teaching universities combined). Another ca. 34,000 students were enrolled in private senior institutions. Total state appropriations for post-secondary education (fiscal year 2001–02) amounted to circa $ 750 million (Commission on Higher Education, 2002b, p. 100).

In order to assess the impact of state appropriations better, we shall look at the revenues and current funds expenditures of two research universities: Clemson, and the University of South Carolina (USC) located in Columbia. Clemson University has an enrollment of circa 17,100 (Fall 2001) and an annual budget of roughly $ 310 million, while the enrollment of the USC at Columbia is circa 23,000 (Fall 2001) and the annual budget is roughly $ 410 million. The revenue and expenditure sheets of the two universities are shown in Tables D.4 and D.5. In the case of Clemson University, state appropriations which are subject to performance budgeting amount to 41.4% of the total budget[16]; and in the case of USC at Columbia, corresponding state appropriations amount to 40.9%.

---

[15]Clemson University, the University of South Carolina at Columbia, and the Medical University of South Carolina.

[16]Additional state appropriations flow in the forms of research grants and contracts.

Table D.4: CLEMSON UNIVERSITY: Current Funds for Educational and General Operations (E&G), in % (Fiscal Year 2000–01) (Commission on Higher Education, 2002b, p. 104).

REVENUES BY SOURCE	% of E&G	EXPENDITURES	% of E&G
Tuition and Fees	29.8	Instruction	34.6
State Appropriations	41.4	Research	19.6
Federal Appropriations	0.0	Public Service	2.9
Local Appropriations	0.0	Acad. Support & Libraries	8.9
Govern. Grants & Contracts		Student Services	3.9
Federal	14.1	Institutional Support	5.2
State	1.5	Operation & Maintenance	7.4
Local	0.2	Scholarships & Fellowships	15.4
Private Gifts, Grants, &c.	9.0	Mandatory Transfers	0.6
Endowment Income	0.4	Non-Mandatory Transfers	1.5
Sales & Services	0.0		
Other Sources	3.5		
Total Revenues	100.0	Total Expenditures	100.0

The original aim of South Carolina's funding system was to fund 100% of state appropriations (amounting, as I have mentioned above, to roughly $ 750 million) on the basis of assessed performance. In the fiscal year 1997–98 $ 4.5 million were distributed, in 1998–99 $ 270 million, and "all appropriated general operating funding in the years thereafter" (Commission on Higher Education, 2002a, p. I.3).

Indicators of Performance Funding. South Carolina's systems is devised with four educational sectors in mind: (i) research universities, (ii) teaching institutions (four-year colleges and teaching universities), (iii) two-year regional campuses, and (iv) technical colleges. To assess performance in these four sectors, Act 359 identifies 37 performance indicators, grouped into nine categories (Commission on Higher Education, 2001, p. 35):

1. Mission Focus:

    (a) expenditures of funds to achieve institutional mission;

    (b) curricula offered to achieve mission;

    (c) approval of mission statement;

    (d) adoption of a strategic plan to support the mission statement;

    (e) attainment of goals of the strategic plan.

Table D.5: USC AT COLUMBIA: Current Funds for Educational and General Operations (E&G), in % (Fiscal Year 2000–01) (Commission on Higher Education, 2002b, p. 105).

REVENUES BY SOURCE	% of E&G	EXPENDITURES	% of E&G
Tuition and Fees	26.7	Instruction	37.4
State Appropriations	40.9	Research	19.2
Federal Appropriations	0.0	Public Service	6.7
Local Appropriations	0.0	Acad. Support & Libraries	10.3
Govern. Grants & Contracts		Student Services	3.5
Federal	17.4	Institutional Support	5.8
State	6.1	Operation & Maintenance	6.8
Local	0.1	Scholarships & Fellowships	10.1
Private Gifts, Grants, &c.	4.8	Mandatory Transfers	0.0
Endowment Income	0.1	Non-Mandatory Transfers	0.3
Sales & Services	3.5		
Other Sources	0.4		
Total Revenues	100.0	Total Expenditures	100.0

2. Quality of Faculty:

   (a) academic and other credentials of professors and instructors;

   (b) performance review system for faculty to include student and peer evaluations;

   (c) post-tenure review for tenured faculty;

   (d) compensation of faculty;

   (e) availability of faculty to students outside the classroom;

   (f) community or public service activities of faculty for which no extra compensation is paid.

3. Instructional Quality:

   (a) class sizes and student-faculty ratios;

   (b) number of credit hours taught by faculty;

   (c) ratio of full-time faculty as compared to other full-time employees;

   (d) accreditation of degree-granting programs;

   (e) institutional emphasis on quality teacher education and reform.

4. Institutional Cooperation and Collaboration:

    (a) sharing and use of technology, programs, equipment, supplies, and source matter experts within the institution, with other institutions, and the business community;

    (b) cooperation and collaboration with private industry.

5. Administrative Efficiency:

    (a) percentage of administrative (in comparison to academic) costs;

    (b) use of best management practices;

    (c) elimination of unjustified duplication of and waste in administrative and academic programs;

    (d) amount of general overhead.

6. Entrance Requirements:

    (a) SAT and ACT scores of student body;

    (b) high school standing, grade point averages, and activities of student body;

    (c) post-secondary non-academic achievement of student body;

    (d) priority on enrolling in-state students.

7. Graduates' Achievements:

    (a) graduation rate;

    (b) employment rate for graduates;

    (c) employer feedback of graduates who were — or were not — employed;

    (d) scores of graduates on post-graduate professional, graduate or employment-related examinations and certification tests;

    (e) number of graduates who continue their education;

    (f) credit hours earned of graduates.

8. User-Friendliness of Institution:

    (a) transferability of credits to and from the institution;

    (b) continuing education programs for graduates and others;

    (c) accessibility to the institution of all citizens of the State.

9. Research Funding:

(a) financial support for reform in teacher education;

(b) amount of public and private sector grants.

After the design of the system in 1996, not all indicators were used during implementation. For each educational sector, a subset of indicators was eventually chosen to be used in the assessment exercise. For the first education sector, i.e. the three research universities, 14 performance indicators were chosen (Commission on Higher Education, 2002a, pp. II.3–II.4)[17].

Model of Performance Assessment. South Carolina uses a simple formula to calculate an overall performance score of an institution:

$$S_i = \sum_{j=1}^{n} a_{ij}, \quad \text{for all } i \in I \tag{D.9}$$

where I is a set of institutions, $j = 1, \ldots, n$ denotes an index of performance indicators; a_{ij} is a measure of indicator attainment, defined on the interval $1 \leq a_{ij} \leq 3$, and associated with institution $i \in I$ and indicator j; and S_i is the calculated performance score of institution i. To normalize S_i on the original interval $[1, 3]$, the Commission on Higher Education calculates

$$\hat{S}_i = \frac{1}{n} S_i \tag{D.10}$$

where $1 \leq \hat{S}_i \leq 3$. The formula D.9 represents a simplified version of a model popular since at least the 1950s. If one defines I to be a set of alternatives — i.e. courses of actions or decision options, if J is a set of objectives to be pursued, $w_{ij} \geq 0$ is a (relative) weight attached to objective $j \in J$ by pursuing (or choosing) $i \in I$, and $a_{ij} \geq 0$ is a measure of attainment of alternative i with regard to objective j, then

$$S_i = \sum_{j \in J} w_{ij} a_{ij}, \quad \text{for all } i \in I \tag{D.11}$$

where S_i denotes a score — or performance measure — of alternative i. That course of action or option i shall be chosen whose performance measure S_i is largest.

In the case where $w_{ij} = 1$, model D.11 reduces to model D.9. Both models are appropriate only if, for any two objectives or indicators $j, k \in J$, j and k can be considered 'independent' (Fishburn, 1964, Chapter 10). If

---

[17] 1b, 1c, 1d/e (combined); 2a and 2d; 3d; 4a/b (combined); 5a; 6a/b (combined); 7a, 7d; 8c; 9a and 9b.

$(a_{i1}, a_{i2}, \ldots, a_{im})$ is a vector of attainment measures of alternative i, and if $v_i(a_{i1}, a_{i2}, \ldots, a_{im})$ and $v_{ij}(a_{ij})$ are value functions, value independence is given, for all $i \in I$, whenever

$$v_i(a_{i1}, a_{i2}, \ldots, a_{im}) = v_{i1}(a_{i1}) + v_{i2}(a_{i2}) + \cdots + v_{im}(a_{im}). \qquad \text{(D.12)}$$

But this is unlikely the case in the present context, and no provisions were made in the South Carolina model to test for value independence[18].

Mission Resource Requirements. In the case of South Carolina's funding system, amounts of funding are calculated in function of mission resource requirements (MRR) and performance scores $\hat{S}_i$ as described above (see definition D.10).

Projected education and general costs E_{ti} for period t and institution i are calculated on the base of the formula (Commission on Higher Education, 2001, p. 6–8)

$$E_{ti} = 1.25[0.3R_{t-1,i} + 0.25P_{t-1,i} + \lambda_i(B_{t-2,i}) + \gamma_i(B_{t-2,i}) + \delta_i(f_i, p_i)] \quad \text{(D.13)}$$

where $R_{t-1,i}$ denote research expenditures, $P_{t-1,i}$ denote public service expenditures, $\lambda_i(B_{t-2,i})$ calculates library resources in relation to the number of students $B_{t-2,i}$ enrolled during period $t - 2$, $\gamma_i(B_{t-2,i})$ calculates student service resources as a function of the number of students enrolled, $\delta_i(f_i, p_i)$ calculates physical plant resources depending on square footage f_i and perimeter length p_i allocated to educational and general operations, and the factor 1.25 is a provision for general administrative costs.

In order to assess mission resource requirements (MRR), the South Carolina model specifies that average institutional revenues, collected to cover tuition and fees during the past three years, have to be deduced from projected education and general costs. Average institutional revenues T_{ti} are given by

---

[18]If one takes the original 37 performance measures, a range of interdependencies are obvious: for example, 2a (academic and other credentials of professors and instructors) and 2d (compensation of faculty) are clearly not independent; the same holds in the case of 3a (class sizes and student-faculty ratios) and 3b (number of credit hours taught by faculty); or for 5a (percentage of administrative costs as compared to academic costs) and 5d (amount of general overhead); or 6a (SAT and ACT scores of student body) and 6b (high school standing, grade point averages, and activities of student body) versus 7a (graduation rate), 7b (employment rate for graduates) and 7d (scores of graduates on post-graduate professional, graduate or employment related examinations and certification tests). The remaining set of 14 indicators retains some of the interdependencies.

$$T_{ti} = \frac{1}{3} \sum_{l=1}^{3} F_{t-l,i} \tag{D.14}$$

where F_{ti} denotes tuition and fees of institution i assessed for period t. Mission resource requirements M_{ti}, i.e. the amount of funding necessary "to continue to operate at acceptable levels" (Commission on Higher Education, 2002a, p. I.7), is then defined as the difference between the projected education and general costs and the previous three-year average of institutional income from tuition and fees:

$$M_{ti} = E_{ti} - T_{ti} \tag{D.15}$$

and

$$M_t = \sum_{i \in I} M_{ti} \tag{D.16}$$

are the MRR for the entire state. Furthermore,

$$p_{ti} = \frac{M_t}{M_{ti}} \tag{D.17}$$

is the assessed share of institution i of the State's total MRR during period t.

Performance Funding. Now, performance funding does not automatically allocate the entire amount of MRR (i.e. of M_{ti}). In order to receive appropriations in the same amount as those of the previous year (i.e. year $t - 1$), an institution has to be assessed — at least to 'achieve standards'. If an institution is being assessed to operate below standards, a reduction in appropriations will occur, and the thus saved monies will be redistributed to other institutions. Funds for reallocation have two sources: (i) newly dedicated State funds, i.e. "current year's appropriations for distribution", and (ii) "disincentive funds", i.e. funds redirected from institutions which were judged to operate below standards. If an institution "does not achieve standards" in year t, 3% of its appropriations of year $t-1$ will be deducted in the appropriations' calculation for year t; likewise, if an institution "substantially does not achieve standards", the corresponding reduction amounts to 5%. These deductions will flow into a reallocation account to be redistributed. If A_{ti} denote the amount of appropriations received by institution i during period t,

$$A_{ti} = 0.97 x_{ti} A_{t-1,i} + 0.95 y_{ti} A_{t-1,i} + (1 - x_{ti} - y_{ti}) A_{t-1,i} \qquad \text{(D.18)}$$

where $x_{ti} = 1$ if institution i did not "achieve standards" during period $t - 1$, 0 else; $y_{ti} = 1$ if institution i "substantially" did not "achieve standards" during period $t - 1$, 0 else; and $x_{ti} y_{ti} = 0$. Furthermore,

$$D_{ti} = 0.03 x_{ti} A_{t-1,i} + 0.05 y_{ti} A_{t-1,i} \qquad \text{(D.19)}$$

are the institutional disincentive funds, funneled into the redistribution fund, and

$$G_t = \sum_{i \in I} D_{ti} + H_t \qquad \text{(D.20)}$$

are the total funds available for redistribution: total disincentive funds plus additional discretionary funds H_t made available by the Government, i.e. "new dollars" appropriated by the legislature.

Institutional appropriations are based on the performance score $\hat{S}_i$ an institution receives (see definition D.10). The score defined on the interval $[1, 3]$ is given the meaning defined in Table D.6. $\hat{S}_i$ is translated into funding percentages b_{ti} by a function $\psi : [1, 3] \rightarrow [0, 100]$ so that $b_{ti} = \psi(\hat{S}_i)$. All institutions are eligible for funds from this account, even those judged to perform below standards[19], and their individual share is given by:

$$U_{ti} = b_{ti}(p_{ti} G_t). \qquad \text{(D.21)}$$

D.3   California's Master Plan

Regulations which characterize higher education in the State of California stand in contrast to those covered previously (see Appendices D.1 and D.2). California's initial Master Plan was devised in 1960 to respond to the "tidal wave" of new student populations, i.e. the children of the "baby boom" after World War II (Kerr, 2001a)[20]. The Master Plan recognized the enor-

---

[19]Also, additional — separate — funds may be set aside for "performance improvements" specifically for institutions which did not meet standards; see (Commission on Higher Education, 2001, p. 36).

[20]Clark Kerr, in his testimony August 24, 1999, before the Joint Committee to Develop a Master Plan for Education, Kindergarten through University, states: "[...] we faced this enormous tidal wave, 600,000 students added to higher education in California in a single decade. There were new campuses to be built, faculty members had to be hired, and so forth, and it looked like an enormous, perhaps impossible, challenge before us".

Table D.6: SOUTH CAROLINA'S FUNDING SYSTEM: Performance Categories by Score and Funding Percentages (Commission on Higher Education, 2002b, p. 105).

PERFORMANCE CATEGORY	Score $\hat{S}_i$ (Range)	Funding b_{ti} (Range)
substantially exceeds standards	2.85 – 3.00	95 – 100%
exceeds standards	2.60 – 2.84	87 – 94%
achieves standards	2.00 – 2.59	67 – 86%
does not achieve standards	1.45 – 1.99	48 – 66%
substantially does not achieve standards	1.00 – 1.44	33 – 47%

Table D.7: ENROLLMENT INDICATORS AND STUDENT POPULATIONS OF THE CALIFORNIA HIGHER EDUCATION SYSTEM, by Level of Higher Education, based on (State of California, 2003).

ENROLLMENT INDICATOR	Community Colleges	California State University	University of California
student population (numbers)	74%	17%	9%
student population (FTE)	45%	33%	22%
FTE to numbers of students	1:4.5	1:1.4	1:1.05

mous role of public higher education in economic and social development, and it provided access to higher education for all high school graduates in the State. It devised a trinary system consisting of Community Colleges, institutions which would be embraced by the State University of California System, and finally institutions which fall under the umbrella of the University of California System. Access to the top two levels of higher education was curtailed by a policy which would draw the top eighth portion of the respective high school classes to the University of California System, and the top third of the respective classes to the State University of California System. Community Colleges had an open access policy.

Today (i.e. 2002), 6.7% of California's population (or 2,355,000 people) attend — part-time or full-time — institutions of higher education, and 5.8% attend public institutions (State of California, 2003). If we focus on enrollment in public institutions and in terms of student numbers, close to three fourth of all students attend Community Colleges, while the remaining quarter enrolls either at the California State University or at the University of California System (see Table D.7). If we concentrate on full-time equivalents (FTE), less than half of all students are enrolled in Community Colleges, a third attends the State University System, and over 20% attend the University of California System. We notice that these figures deviate some from the normative shares mentioned before, and this is so because the percentages of full-time students are lower in community colleges and in institutions of the State University System than in institutions of the University of California System.

Ever since, the Californian Higher Education System has been heralded as being exemplary within the US if not the world. The trinary system was based on a social contract, i.e. a partnership model

> "[...] in which the state commits to an adequate and stable level of funding for higher education in exchange for a commitment by the institutions to achieve specific outcomes in areas that further state goals (e.g., providing access to all eligible students, reducing 'time-to-degree', increasing the production of graduates in high-need areas like teaching and engineering/computer science, etc.) [...] State goals are made explicit and institutional progress is monitored. By linking achievement of the goals to explicit state commitments on resources, it makes clear that reducing resources will have particular and usually adverse consequences for the state"[21].

This partnership model provided for the control of (i) the student populations of the three levels of higher education and (ii) the corresponding funds which would flow into the higher education system.

Some 40 years after the original Master Plan, a new plan is being drafted (Alpert, Alquist, & Strom-Martin, 2002)[22]. This new draft of a Master Plan is not restricted to higher education as such, but covers the entire educational spectrum, from pre-Kindergarten to University. This much broader spectrum evolved because various aims of higher education — equal opportunity, broader access of economically disadvantaged students, etc. — cannot be pursued without looking at opportunities and barriers which show up much earlier in the educational pipeline. Furthermore, higher education is also responsible for the education and reeducation of teachers, faculty, counselors, staff and administrators, and for research findings in the fields of teaching, learning, curriculum development, families, environment, and social services delivery; hence, higher education is also indirectly responsible for the quality of primary and secondary education.

---

[21]University of California, "A Perspective on Developing a New Master Plan", Annex to a letter of Richard C. Atkinson, President of the University of California System, to Senator Alpert, May 8, 2002. We should note here, in passing, that this social contract is not based on a performance funding scheme.

[22]http://www.ucop.edu/acadinit/mastplan/current.htm.

The current draft of the Master Plan of California contains 55 major recommendations. The first 21 pertain to the question as to how to assure and improve "access to high quality education" on all levels. In this context, a range of issues are being covered: conditions which are conducive to learning, particularly in the early phases of child development; access to qualified and "inspiring" teachers; access to rigorous, successful curricula on all levels of education; participation in California's public universities; access to modern textbooks and instructional material, and access to adequate learning support services; access to and provision of qualified administrators and educational personnel serving in schools and campuses; and access to a physical school or campus environment that is "safe, well-equipped, and well-maintained". The next seven major recommendations address the question of "achievement of students". Issues such as the assessment of students' needs and educational progress are being covered; the "alignment and coordination of curricula, assessment, admissions, and placement" in support of transfer processes and the transition between grade levels and school districts, between high school and college, and between colleges and universities; and the professional development and preparation of teachers and faculty. The following 16 major recommendations pertain to "accountability for learner outcomes and institutional performance". Here, accountability systems and responsibilities are delineated, from those of the Governor, to those of regional offices of education, to those of governing boards and education commissions. The last 11 major recommendations pertain to the "affordability of a high quality education system". In this context issues such as early child care and education are addressed, quality monitoring, tax measures to secure educational income, the stability of resource allocation, student charges, space planning and the multiple usage of facilities, as well as shared responsibilities.

The draft of the new Master Plan does not specify outcomes or specific means of development. Rather, the plan is intended to act as a broad framework for policy development, with a longer planning horizon in mind. The policies, in turn, would guide educational development and management, and they could be adapted or changed as required by changing conditions. Specifically, and in stark contrast to schemes based on performance-funding, the California Master Plan (Alpert et al., 2002, pp. 79–92)

- would commit the State "to provide an adequate base funding to meet the basic operational needs of its public colleges and universities";

- intends to align "the allocation and expenditures of moneys with the actual costs of providing the educational services for which they are spent";

- recommends that policies be adopted "to provide more stability for finance and dampen the 'boom and bust' of swings of state appropriations for postsecondary education".

References

Abbott, A. (1988). *The System of Professions: An Essay on the Division of Expert Labor.* The University of Chicago Press.

Abbott, A. (2001). *Chaos of Disciplines.* The University of Chicago Press.

Adams, J. (2002). Research Assessment in the UK. *Science, 296*(5569), 805.

Adams, J., & Smith, D. (2003). *Funding Research Diversity: The Impact of Further Concentration on University Research Performance and Regional Research Capacity.* Universities UK and Evidence, Ltd.

Adams, R. M. (Ed.). (2002). *Trends in American & German Higher Education.* American Academy of Arts & Sciences.

Akerlof, G. A., & Kranton, R. E. (2002). Identity and Schooling: Some Lessons for the Economics of Education. *Journal of Economic Literature, XL,* 1167–1201.

Algemene Rekenkamer. (2003, February 19). *Irregularities in the Funding of Higher Education.* www.rekenkamer.nl.

Alpert, D., Alquist, E., & Strom-Martin, V. (2002, July,). *The California Master Plan for Education (Draft).* Joint Committee to Develop a Master Plan for Education — Kindergarten through University, www.ucop.edu/acadinit/mastplan/0207302NDDRAFTMASTERPLAN.PDF.

Altbach, P. G., Gumport, P. J., & Johnstone, D. B. (Eds.). (2001). *In Defense of American Higher Education.* Johns Hopkins University Press.

Andrey Allakhverdov and Vladimir Pokrovsky. (2004). Russian Universities want their Share of the Research Pie. *Science, 304*(5673), 953.

Arbeitskreis Kapital und Wirtschaft. (2004, Januar). *Neue Wege zur Hochschulfinanzierung.* Herausgegeben vom AKW, in Zusammenarbeit mit Avenir Suisse und economie-suisse.

Aronowsky, J. S. (Ed.). (1969). *Progress in Operations Research: Relationship between Operations Research and the Computer* (Vol. III). John Wiley & Sons.

Arrow, K. J. (1963 (1951)). *Social Choice and Individual Values* (Vol. 12). John Wiley & Sons.

Arrow, K. J., Cottle, R. W., Eaves, B. C., & Olkin, I. (Eds.). (1996). *Education in a Research University.* Stanford University Press.

Astin, A. W. (1985). *Achieving Educational Excellence: A Critical Assessment of Priorities and Practices in Higher Education.* Jossey-Bass Publishers.

Astin, A. W. (1993). *What Matters in College? Four Critical Years Revisited.* Jossey-Bass Publishers.

Balter, M. (1998). CNRS Researchers Take up the Fight Against Allègre's Reforms. *Science*, *282*(5307), 2162–2163.

Balter, M. (1999). Claude Allègre: Back to the Wall, But Still Fighting. *Science*, *283*(5407), 1442–1443.

Balter, M. (2001). French Universities: Reform Plan Seen as Halting Step. *Science*, *292*(5518), 829.

Barash, D. P. (2004). Caught Between Choices: Personal Gain vs. Public Good. *The Chronicle of Higher Education*, B12–B14.

Barro, R. J. (2001). Human Capital and Growth. *AEA Papers and Proceedings*, *91*(2), 12–17.

Bartlett, T. (2004). What's Wrong With Harvard. *The Chronicle of Higher Education*, *L*(35), A14–A16.

Barzelay, M. (2001). *The New Public Managment: Improving Research and Policy Dialogue* (Vol. 3). University of California Press.

Bauer, M. (1996). Quality as Expressed in a Swedish Reform of Higher Education and as Viewed by University Teachers and Leadership. *Tertiary Education and Management*, *2*(1), 76–85.

Bauer, M., Askling, B., Marton, S. G., & Marton, F. (1999). *Transforming Universities: Changing Patterns of Governance, Structure and Learning in Swedish Higher Education* (Vol. 48). Jessica Kingsley Publishers.

Bell, D. (Ed.). (1967). Toward the Year 2000: work in progress. *Dædalus*, *96*(3).

Ben-David, J. (1972). *American Higher Education: Directions Old and New*. McGraw-Hill Book Company.

Ben-David, J. (1991). *Scientific Growth: Essays on the Social Organization and Ethos of Science*. University of California Press.

Bergier, J.-F., & Tobler, H. W. (Eds.). (1980). *Eidgenössische Technische Hochschule Zürich: 1955-1980, Festschrift zum 125jährigen Bestehen*. Verlag Neue Zürcher Zeitung.

Bils, M., & Klenow, P. J. (2000). Does Schooling Cause Growth? *The American Economic Review*, *90*(5), 1160–1183.

Bleiklie, I., Høstaker, R., & Vabø, A. (2000). *Policy and Practice in Higher Education: Reforming Norwegian Universities* (Vol. 49). Jessica Kingsley Publishers.

Bok, D. (2003). *Universities in the Marketplace: The Commericialization of Higher Education*. Princeton University Press.

Bollag, B. (2001). European Governments are Urged to Speed Alignment of Higher Education Systems. *The Chronicle of Higher Education*.

Bonaccorsi, A. (2005, January 7–9,). *Better Politics vs. Better Institutions in European Science*. Paper presented to the PRIME General Conference, Manchester.

Bonjour, D., Cherkas, L., Haskel, J., Hawkes, D., & Spector, T. (2002, April). *Returns to Education: Evidence from UK Twins*. Centre for the Economics of Education, London School of Economics and Political Science.

Bonner, T. N. (2002). *Iconoclast: Abraham Flexner and a Life in Learning*. Johns Hopkins University Press.

Boston, J., Dalziel, P., & St John, S. (Eds.). (1999). *Redesigning the Welfare State in New Zealand: Problems, Policies, Prospects*. Oxford University Press.

Boulding, K. E. (1961). *The Image: Knowledge in Life and Society.* The University of Michigan Press.

Boulding, K. E. (1968). *Beyond Economics: Essays on Society, Religion and Ethics.* The University of Michigan Press.

Bourdieu, P. (1988 (1984)). *Homo Academicus.* Stanford University Press (Les Editions de Minuit).

Bowen, H. R., & Fincher, C. (1996). *Investment in Learning: The Individual and Social Value of American Higher Education.* Transaction Publishers.

Bowles, S., Gintis, H., & Osborne, M. (2001). The Determinants of Earnings: A Behavioral Approach. *Journal of Economic Literature, XXXIX,* 1137–1176.

Boyer, M., & Kihlstorm, R. (Eds.). (1983). *Bayesian Models of Econometrics.* North Holland.

Braun, D., & Merrien, F.-X. (Eds.). (1999). *Towards a New Model of Governance for Universities? A Comparative View* (Vol. 53). Jessica Kingsley Publishers.

Breneman, D. W. (2001). An Essay on College Costs. In A. F. Cunningham, J. V. Wellman, M. E. Clinedinst, J. P. Merisotis, & C. D. Carroll (Eds.), (Vol. 2, pp. 13–20). National Center for Education Statistics, U.S. Department of Education, Office of Educational Research and Improvement.

Breu, M. (2004). Kurt Wüthrich über das EU-Forschungsförderungssystem. *ETHlife* (13. Januar).

Brudney, J. L., Jr., L. J. O., & Rainey, H. G. (Eds.). (2000). *Advancing Public Management: New Developments in Theory, Methods, and Practice.* Georgetown University Press.

Bundesminister für Bildung und Forschung. (2001). *Grund- und Strukturdaten 2000/2001.* Bonn: Bundesministerium für Bildung und Forschung (BMBF).

Bundesminister für Bildung und Forschung. (2002). *Basic and Structural Data 2001/2002.* Bonn: Federal Ministry of Education and Research (BMBF).

Bundesminister für Bildung und Wissenschaft. (1991). *Grund- und Strukturdaten 1991/92.* Karl Heinrich Bock.

Burd, S. (2003). Education Department Wants to Create Grant Program Linked to Graduation Rates. *The Chronicle of Higher Education, 49*(17), A31.

Burke, J. C., & Minassians, H. (2002). *Performance Reporting: The Preferred 'No Cost' Accountability Program.* The Nelson A. Rockefeller Institute of Government, State University of New York.

Burke, Joseph C. and Associates (Ed.). (2002). *Funding Public Colleges and Universities for Performance: Popularity, Problems, and Prospects.* The Rockefeller Institute Press.

Burke, Joseph C. and Associates (Ed.). (2004). *Achieving Accountability in Higher Education: Balancing Public, Academic, and Market Demands.* Jossey-Bass.

Burke, Joseph C. and Terry A. Lessard. (2002). Performance Funding: Campus Reactions. In Burke, Joseph C. and Associates (Ed.), (pp. 61–82). The Rockefeller Institute Press.

Burton, N. W., & Ramist, L. (2001). *Predicting Success in College: SAT Studies of Classes Graduating Since 1980.* College Entrance Examination Board.

Bush, V. (1945). *Science the Endless Frontier, A Report to the President.* US Government Printing Office.

Butler, D. (2004). Battle Lines are Drawn as French Researchers Resign en Masse. *Nature*, *428*(18 March), 241.

Butler, L. (2003). Modifying Publication Practices in Response to Funding Formulas. *Research Evaluation*, *12*(1), 39–46.

Cabinet Office. (1999, March). *Next Steps Report 1998*. Minister of Cabinet Office.

Carayol, N., & Matt, M. (2003, December). *Individual and Collective Determinants of Academic Scientists' Productivity*. Université Louis Pasteur, Strasbourg (France).

Carayol, N., & Matt, M. (2004a). Does Research Organization Influence Academic Production? Laboratory Level Evidence from a Large European University. *Research Policy*, *33*, 1081–1102.

Carayol, N., & Matt, M. (2004b). The Exploitation of Complementarities in Scientific Production Process at the Laboratory Level. *Technovation*, *24*, 455–465.

Carnevale, A. P., Johnson, N. C., & Edwards, A. R. (1998). Performance-Based Appropriations: Fad or Wave of the Future? *The Chronicle of Higher Education*, B6.

Casassus, B. (2005). Cracks in the Monolith: CNRS Begins a Long-Awaited Reform. *Science*, *308*, 1243.

Cave, M., Hanney, S., & Kogan, M. (1991). *The Use of Performance Indicators in Higher Education: A Critical Analysis of Developing Practice* (Vol. 3). Jessica Kingsley.

CEST. (2002). *La Suisse et la 'Champions League' internationale des institutions de recherche 1994–99: Contribution au benchmarking international des institutions de recherche (CEST 2002/6)*. Centre d'Etudes de la Science et de la Technologie (CEST).

Chevailier, T. (2004). Higher Education and Markets in France. In P. Teixeira, B. Jongbloed, D. Dill, & A. Amaral (Eds.), (pp. 311–326). Kluwer Academic Publishers.

Clark, B. R. (1983). *The Higher Education System: Academic Organizations in Cross-National Perspective*. University of California Press.

Clark, B. R. (1997). Diversification, Competitive Autonomy, and Institutional Initiative in Higher Education Systems. In M. Herbst, G. Latzel, & L. Lutz (Eds.), (pp. 37–41). Verlag der Fachvereine (vdf).

Clark, B. R. (1998). *Creating Entrepreneurial Universities: Organizational Pathways of Transformation*. Pergamon.

Clark, B. R. (2004a). Delineating the Character of the Entrepreneurial University. *Higher Education Policy*, *17*, 355–370.

Clark, B. R. (2004b). *Sustaining Change in Universities: Continuities in Case Studies and Concepts*. Society for Research into Higher Education (SRHE) & Open University Press.

Clarke, C. (2003, January). *The Future of Higher Education*. UK Secretary of State for Education and Skills.

Clery, D. (2006). Despite a Chilly Reception, the 'European MIT' Advances. *Science*, *311*(5765), 1227.

Clotfelter, C. T., Ehrenberg, R. G., Getz, M., & Siegfried, J. J. (Eds.). (1991). *Economic Challenges of Higher Education*. The University of Chicago Press.

Coglianese, C., Nash, J., & Olmstead, T. (2002, December). *Performance-Based Regulation: Prospects and Limitations in Health, Safety and Environmental Protection*. John F. Kennedy School of Government, Harvard University, RWP02-050.

Coleman, J. S. (1961). *The Adolescent Society: The Social Life of the Teenager and its Impact on Education.* The Free Press.

Commission on Higher Education. (2001). *Mission Resource Requirements, Fiscal Year 2001–2002.* Division of Finance, Facilities and Management Information Systems.

Commission on Higher Education. (2002a, November). *Performance Funding Workbook: A Guide to South Carolina's Performance Funding System for Public Higher Education.* Division of Planning, Assessment and Performance Funding.

Commission on Higher Education. (2002b, September). *South Carolina: Higher Education Statistical Abstract.* Division of Finance, Facilities and Management Information Systems.

Commission on National Investment in Higher Education. (1997). *Breaking the Social Contract: The Fiscal Crisis in Higher Education.* Council for Aid to Education, Rand Corporation.

Committee on Science, Engineering, and Public Policy. (2000). *Experiments in International Benchmarking of US Research Fields.* National Academy Press.

Committee on Science, Engineering, and Public Policy. (2001a). *Implementing the Government Performance and Results Act for Research: A Status Report.* National Academy Press.

Committee on Science, Engineering, and Public Policy. (2001b). *Implementing the Government Performance and Results Act for Research.* National Academy Press.

Congress of the United States, Joint Economic Committee. (1969). *The Analysis and Evaluation of Public Expenditures: The PPB System* (Vols. 1, 2, 3). United States Government Printing Office.

Council of Economic Advisors. (1971). *Economic Report of the President, Transmitted to the Congress.* United States Government Printing Office.

Crewe, I. (Ed.). (2004, January). *Achieving our Vision: 2004 Spending Review Submission for England and Northern Ireland.* Universities UK.

Cunningham, A. F., Wellman, J. V., Clinedinst, M. E., Merisotis, J. P., & Carroll, C. D. (Eds.). (2001). *Study of College Costs and Prices, 1988–89 to 1997–98* (Vol. 2). National Center for Education Statistics, U.S. Department of Education, Office of Educational Research and Improvement.

Da Pozzo, F., Maye, I., Roulin-Perriard, A., & von Ins, M. (2001, December). *List of the Worldwide 'Champions League' of Research Institutions 1994-1999.* Centre d'études de la science et de la technologie (CEST).

Da Pozzo, F., Maye, I., Roulin Perriard, A., & von Ins, M. (2003). *Place scientifique suisse 2001: Développements de la recherche en comparaison internationale sur la base d'indicateur bibliométriques 1981–2001.* Centre d'études de la science et de la technologie (CEST 2003/2).

Da Pozzo, F., Maye, I., Roulin Perriard, A., & von Ins, M. (2004). *ETH Zürich in the 'Champions League': 1998-2002 versus 1981-1985.* CEST Scientometric Focus, Centre d'études de la science et de la technologie , www.cest.ch/Publikationen/2004/Scientometrics_Focus_Dec_04.pdf.

Da Pozzo, F., & Roulin Perriard, A. (2003). Performance des Forschungsplatzes Schweiz: Trend-Indikatoren 1981–2001. *Die Volkswirtschaft* (12), 60–63.

de Boer, & others (Eds.). (2002). *Academia in the 21st Century: An Analysis of Trends and Perspectives in Higher Education and Research.* Adviesraat voor her Wetenschaps- en Technologiebeleid (AWT).

Dearden, L. (1998, W98/14). *Ability, Families, Education and Earnings in the UK.* IFS Working Paper.

di Mento, M. (2005). Yale gets $ 100-Million for School of Music. *The Chronicle of Philanthropy* (November 10), 12.

Djerassi, C. (2004). Asian Brains: US v. Europe. *Science, 305*(5684), 609.

Doerig, H.-U. (2004). *Neue Wege zur Hochschulfinanzierung.* Arbeitskreis Kapital und Wirtschaft.

Dorfman, R. (Ed.). (1965). *Measuring Benefits of Government Investments.* The Brookings Institution.

Dorfman, R., Samuelson, P. A., & Solow, R. M. (1958). *Linear Programming and Economic Analysis.* McGraw-Hill.

Duderstadt, J. J. (2000). *A University for the 21st Century.* The University of Michigan Press.

Duke, C. (1992). *The Learning University: Towards a New Paradigm?* The Society for Research into Higher Education (SRHE) & Open University Press.

Edwards, K. (1999, June). *The European Space for Higher Education.* Paper presented at the University of Bologna to the European Ministers of Education.

Elton, L. (1996). Task Differentiation in Universities: Towards a New Collegiality. *Tertiary Education and Management, 2*(2), 138–145.

Erhardt, M., & Müller-Böling, D. (1998, Mai). *Modell für einen Beitrag der Studierenden zur Finanzierung der Hochschulen (Studienbeitragsmodell).* Stifterverband für die Deutsche Wissenschaft und Centrum für Hochschulentwicklung (CHE).

ETHZ. (1991, 23. Januar). *Planung 1992-95 (Mehrjahresplan).* Vizepräsidium Planung & Entwicklung.

ETHZ. (1997, 14. April). *Akademische Vision 2011 der ETH Zürich.* Planungskommission.

Etzioni, A. (1975). *A Comparative Analysis of Complex Organizations.* The Free Press.

Etzkowitz, H. (1999). Academia Agonistes: The 'Triple Helix' of Government-University-Industry Relationships in the United States. In D. Braun & F.-X. Merrien (Eds.), (Vol. 53, pp. 78–99). Jessica Kingsley Publishers.

Etzkowitz, H., & Leydesdorff, L. (Eds.). (2001 (1997)). *Universities and the Global Knowledge Economy: A Triple Helix of University-Industry-Government Relations.* Continuum.

Evans, L., Grimes, A., Wilkinson, B., & Teece, D. (December 1996). Economic Reform in New Zealand 1984-95: The Pursuit of Efficiency. *Journal of Economic Literature, XXXIV,* 1856-1902.

Fishburn, P. C. (1964). *Decision and Value Theory.* John Wiley & Sons.

Fishburn, P. C. (1973). *The Theory of Social Choice.* Princeton University Press.

Fiske, E. B., & Ladd, H. (2000). *When Schools Compete: A Cautionary Tale.* Brookings Institution Press.

Flexner, A. (1930). Universities: American, English, German. In C. Kerr (Ed.), *Abraham Flexner: Universities, American, English, German* (pp. xxxiii–381). Oxford University Press.

Freeland, R. M. (1992). *Academia's Golden Age: Universities in Massachusetts 1945-1970.* Oxford University Press.

Freeman, R. J., & Shoulders, C. D. (1999). *Governmental and Nonprofit Accounting: Theory and Practice.* Prentice Hall.

Frey, R. L. (1997). Universität — Wirtschaft — Staat: Leistungsfähige Hochschulen zur Stärkung der regionalen Wettbewerbsfähigkeit. In M. Herbst, G. Latzel, & L. Lutz (Eds.), (pp. 59–70). Verlag der Fachvereine (vdf).

Fritzell, A. (1998). *The Current Swedish Model of University Governance: Background and Description.* National Agency for Higher Education.

Fröhlicher-Güggi, S. (Ed.). (2002). *Jüngste Entwicklungen an den Schweizer Hochschulen: Universitäten und Fachhochschulen — eine gelungene Integration?* Neuchâtel: Bundesamt für Statistik.

Frost, S., Chopp, R., & Pozorski, A. L. (2004). Advancing Universities: The Global City as Guide for Change. *Tertiary Education and Management, 10*(1), 73–86.

Fujita, M., Krugman, P., & Venables, A. J. (2001). *The Spatial Economy: Cities, Regions, and International Trade.* MIT Press.

Fujita, M., & Thisse, J.-F. (2002). *Economics of Agglomeration: Cities, Industrial Location, and Regional Growth.* Cambridge University Press.

Gans, H. (Ed.). (1979). *On the Making of Americans.* University of Pennsylvania Press.

Gawande, K., & Wheeler, T. (1999). Measure of Effectiveness for Governmental Organizations. *Management Science, 45*(1), 42–58.

Geiger, R. L. (1993). *Research and Relevant Knowledge: American Research Universities since World War II.* Oxford University Press.

Geoghegan, M. C., & Ackoff, R. L. (1989). Productivity and Learning. *Systems Practice, 2*(1), 7–10.

Geuna, A., & Martin, B. R. (2003). University Research Evaluation and Funding: An International Comparison. *Minerva, 41*(4), 277–304.

Glotz, P. (2004). Warten auf den Urknall. *Weltwoche* (3).

Gore, A. (1993). *Creating a Government That Works Better and Costs Less: The Report of the National Performance Review.* Plume.

Gore, A. (1996). *The Best Kept Secrets in Government: How the Clinton Administration Is Reinventing the Way Washington Works; Fourth Report of the National Performance Review.* Random House.

Graham, H. D., & Diamond, N. (1997). *The Rise of the American Research Universities: Elites and Challengers in the Postwar Era.* Johns Hopkins University Press.

Gray, H. (Ed.). (1999). *Universities and the Creation of Wealth.* The Society for Research into Higher Education & Open University Press.

Griliches, Z. (2000). *R&D, Education, and Productivity: A Retrospective.* Harvard University Press.

Grove, E. W. (1973). Comments to Mancur Olson's Paper. In M. Moss (Ed.), (Vol. 38, pp. 394–397). National Bureau of Economic Research and Columbia University Press.

Grübler, A. (1998). *Technology and Global Change.* The International Institute for Applied Systems Analysis (IIASA): Cambridge University Press.

Gugerli, D., Kupper, P., & Speich, D. (2005). *Die Zukunftsmachine: Konjunkturen der ETH Zürich 1855–2005*. Chronos Verlag.

Hammer, M., & Champy, J. (1993). *Reengineering the Corporation: A Manifesto for Business Revolution*. HarperBusiness.

Hammerstein, N. (1999). *Die Deutsche Forschungsgemeinschaft in der Weimarer Republik und im Dritten Reich: Wissenschaftspolitik in Republik und Diktatur*. C.H. Beck.

Hammerstein, N. (2000). *Res publica litteraria: Ausgewählte Aufsätze zur frühgeschichtlichen Bildungs-, Wissenschafts- und Universitätsgeschichte*. Duncker & Humblot.

Hanft, A. (Ed.). (2001). *Grundbegriffe des Hochschulmanagements*. Luchterhand Verlag.

Hanushek, E. A., & Kimko, D. D. (2000). Schooling, Labor-Force Quality, and the Growth of Nations. *The American Economic Review*, *90*(5), 1184–1208.

Harbison, F., & Myers, C. (Eds.). (1965). *Manpower and Education*. McGraw-Hill.

Haveman, R., & Wolfe, B. (1995). The Determinants of Children's Attainments: A Review of Methods and Findings. *Journal of Economic Literature*, *XXXIII*, 1829–1878.

Hebel, S. (2003). Private Colleges Face Cuts in Public Dollars: Direct taxpayer support and student-aid programs are in jeopardy as states struggle to close deficits. *The Chronicle of Higher Education*, *XLIX*(47), A19–A20.

Heckman, J., Heinrich, C., & Smith, J. (1997). Assessing the Performance of Performance Standards in Public Bureacracies. *American Economic Review*, *87*, 389–395.

Helfenstein, U. (2001, August). *Die Matrikel der Universität Zürich, 1833 bis 1914*. www.matrikel.unizh.ch/pages/0.htm.

Henkel, M., & Little, B. (Eds.). (1999). *Changing Relationships between Higher Education and the State* (Vol. 45). Jessica Kingsley Publishers.

Herbst, M. (1970). *A Short Definition of Systems Analysis*. unpublished report, University of North Carolina at Chapel Hill, Department of City & Regional Planning.

Herbst, M. (1997). Die Hochschule zwischen Tradition und Erneuerung. In M. Herbst, G. Latzel, & L. Lutz (Eds.), (pp. 173–193). Verlag der Fachvereine (vdf).

Herbst, M. (1999). Change Management: A Classification. *Tertiary Education and Management*, *5*, 125–139.

Herbst, M. (2004a). *Governance and Management of Research Universities: Funding and Budgeting as Instruments of Change*. Centre d'études de la science et de la technologie (CEST 2004/4, www.cest.ch/en/publikationen/cest_reihe.htm).

Herbst, M. (2004b). The Production-Morphology Nexus of Research Universities: The Atlantic Split. *Higher Education Policy*, *17*(1), 5–21.

Herbst, M. (November 2, 2005). Zur Rangordnung von Universitäten: ein Jahrmarkt der Eitelkeiten? *Tages-Anzeiger*, 11.

Herbst, M., Hugentobler, U., & Snover, L. (2002). *MIT and ETH Zürich: Structures and Cultures Juxtaposed*. Centre d'études de la science et de la technologie (CEST 2002/9, www.cest.ch/en/publikationen/cest_reihe.htm).

Herbst, M., Latzel, G., & Lutz, L. (Eds.). (1997). *Wandel im tertiären Bildungssektor: Zur Position der Schweiz im internationalen Vergleich*. Verlag der Fachvereine (vdf).

Herbst, M., & Schmitt, G. (2001). Virtueller Campus. In A. Hanft (Ed.), (pp. 470–478). Luchterhand Verlag.

HERO (Ed.). (December 2001). *Research Assessment Exercise 2001: The Outcome.* Higher Education & Resarch Opportunities in the United Kingdom.

Higher Education Funding Council for England. (2001). *A Guide to the 2001 Research Assessment Exercise.* HEFCE.

Higher Education Funding Council for England. (2002a, April). *An Introduction to the Higher Education Funding Council for England.* Guide 02/17.

Higher Education Funding Council for England. (2002b, April). *Funding Higher Education in England: How HEFCE allocates its funds.* Guide 02/18.

Higher Education Funding Council for England. (2003, June). *Funding Higher Education in England: How HEFCE allocates its funds.* Guide 03/29.

HM Treasury (Ed.). (July 2002). *Investing in Innovation: A Strategy for Science, Engineering and Technology.* The Public Enquiry Unit.

Hoenack, S. A. (1983). *Economic Behavior Within Organizations.* Cambridge University Press.

Holstrom, B. (1983). On the Theory of Delegation. North Holland.

Hölttä, S., & Nuotio, J. (1995). Academic Leadership in a Self-Regulative Environment: A challenge for Finnish universities. *Tertiary Education and Management, 1*(1), 12–20.

Hopkins, D. S. (Ed.). (1981). *Planning Models for Colleges and Universities.* Stanford University Press.

Huisman, J. (2001). The Netherlands. In J. Huisman & F. Kaiser (Eds.), (pp. 27–33).

Huisman, J., & Kaiser, F. (2001a). Comparative Analysis. In J. Huisman & F. Kaiser (Eds.), (pp. 19–26).

Huisman, J., & Kaiser, F. (Eds.). (2001b, January). *Fixed and Fuzzy Boundaries in Higher Education: A Comparative Study of (binary) Structures in Nine Countries.* Adviesraad voor het Wetenschaps- en Technologiebeleid (AWT), Den Haag.

Hurley, J. (1997). *Organisation and Scientific Discovery.* John Wiley & Sons.

Johnes, J., & Taylor, J. (1990). *Performance Indicators in Higher Education: UK Universities.* The Society for Research into Higher Education & Open University Press.

Jones, L. R., & Kettl, D. F. (2003). Assessing Public Management Reform in an International Context. *International Public Management Review, 4*(1), 1–18.

Jones, L. R., Schedler, K., & Wade, S. W. (Eds.). (1997). *International Perspectives on the New Public Management.* JAI Press.

Kahn, H., & Wiener, A. J. (1967). The Next Thirty-Three Years: A Framework for Speculation. In D. Bell (Ed.), (Vol. 96, pp. 705–732).

Kahn, P. (1996). The Decline of German Universities. *Science, 273*(5272), 172–174.

Kaplan, R. S., & Norton, D. P. (1996). *The Balanced Scorecard: Translating Strategy into Action.* Harvard Business School Press.

Karabel, J. (2005). *The Chosen: The Hidden History of Admission and Exclusion at Harvard, Yale, and Princeton.* Houghton Mifflin.

Karmel, P. (2003). Higher Education at the Crossroads: Response to an Australian Ministerial Discussion Paper. *Higher Education, 45,* 1–18.

Keeney, R. L., & Raiffa, H. (1976). *Decisions with Multiple Objectives: Preferences and Value Tradeoffs.* John Wiley & Sons.

Keller, P., & Keller, M. (2001). *Making Harvard Modern: The Rise of America's University.* Oxford Press.

Kells, H. R. (1986). The Inadequacy of Performance Indicators for Higher Education: The Need for a More Comprehensive and Developmental Construct. *Higher Education Management,* 2(3), 258–270.

Kells, H. R. (1995). *Self-Study Processes: A Guide to Self-Evaluation in Higher Education* (4th ed.). American Council on Education and Oryx Press.

Kelly, P. J. (2005, November). *As America Becomes More Diverse: The Impact of State Higher Education Inequality.* National Center for Higher Education Management Systems (NCHEMS).

Kelly, U., Marsh, R., & McNicoll, I. (2002, May). *The Impact of Higher Education Institutions on the UK Economy.* Universities UK.

Kennedy, D. (1997). *Academic Duty.* Harvard University Press.

Kerr, C. (Ed.). (1994). *Abraham Flexner: Universities, American, English, German.* Transaction Publishers (Oxford University Press).

Kerr, C. (2001a). *The Gold and the Blue: A Personal Memoir or the University of California, 1949-1967* (Vol. 1 [Academic Triumphs]). University of California Press.

Kerr, C. (2001b). *The Gold and the Blue: A Personal Memoir or the University of California, 1949-1967* (Vol. 2 [Political Turmoil]). University of California Press.

Kettl, D. F. (2000). *The Global Public Management Revolution: A Report on The Transformation of Governance.* Brookings Institution Press.

Kettl, D. F. (2002). *The Transformation of Governance: Public Administration for the Twenty-First Century America.* Johns Hopkins University Press.

King, D. A. (2004). The Scientific Impact of Nations: What Different Countries get for their Research Spending. *Nature,* 430, 311–316.

Kleiber, C. (Ed.). (1999). *Die Universität von morgen: Visionen, Fakten, Einschätzungen.* Gruppe für Wissenschaft und Forschung (GWF), Eidgenössisches Departement des Innern.

Klemperer, A. (2001). Sweden. In J. Huisman & F. Kaiser (Eds.), (pp. 95–102).

Klitgaard, R., & Light, P. C. (2005). *High-Performance Government: Structure, Leadership, Incentives.* Rand Corporation.

Kogan, M., & Hanney, S. (2000). *Reforming Higher Education* (Vol. 50). Jessica Kingsley Publishers.

Koller, T., & Imboden, D. M. (2001, 25. Januar). *Die Umweltnaturwissenschaften: Beispiel einer bottom-up-Bewegung zur Schaffung neuer Lehr- und Forschungseinheiten.* unpublished report, Department of Environmental Sciences, ETHZ.

Koopmans, T. C. (1957). *Three Essays on the State of Economic Science.* McGraw-Hill.

Krägenow, T., Jaklin, P., & Nink, K. (2004, January). SPD-Generalsekretär entfacht Streit um Elite-Universität. *Financial Times Deutschland.*

Krueger, A. B., & Lindahl, M. (2001). Education for Growth: Why and For Whom? *Journal of Economic Literature, XXXIX,* 1101–1136.

Lampe, D. (Ed.). (1988). *The Massachussetts Miracle: High Technology and Economic Revitalization.* The MIT Press.

LaRocque, N. (2003, January). *Who Should Pay? Tuition fees and tertiary education financing in New Zealand.* Education Forum.

Lattuca, L. R. (2001). *Creating Interdisciplinarity: Interdisciplinary Research and Teaching among College and University Faculty.* Vanderbilt University Press.

Leszczensky, Michael (Ed.). (2003a, Dezember). *Internes und externes Hochschulcontrolling* (No. A8). Hochschul-Informations-System (HIS), Kurzinformationen.

Leszczensky, Michael. (2003b, Februar). *Paradigmenwechsel in der Hochschulfinanzierung* (No. A1). Hochschul-Informations-System (HIS), Kurzinformationen.

Levin, S. G., & Stephan, P. E. (1999). Are the Foreign Born a Source of Strength for US Science? *Science, 285*(5431), 1213–1214.

Levine, A. E. (Ed.). (1993). *Higher Learning in America: 1980–2000.* Johns Hopkins University Press.

Liefner, I. (2003). Funding, Resource Allocation, and Performance in Higher Education. *Higher Education, 46,* 469–489.

Light, P. C. (1997). *The Tides of Reform: Making Government Work, 1945–1995.* Yale University Press.

Light, P. C. (2002). *Pathways to Nonprofit Excellence.* Brookings Institution Press.

Lindner, A. (Ed.). (2003). *Gewogen und für zu leicht befunden? Neue Herausforderungen für die Forschung in Deutschland und in Europa.* Stifterverband für die Deutsche Wissenschaft.

Little, W., Fowler, H., Coulson, J., & Onions, C. (Eds.). (1967 (1933)). *The Shorter Oxford English Dictionary on Historical Principles.* Oxford Univesity Press.

Lotka, A. J. (1926). The Frequency Distribution of Scientific Productivity. *Journal of the Washington Academy of Sciences, 16,* 317–323.

Macedo, D. (Ed.). (2000). *Chomsky on Miseducation.* Rowman & Littlefield.

March, J. G., Schulz, M., & Zhou, X. (2000). *The Dynamics of Rules: Change in Written Organizational Codes .* Stanford University Press.

Massy, W. F. (1990). A Paradigm for Research on Higher Education. In J. C. Smart (Ed.), (Vol. VI, pp. 1–34). Agathon Press.

Massy, W. F. (Ed.). (1996). *Resource Allocation in Higher Education.* The University of Michigan Press.

Massy, W. F. (2003). *Honoring the Trust: Quality and Cost Containment in Higher Education.* Anker Publishing Company.

Massy, W. F. (2004). Markets in Higher Education: Do they Promote Internal Efficiency? In P. Teixeira, B. Jongbloed, D. Dill, & A. Amaral (Eds.), (pp. 13–35). Kluwer Academic Publishers.

McCaughey, R. A. (2003). *Stand, Columbia: A History of Columbia University in the City of New York, 1754–2004.* Columbia University Press.

McNay, I. (1999). Changing Cultures in UK Higher Education. In D. Braun & F.-X. Merrien (Eds.), (Vol. 53, pp. 34–58). Jessica Kingsley Publishers.

McQueen, D. H. (1992, Fall). *International Comparison of Technically Oriented Universities.* Office of Planning & Development, ETH Zürich, unpublished Report.

Medawar, J., & Pike, D. (2000). *Hitler's Gift: Scientists Who Fled Nazi Germany*. Richard Cohen Books and European Jewish Publication Society.

Merton, R. K. (1973). *The Sociology of Science: Theoretical and Empirical Investigations*. The University of Chicago Press.

Merton, R. K. (1996). *On Social Structure and Science*. The University of Chicago Press.

Merton, R. K., & Barber, E. (2004). *The Travels and Adventures of Serendipity*. Princeton University Press.

Ministry of Education. (1997). A Future Tertiary Education Policy for New Zealand: Green Paper. *Tertiary Education Review, Government of New Zealand*.

Mittelstraß, J. (1994). *Die unzeitgemäße Universität*. Suhrkamp Verlag.

Mora, J.-G. (2001). Governance and Management in the New University. *Tertiary Education and Management*, 7(2), 95–110.

Morey, D., Maybury, M., & Thuraisingham, B. (Eds.). (2000). *Knowledge Management: Classic and Contemporary Works*. MIT Press.

Moss, M. (Ed.). (1973). *The Measurement of Economic and Social Performance* (Vol. 38). National Bureau of Economic Research and Columbia University Press.

Mühlethaler, J. (2004). Berufliche Doppelaufgabe auf dem Prüfstand: Ein Interview mit Bruno Staffelbach. *Neue Zürcher Zeitung* (64), 67.

Mullis, I. M., Martin, M. O., Gonzales, E. J., O'Connor, K. M., Chrostowsky, S. J., Gregory, K. D., Garden, R. A., & Smith, T. A. (2001). *Mathematics Benchmarking Report TIMSS 1999 — Eighth Grade: Achievement for U.S. States and Districts in an International Context*. The International Study Center, Lynch School of Education; and The International Association for the Evaluation of Educational Achievement.

Murphy, K. M., Shleifer, A., & Vishny, R. W. (1991). The Allocation of Talent: Implications for Growth. *Quarterly Journal of Economics*, 102(2), 503–530.

National Research Council. (1995). *Research-Doctorate Programs in the United States: Continuity and Change*. National Academy Press.

National Research Council. (2000). *The Digital Dilemma: Intellectual Property in the Information Age*. National Academy Press.

Neave, G. (2002). On Looking through the Wrong End of the Telescope: Being sundry observations of the State of Academic in the 21st century from an historical perspective. In de Boer & others (Eds.), (pp. 55–79). Adviesraat voor her Wetenschaps- en Technologiebeleid (AWT).

Newell, A. (1969). Heuristic Programming: Ill-Structured Problems. In J. S. Aronowsky (Ed.), (Vol. III, pp. 360–414). John Wiley & Sons.

Nowotny, H., & Felt, U. (2002). *After the Breakthrough: The Emergence of Superconductivity as a Research Field*. Cambridge University Press.

Nyborg, P. (2000, March 9–10). *Opening Session: A Norwegian Contribution*. Higher Education in the Digital Age, UC Berkeley.

OECD. (2001). *Knowledge and Skills for Life: First Results from PISA 2000*. Programme for International Student Assessment, OECD Publications.

OECD. (2003). *Education at a Glance: OECD Indicators 2003*. Centre for Educational Research and Innovation, OECD Publications.

Olson, M. (1973). Evaluating Performance in the Public Sector. In M. Moss (Ed.), (Vol. 38, pp. 355–384). National Bureau of Economic Research and Columbia University Press.

Orlans, H. (1967). Educational and Scientific Institutions. In D. Bell (Ed.), (Vol. 96, pp. 823–831).

Osborne, D., & Gaebler, T. (1993). *Reinventing Government: How the Entrepreneurial Spirit is Transforming the Public Sector.* Plume–Penguin.

Pavitt, K. (2003). From Competence to Rigidity. In A. Lindner (Ed.), (pp. 10–13). Stifterverband für die Deutsche Wissenschaft.

Pearce, D. W. (Ed.). (1989). *The MIT Dictionary of Modern Economics.* MIT Press.

Pechar, H., & Wrobleski, A. (2001). Weniger Scheinimmatrikulationen, gleichbleibende Studienaktivität: Über die Auswirkungen der Studiengebühren auf die Zahl der Studentinnen und Studenten an österreichischen Universitäten. *Beiträge zur Hochschulforschung* (2), 219–241.

Pelz, D. C., & Andrews, F. M. (1976). *Scientists in Organizations: Productive Climates for Research and Development.* Institute for Social Research, University of Michigan.

Peters, T. J., & Waterman, R. H. (1988 (1982)). *In Search of Excellence: Lessons from America's Best Run Companies.* Warner Books.

Pollitt, C., & Bouckaert, G. (2000). *Public Management Reform: A Comparative Analysis.* Oxford University Press.

Ratcliff, J. L. (1996). A Rationale for a Differentiated System of Higher Education: The Person-Environment Fit Model of Student Learning. *Tertiary Education and Management, 2*(2), 127–137.

Rhodes, F. H. (2001). *The Creation of the Future: The Role of the American University.* Cornell University Press.

Rhodes, F. H. (2004). Governance of US Universities and Colleges. In L. E. Weber & J. J. Duderstadt (Eds.), (pp. 213–226). Economica.

Richter, W. F. (2003). Hochschulforschung im Vergleich: Strukturprobleme und ein Vorschlag zu deren Lösung. *Forschung & Lehre* (12).

Ringer, F. K. (1990 (1969)). *The Decline of the German Mandarins: The German Academic Community, 1890-1933.* Wesleyan University Press.

Robins, K., & Webster, F. (Eds.). (2003). *The Virtual University? — Knowledge, Markets, and Management.* Oxford University Press.

Rudenstine, N. L. (2001). *Pointing our Thoughts: Reflections on Harvard and Higher Education, 1991–2001.* Harvard University.

Rusterholz, P., & Liechti, A. (Eds.). (1998). *Universität am Scheideweg: Herausforderungen, Probleme, Strategien.* Akademische Kommission der Universität Bern, Verlag der Fachvereine (vdf).

Saxenian, A. (1994). *Regional Advantage: Culture and Competition in Silicon Valley and Route 128.* Harvard University Press.

Schalenberg, M. (2002). *Humboldt auf Reisen? Die Rezeption des 'deutschen Universitätsmodells' in den französichen und britischen Reformdiskursen (1810-1870).* Schwabe & Co.

Schedler, K., & Reichard, C. (Eds.). (1998). *Die Ausbildung zum Public Manager.* Verlag Paul Haupt.

Schick, A. (1996). *The Spirit of Reform: Managing in the New Zealand State Sector in a Time of Change*. New Zealand State Services Commission.

Schmidt, P. (1996). More States Tie Spending on Colleges to Meeting Specific Goals. *The Chronicle of Higher Education*, A23.

Schmidt, P. (2002a). Missouri's Financing System is Praised, but More for Longevity Than for Results. *The Chronicle of Higher Education*, A20–22.

Schmidt, P. (2002b). Most States Tie Aid to Performance, Despite Little Proof That It Works: College leaders doubt their institutions improve, but the systems are a fact of life. *The Chronicle of Higher Education*, A20–22.

Schmidtlein, F. A. (1999). Assumptions Underlying Performance-Based Budgeting. *Tertiary Education and Management*, 5(2), 159–174.

Schmidtlein, F. A. (2004). Assumptions Commonly Underlying Government Quality Assessment Practices. *Tertiary Education and Management*, 10(1), 1–23.

Schultze, C. L., Hamilton, E. K., & Schick, A. (1970). *Setting National Priorities: The 1971 Budget*. The Brookings Institution.

Schwendener, R. (2004, May 27). *Mid-level Employment: A Construction Site*. ETHlife international (`www.ethlife.ethz.ch/e/articles/campuslife/BefristeteMibau.html`).

Schwinges, R. C. (Ed.). (2001). *Humboldt International: Der Export des deutschen Universiätsmodells im 19. und 20. Jahrhundert* (Vol. 3). Schwabe & Co.

Selingo, J. (2004). US Public's Confidence in Colleges Remains High. *The Chronicle of Higher Education*, L(35), A1, A10–A13.

Senge, P. M. (2000). The Leader's Work: Building Learning Organizations. In D. Morey, M. Maybury, & B. Thuraisingham (Eds.), (pp. 19–51). MIT Press.

Shattock, M. (2003). *Managing Successful Universities*. Open University Press.

Shleifer, A. (1998). State versus Private Ownership. *Journal of Economic Perspectives*, 12(4), 133–150.

Simon, H. A. (1957). *Models of Man: Mathematical Essays on Rational Human Behavior in a Social Setting*. John Wiley & Sons.

Snyder, T. D., & Hoffman, C. M. (2003). *Digest of Education Statistics, 2002*. National Center for Education Statistics.

SPD. (2004, 6. Januar). *Unser Land gerecht erneuern: Beschluss des Parteivorstandes*. Willy-Brandt-Haus Materialien: Weimarer Leitlinien Innovation.

Spence, A. M. (1974). *Market Signaling: Informational Transfer in Hiring and Related Screening Processes*. Harvard University Press.

Sporn, B. (1999). *Adaptive University Structures: An Analysis of Adaptation to Socioeconomic Environments of US and European Universities* (Vol. 54). Jessica Kingsley.

Sporn, B., & Aeberli, C. (2004). *Hochschule Schweiz: Ein Vorschlag zur Profilierung im internationalen Umfeld*. Avenir Suisse.

Starr, M. K., & Zeleny, M. (Eds.). (1977). *Multiple Criteria Decision Making* (Vol. 6). North-Holland.

State of California. (2003). *California Statistical Abstract*. `www.dof.ca.gov`.

Stembeck, T. (2004). Gegen hohe Studiengebühren kann man sich versichern. *NZZ am Sonntag* (February 29), 19.

Teixeira, P., Jongbloed, B., Dill, D., & Amaral, A. (Eds.). (2004). *Markets in Higher Education: Rhetoric or Reality?* Kluwer Academic Publishers.

Teixeira, P., Rosa, M. J., & Amaral, A. (2004). Is there a Higher Education Market in Portugal? In P. Teixeira, B. Jongbloed, D. Dill, & A. Amaral (Eds.), (pp. 291–310). Kluwer Academic Publishers.

The Editor. (2003). Almanac Issue 2003–4. *The Chronicle of Higher Education*, *L*(1).

The Graduate School. (1979, April). *Record of the University of North Carolina at Chapel Hill (Session 1979–80)*. Graduate School Series Nr. 99.

The National Summit on Competitiveness. (2005, December 6). *Investing in US Innovation.* A National Gathering of Executives Concerned about America's Future Competitiveness.

Trow, M. (1970). Reflections on the Transition from Elite to Mass Higher Education. *Dædalus*, *90*, 1–42.

Trow, M. (1979). Aspects of Diversity in Higher Education. In H. Gans (Ed.), (pp. 271–290). University of Pennsylvania Press.

Trow, M. (1993). Federalism in American Higher Education. In A. E. Levine (Ed.), (pp. 39–66). Johns Hopkins University Press.

Trow, M. (1996). Trust, Markets and Accountability in Higher Education: A Comparative Perspective. *Higher Education Policy*, *9*(4), 309–324.

Trow, M. (1997). Reflections on Diversity in Higher Education. In M. Herbst, G. Latzel, & L. Lutz (Eds.), (pp. 15–36). Verlag der Fachvereine (vdf).

Trow, M. (2003a). In Praise of Weakness: Chartering, the University of the United States, and Dartmouth College. *Higher Education Policy*, *16*(1), 9–26.

Trow, M. (2003b). Some Consequences of the New Information and Communication Technologies for Higher Education. In K. Robins & F. Webster (Eds.), (pp. 301–317). Oxford University Press.

Tzermias, N. (2004, 19. Januar). Braucht Italiens Wirtschaft ein 'MIT'? 'Flucht der Gehirne' beunruhigt die Apeninenrepublik. *Neue Zürcher Zeitung* (14), 13.

United States General Accounting Office. (2000a, June). *Department of Education: Fiscal Year 1999 Performance Report and Fiscal Year 2001 Performance Plan.* GAO/HEHS-00-128R.

United States General Accounting Office. (2000b, June). *Department of Transportation: Fiscal Year 1999 Performance Report and Fiscal Year 2001 Performance Plan.* GAO/RCED-00-201R.

United States General Accounting Office. (2000c, June). *Environmental Protection Agency: Fiscal Year 1999 Performance Report and Fiscal Year 2001 Performance Plan.* GAO/RCED-00-203R.

United States General Accounting Office. (2000d, June). *Health and Human Services: Fiscal Year 1999 Performance Report and Fiscal Year 2001 Performance Plan.* GAO/HEHS-00-127R.

United States General Accounting Office. (2000e, June). *National Science Foundation: Fiscal Year 1999 Performance Report and Fiscal Year 2001 Performance Plan.* GAO/RCED-00-205R.

United States General Accounting Office. (2001a, June). *Department of Education: Status of Key Outcomes and Addressing Major Management Challenges.* GAO-01-807.

United States General Accounting Office. (2001b, June). *Department of Transportation: Status of Key Outcomes and Addressing Major Management Challenges.* GAO-01-834.

United States General Accounting Office. (2001c, June). *Environmental Protection Agency: Status of Key Outcomes and Addressing Major Management Challenges.* GAO-01-774.

United States General Accounting Office. (2001d, June). *Health and Human Services: Status of Key Outcomes and Addressing Major Management Challenges.* GAO-01-748.

United States General Accounting Office. (2001e, June). *National Science Foundation: Status of Key Outcomes and Addressing Major Management Challenges.* GAO-01-785.

Ursprung, H. (1997). *Die Zukunft erfinden: Wissenschaft im Wettbewerb.* Verlag der Fachvereine (vdf).

van Vught, F. A. (Ed.). (1989). *Governmental Strategies and Innovation in Higher Education.* Jessica Kingsley.

van Vught, F. A. (1997). Relevant Issues for Higher Education Policy-Research. In M. Herbst, G. Latzel, & L. Lutz (Eds.), (pp. 149–157). Verlag der Fachvereine (vdf).

van Vught, F. A. (2004). Closing the European Knowledge Gap? Challenges for the European Universities of the 21st Century. In L. E. Weber & J. J. Duderstadt (Eds.), (pp. 89–106). Economica.

Vignoles, A., Levacic, R., Walker, J., Machin, S., & Reynolds, D. (2000, September). *The Relationship Between Resource Allocation and Pupil Attainment: A Review.* Centre for the Economics of Education, London School of Economics and Political Science.

von Maravic, Patrick and Christoph Reichard. (2003). New Public Management and Corruption: International Public Management Network (IPMN), Dialogue and Analysis. *International Public Management Review, 4*(1), 84–129.

Watt, C., Lancaster, C., Gilbert, J., & Higerd, T. (2004). Performance Funding and Quality Enhancement at three Research Universities in the United States. *Tertiary Education and Management, 10*(1), 61–72.

Weber, K. (1999). Switzerland: Discussion of University Reform and its Implementation. In D. Braun & F.-X. Merrien (Eds.), (Vol. 53, pp. 141–162). Jessica Kingsley Publishers.

Weber, L. E. (2004). Financing the Research University: A European Perspective. In L. E. Weber & J. J. Duderstadt (Eds.), (pp. 179–196). Economica.

Weber, L. E., & Duderstadt, J. J. (2004a). Challenges and Possible Strategies for Research Universities and the United States. In L. E. Weber & J. J. Duderstadt (Eds.), (pp. 239–254). Economica.

Weber, L. E., & Duderstadt, J. J. (Eds.). (2004b). *Reinventing the Research University.* Economica.

Weber, L. E., & Zgaga, P. (2004). Reinventing the European Higher Education and Research Sector: the Challenge for Research Universities. In L. E. Weber & J. J. Duderstadt (Eds.), (pp. 29–49). Economica.

Weisz, G. (1983). *The Emergence of Modern Universities in France, 1863-1914.* Princeton University Press.

Whalen, E. L. (1991). *Responsibility Center Budgeting: An Approach to Decentralized Management for Institutions of Higher Education.* Indiana University Press.

Wildavsky, A. (1997). *But Is It True?: A Citizen's Guide to Environmental Health and Safety Issues.* Harvard University Press.

Wilson, J. Q. (1989). *Bureaucracy: What Government Agency Do and Why they Do it.* Basic Books.

Wolf, C. (1993). *Markets or Governments: Choosing between Imperfect Alternatives.* MIT Press.

Wood, W. B., & Gentile, J. M. (2003). Teaching in a Research Context. *Science, 302*(5650), 1510.

Woodfield, A., & Gunby, P. (2003). The Marketization of New Zealand Schools: Assessing Fiske and Ladd. *Journal of Economic Literature, XLI,* 863–884.

Woolf, S. (2003). On University Reform in Italy: Contradictions and Power Relations in Structure and Function. *Minerva, 41,* 347–363.

Wüthrich, K. (2003). Interview: Forschungsstandort Schweiz — Quo vadis? *Leader: Die Zeitung des Technopark Zürich* (March), 4–7.

Yorke, M. (1998). Performance Indicators Relating to Student Development: can they be trusted? *Quality in Higher Education, 4*(1), 45–62.

Yorke, M. (1999). *Leaving Early: Undergraduate Non-Completion in Higher Education.* Taylor & Francis.

Zehnder, C. A. (2001, August 22). *Der Weg zum Diplomstudiengang Informatik 1970–1981.* unpublished report, Department of Computer Science, ETHZ.

Zemsky, R. (2004). On Classifying Universities: Policy, Function and Market. In L. E. Weber & J. J. Duderstadt (Eds.), (pp. 109–117). Economica.

Ziegele, F., Erhardt, M., & Müller-Böling, D. (1998). *Modell für einen Beitrag der Studierenden zur Finanzierung der Hochschulen (Studienbeitragsmodell).* Stifterverband für die Deutsche Wissenschaft, und Centrum für Hochschulentwicklung (CHE).

Zuckerman, H. (1996 (1977)). *Scientific Elite: Nobel Laureates in the United States.* Transaction Publishers.

Index

Printed in the United States
131963LV00002B/33/P

9 781402 095023